Roads to
the Learning Society

Roads to the Learning Society

Lois Lamdin
Editor

cael

The Council for Adult and Experiential Learning
Chicago

ISBN: 0-9628073-1-1

Cael
The Council for Adult and Experiential Learning
223 West Jackson Boulevard, Suite 510
Chicago, Illinois 60606

Editing and production services by Winthrop Publishing Company, a division of Winthrop Marketing, Inc.

Manufactured in the United States of America

To Morris T. Keeton

"and gladly wolde he lerne, and gladly teche."

— *Chaucer*
Prologue, Canterbury Tales

Contents

Preface

Roads to the Learning Society
(Prefatory Notes to the Second Edition)

The essays comprising this book first appeared in a limited printing presented to Morris Keeton as a *Festschrift* upon his retirement from the presidency of CAEL in 1989. A *Festschrift* seemed the logical, perhaps the inevitable, way to salute the man who has for so long been mentor to us all. A group of friends and colleagues wanted, in a manner meaningful to Morris, to acknowledge his pervasive influence on our lives, our careers and our ideologies. How better to express that appreciation than in the coin of his own realm—ideas?

The alacrity that characterized the reactions to invitations for contributions to this volume bore witness, if indeed proof is still needed at this juncture of his life, to the esteem in which Morris is held by his colleagues. The response of these contributors, all active people, busy with multiple professional commitments, was immediate, spirited, even joyous. Without exception, they *wanted* an opportunity to attest, for the record and via the printed word, the impact Keeton had made on their thinking about issues central to their intellectual and professional lives.

In the almost two years since that first, limited edition, many who had occasion to read it requested that the book be made more widely available. The consensus seemed to be that the authors represented herein constitute a gathering of giants in adult education whose collective contributions span most of the major issues in the field. Those readers felt that the caliber of the essays was such, and their cumulative effect potentially so powerful, that republication for a larger audience was warranted.

The essays in this edition are essentially the same as in the original, as is the format and organization of the volume. This edition, unlike the original, benefits from overview by Morris Keeton himself. Grateful beneficiary of this tribute though he be, he remains ever the unsentimental editor. Gimlet-eyed wielder of the redactor's fine-tooth comb, he helped find errors which slipped through the first time. For this, and for much else, I am grateful.

— LL

Introduction

The point about Morris T. Keeton is that he never met an idea he didn't like, or at least didn't think he could tame to his purposes. That is not to say he is not discriminating—he is—but that he has an uncanny alchemical ability to find the gold in the dross and to refine it until the rest of us can perceive its shine.

The Keeton hegemony, as noted in many of the essays that follow, has been a potent one. One man's influence has spread not only throughout his own organizations, most notably Antioch College and the Council for Adult and Experiential Learning, but throughout the world of those who are concerned with the meaning of learning, with broader recognition of learning no matter where or how it is acquired, with understanding the messages of adult development theory, and with the issues of social equity that are bound up with expanded access to education. These are indeed some of the roads to the learning society that has been Morris's lifelong goal.

While none of the contributors to this volume received any suggestions as to what they might write about, their collected essays fell easily into four sections, sections that can serve as signposts to the major roads to that learning society. If today the learning society is in the process of becoming a reality in the United States, then Keeton and these authors have been among the most active agents in its coming to fruition.

In the first section, *Innovation and Innovators,* Zelda Gamson writes about CAEL and Keeton as instruments of social movement and change and discusses the extent of their influence on traditional higher education. In a similar vein, **Jim Hall** in "The Genetics of Innovation" looks at the philosophical and intellectual background of Keeton's thinking, and fits this into a history of innovation in American colleges and universities.

Malcolm Knowles writes about Keeton and Edward Lindeman, two "heroes" who have given the concepts of experiential learning and non-traditional study intellectual respectability; while **Bill Warren** steps back to take a wry look at the nature of innovation itself, concluding that "innovation has entered a gentler age, preferring to provide exemplary alternatives rather than to transform institutions overnight."

Norman Evans turns to the nature of the man, Keeton himself, of what it is in his character that has enabled his vision to reach across the Atlantic to influence the progress of assessment of prior experiential learning in Great Britain. He finds his metaphor for the man from observing Keeton as he played with Evans' granddaughter: "friendly navigator, pilot, co-worker, guide and sometimes passenger." And finally, **John Valley** looks at "the uncompleted tasks," those changes that still need to be made if all learners are to gain access to education. He calls upon Keeton to pick up these further challenges.

The contributors to the second section of this book, *Experiential Learning,* offer provocative insights into that broadest of "roads" with which Keeton's name is synonymous, the encouragement and recognition of learning that occurs outside the structure of the classroom. **Joan Knapp** looks at the history of portfolio assessment, tracing where it's been and where it's going, with reflections on personal and professional relationships pertinent to its development. **John Strange** makes a witty and impassioned plea for an expansion of experiential learning into the liberal arts, with some "Strange" graphs to illustrate the distance between what should be and what is in current educational practice.

Jackson Kytle, from his base at Antioch College, writes of the "Power and Problematics of Experience-Based Curriculum Methods," addressing both the distance we have come and the pitfalls on the road we yet must follow. And coming back from a year as Empire State College mentor in Israel, **Elana Michelson** looks with a fresh eye at some of the issues in assessing prior learning from a cross-cultural perspective. She adds a new twist to the meaning of a secular humanist liberal arts education.

Section three, *Adult Development Theory: Implications for Teaching and Professional Development,* begins with **Arthur Chickering's** moving article on how, as a young instructor attempting to make Psych 101 a more powerful learning experience, he encountered an array of issues regarding learning styles, self-directed learning, stage changes in ego development, and social control, among others. From this and subsequent experiences, he has derived a set of "good practice" guidelines to enable students to take charge of their own continued development.

Barry Sheckley and **George Allen** clarify and amplify the relationship between experiential learning and adult development, and extend their theory to the area of professional competence. They argue that the basic grasping/transforming process that underlies learning can be extended by designing learning programs that reduce the gap between the student's current and potential levels of development.

David Kolb formulates the eight arenas of life challenge that constitute a lifelong learning agenda for advanced professionals and, indeed, all adults. He ends with a moving vision of a community of learners "actively involved in creating humanity's common future."

On the level of current institutional practice, **Urban Whitaker** looks at the "nonsense" that surrounds residence requirements for degree study, pointing out the differences between theory and reality in many colleges and universities. And **Bessie Blake** addresses the question of how we can ease the struggle of non-traditional students to survive in the climate of academia, arguing that we can provide retention strategies that work for these adult learners.

The road described in section four, *Towards the Learning Society,* might be termed "Access." In different ways, each of these articles is concerned with opening up learning opportunities to a broader constituency, those who traditionally have been under served by the educational establishment, and who now, in a world dominated by communications and technology, are in greater danger than ever before of losing their precarious foothold on the economic ladder.

Patricia Cross leads off with a discussion of the "four villages of experiential learning," moving from the assessment and accrediting of learning from life and work; to experiential learning as the basis for bringing about change in higher education; to experiential learning as the basis for social change; and finally, to learning approaches that increase self-awareness and group effectiveness.

Norman Evans, in his second appearance in this volume, discusses the implications of the British "Youth Access" scheme as a tentative solution to workforce problems. "Youth Access" is based upon recognition of the relationship between learning and experience, quality assurance (making certain that the achievements of the students are acceptable to higher education institutions), and the integrity of learning achievements no matter where they have been acquired.

The final two articles in this volume look at CAEL's current joint ventures to reveal how Keeton's lifetime commitment to adult development, experiential learning, creating institutional change and providing access to new learners is being put into practice to provide for the growth and development of the American workforce.

Elinor Greenberg writes about the challenges that link America's future to education and of the institutional changes that must be put into place if we are to address the needs of the class of the year 2000. **Pamela Tate** and **Lois Lamdin** look at current joint ventures with labor, industry, government and institutions of postsecondary education, delineating how these may suggest solutions to some of the major issues facing us in training the American workforce. They go on to suggest some experientially-derived guidelines for policy-making at state and national levels.

What a close-knit world this band of innovators and practitioners inhabits! Throughout the volume there is a bedrock continuity of language and context, a continual cross-referencing among themselves and mutual concerns:

— that people's non-institutionally-derived learning should be recognized and honored;

— that the changing developmental needs of adults should be addressed;

— that new populations, minorities, women, service and technical workers, should have access to education appropriate to their needs;

— that educational institutions should become more responsive to adult students.

Keeton's influence has spread only partially because of the power of his ideas. This modest, self-effacing man, with a mind of steel and a will to match, seemingly reserved in personal relationships, has forged enduring friendships with an astounding number and variety of colleagues who regard him fondly as mentor, ally and confidant. These colleagues have joined him in carrying the Keeton message across this country and Canada and as far away as Europe, England and Australia, thereby transforming the landscape of postsecondary education.

Roads to
the Learning Society

Part I

Innovation and Innovators

1

CAEL and Change Movements in Higher Education

Zelda F. Gamson

Morris Keeton's greatest creation has been CAEL, his life's work from 1974 to 1989. Early in 1983, Keeton invited me to study his organization. I knew him by reputation and through our common bond with Antioch College. I was a member at the time of the Study Group on the Conditions of Excellence in American Higher Education, appointed by the National Institute of Education, which was to issue a major report on ways to improve higher education (U.S. Department of Education, 1984. I had also written about and taught courses on change in higher education. CAEL offered me the opportunity to study change in higher education from the angle of an organization unconnected to a college or university.

From 1983 through 1987, I immersed myself in CAEL. The more I came to know CAEL, the more I was struck by its resemblance to certain kinds of organizations outside of higher education. Such organizations passionately promote social change of one kind or another—for civil rights, against abortion. They are organized in a loose, decentralized way and often spread geographically across the country. They are led by a core group of activists who pursue a set of programs to promote their change agenda. They have members who must be mobilized from time to time; influential outsiders, especially those with resources and power, are also crucial for such organizations.

As a sociologist, I recognized these kinds of organizations as "social movement organizations." The study of social movements is a highly developed area in sociology, and I found its ideas increasingly helpful as I came to terms with the significance of CAEL in higher education. What follows is based on the final chapter of my history of CAEL, *Higher Education and the Real World* (Gamson, 1989), which analyzes CAEL as a social movement organization.

CAEL began at a time of great ferment in higher education. The legitimacy of learning outside the classroom and the notion that content and pedagogy should be relevant to students' concerns, alongside the belief that more people—blacks and other minorities, women and adults—had a right to a higher education were legacies of the 1960s which shaped the 1970s. The task of the 1970s was to make some of these ideas work.

There were resources to do it. Any college or university bent on starting a new program or improving existing ones stood a good chance of raising at least start-up money from the foundations or the federal government. Foundations, most prominently the Carnegie Corporation, the Lilly Endowment, the Ford Foundation, the W. K. Kellogg Foundation, the Exxon Education Foundation, the Rockefeller Foundation, the Danforth Foundation and the Mellon Foundation were more than ready to support various improvement efforts.

The federal government was also encouraging improvement in higher education during this period. The passage of the Higher Education Act of 1965 and then the Education Amendments of 1972 expanded the federal role in improving higher education and increasing access to it. The greatest expenditures were for direct grants and loans to students, but there was also a variety of programs for institutions, special programs for minorities and under-prepared students, and projects targeted to particular subjects like science.

Into this scene entered the Fund for the Improvement of Postsecondary Education (FIPSE), whose budget of $10 million when it was founded in 1973 did not match the resources of the foundations or other federal programs but whose attention was squarely focused on reforming higher education. Its staff spent much time around the country carrying word of what was going on from innovator to innovator, people who were often geographically and socially marginalized (Gamson, 1979; Fund for the Improvement of Postsecondary Education, 1983).

An infrastructure that would bring these scattered innovators together had already begun to emerge when the FIPSE staff began its travels. Some people, especially administrators, had already discovered *Change*, a bi-monthly magazine founded by the Union of the Experimenting Colleges and Universities in 1969 that was devoted entirely to higher education, and *The Chronicle of Higher Education*, a weekly newspaper which began publishing in 1966. Jossey-Bass, a publishing house which specialized in higher education, opened in 1967.

While disciplinary associations and organizations representing prestigious institutions remained outside the growing infrastructure for change, other higher education associations became visible proponents of change during the early 1970s. The American Association for Higher Education (AAHE), a department of the National Education Association which became an independent organization in 1969, served as a meeting ground for administrators and faculty members from a variety of disciplines to talk about innovation. The Council for the Advancement of Small Colleges (CASC; later, the Council of Independent Colleges) provided technical assistance to its members on ways of improving undergraduate education. The Association of American Colleges (AAC) was a voice for liberal education. AAHE, AAC, and CASC set the tone for other higher education associations and regional consortia, which became increasingly active in the 1970s. They could call on a variety of consultants and experts who operated in and around colleges and universities.

The time was ripe for the formation of a social movement for change in higher education. Much has been written about the conditions which are conducive to the formation of social movements: a combination of sentiments and ideologies in support of change, organizations ready to carry out programs for change, resources to help them do it, and the right opportunities for them to act. Several important conditions for the formation of a social movement were already present in higher education when CAEL entered the scene. Non-traditional educators had a general ideology about improving higher education which received space in the higher education media. Through the higher education associations and regional consortia, a growing cadre of people had developed expertise in carrying out some of the movement's programs with ample support from outside sympathizers in the foundations and federal government.

One critical element, however, was missing: a sense of collective identity among the advocates of change. There were several different submovements for change in higher education. Those concerned about increasing access for different groups—minorities, women, adults—pursued programs focused on those groups. The "sixties" innovators were disconnected from one another and culturally split off from the "seventies" innovators. Those who were working on changes in curriculum did not communicate with those working on changes in the extra-curriculum. Individualistic and freewheeling, people in the various submovements for change in higher education operated in different institutional sectors. This meant that they did not have a vehicle for mobilizing a potential constituency in the new programs and institutions already primed to respond to their change programs.

Enter CAEL

CAEL became one of the vehicles for bringing the different submovements together. At the time it was founded it took ideas from several social movements for change in higher education and combined them in new ways. With support from the emerging national infrastructure for change, CAEL attracted large pools of resources. Most of the foundations with an interest in higher education have given money to CAEL, some of them several times: the W. K. Kellogg Foundation, FIPSE, the Carnegie Corporation, the Lilly Endowment, and the Ford Foundation. What explains CAEL's appeal to foundations? The foundations actively seek innovation and promote their own agendas. Foundation people referred to Morris Keeton as a "responsible innovator." Keeton succeeded in articulating not only a practical program that was consistent with their agendas; he was also able to communicate a vision of success.

This vision drew support from the national higher education establishment. CAEL had enough resources to cultivate various members of the establishment by inviting them to work on its myriad task groups, advisory committees, research projects, publications, or conferences. At one time or another, CAEL worked with most of the important higher education associations in Washington, most particularly the American Council on Education (ACE). In touch with campuses through its networks, CAEL itself was not bound by the constraints of academic organization. It became a key link between the national infrastructure for change and campus-based innovators. Without the innovators, the infrastructure had no clients. Without the infrastructure, the innovators had no resources.

CAEL is a unique organization in higher education. Influential figures on the national scene have been fascinated by CAEL. As one of them put it:

> CAEL can bridge the world of traditional institutions and organizations for adults. [It can] bring together traditional academic institutions, institutions that serve adults, and organizations comprised of adults, e.g., unions. Bridges and relationships are important among these groups...brokering and advocacy, creating a structure for new relationships.
>
> CAEL is a seminal organization, a pioneering organization. It's the conscience of higher education, forging ahead and exploring areas that the higher education community has ignored or is unwilling to explore...CAEL is pushing out at the frontiers, asking important questions we don't ask or are afraid to ask, or don't have time to ask (Talburtt, 1986, p. 17)

How did CAEL carve out a space for itself in the higher education arena? The answer to this question will teach us a good deal about the openness of higher education to change. For much of its history, CAEL operated as a social movement organization. A *social movement* occurs when a group of people want to change the social structure or the distribution of rewards in society at large or in a segment of society (McCarthy and Zald, 1977). A social movement *organization* is a formal organization which tries to implement the goals of a social movement; it is not simply focused on doing something different for its members or on providing services to a clientele (McCarthy and Zald, 1977; Zald and Ash, 1966).

While CAEL certainly was an innovative organization in its own right and provided its members with a repertoire of experiences that was unusual in higher education, this was not its *raison d'*être. From the beginning, CAEL was bent on changing colleges and universities. Let us go over CAEL's history to see how exactly it operated as a social movement organization.

Defining the Agenda: "Assessment" as an Organizing Framework

CAEL took several ideas that were in the air when it was founded, applied them to a new domain, and used them to establish its own domain. It did this, first, by defining its collective agenda around the idea of assessment.

"Assessment" turned out to be an extraordinarily robust tool. Ideologically, it put CAEL and its somewhat ragged troops on the high ground; they were for non-traditional approaches, to be sure, but with *discipline* and *quality*. Focusing on the assessment of learning from experience, as the first CAEL project did, was a fruitful entry point into many other aspects of higher education—admissions, counseling, teaching, curriculum, faculty development.

"Assessment" was also subversive. If the basic premise was granted that people learned outside of school settings and that this learning could be assessed for academic credit, then it followed that there should be ways of equating such learning to what went on in regular school settings. But CAEL's research demonstrated how difficult it was to equate courses in the same subject taught at different schools or even by different instructors in the same school, let alone comparing course learning with learning from experience.

The only sensible way to award credit for learning from experience was to assess what was learned rather than how it was learned, i.e., to focus on outcomes. The outcomes approach held particular appeal for the schools connected to CAEL, many of which were operating without the kinds of resources available to traditional colleges and universities. If it were true, as Morris Keeton claimed, that colleges and universities used "the same labels (Associate of Arts Degree or Bachelor of Arts degree, and so on) for enormously different outcomes," then quality was not only a problem for non-traditional education. What was sauce for the goose should be sauce for the gander.

The argument that they were willing to be judged not on "inputs" but on "outcomes" had already been taken up by the movement for competence-based education (Grant and Associates, 1975) and would be raised under another guise a decade later under the banner of "value-added" education (Astin, 1985). By the time "value added" came along, the point had been generalized to all of higher education.

CAEL's specific concern with assessment—the assessment of prior learning—became an important selling point as it began operating at the boundaries between higher education and other organizations. The idea of getting credit for what you learned in life appealed to homemakers and insurance agents, employers and unions. It captured the attention of politicians and business people who were interested in education's effects on economic productivity. It became the center of interest in CAEL's work in Great Britain and Quebec.

CAEL articulated its view of assessment in an extraordinary outpouring of publications, which began to appear the moment the organization began operating. This literature itself signalled the reach of the assessment issue, and of CAEL's own ambitions. Both the rate and scope of CAEL's publications became mobilizing tools in their own right. As Morris Keeton put it, "If you want to shape things in higher education, you need literature."

Broadening the Scope of Action:
From Institutions to Their Environment

To what change goals would this literature point? Goals provide meaning and direction to organizations. They are the "shaping content of concern" (Zald, 1979, p. 21). Goals may be latent or explicit. They may be single or multiple. They may focus on ideas, practices, or structures. Goals may be directed at influencing those they wish to change, or they may aim at replacing them.

At the beginning, CAEL's goals were latent and rather limited. As time passed, they became more explicit. They also expanded to include new arenas and actors. Throughout, however, CAEL focused more on ideas and practices than on structures. CAEL did not challenge the fundamental organization of colleges and universities or the way they were governed or funded. Despite Keeton's claims that CAEL would become the "new establishment," CAEL was more interested in influencing authorities than in replacing them. Nor did CAEL challenge the fundamental structure of higher education or the resource base on which it rested. It did not question the departmental structure, disciplinary specialization, or enrollment-driven funding for undergraduate education, facts of life in colleges and universities which affect much else.

CAEL had multiple goals; these goals were enshrined in its original title as a project with the Educational Testing Service from 1974 to 1977: The Cooperative Assessment of Experiential Learning. As time passed some aspects of these initial preoccupations were heightened at the expense of others, but hardly anything in CAEL's original menu was dropped. Instead, new goals were added as new resources and interests became available.

Goals in social movement organizations change in response to the ebb and flow of sentiments and resources within larger social movements (Zald and Ash, 1966). When experiential learning stopped attracting the attention of educators and the support of foundations, CAEL broadened its scope to include a variety of programs to make higher education more accessible to adults—computer-based counseling, telecommunications, information services, work-site education, new ways of assessing potential for college-level work. CAEL's name changes signify its growing scope: from the *assessment* (1974–1977) to the advancement (1977–1985) of experiential learning to *adult* (1985–present) and experiential learning.

CAEL's ever-broadening scope was not accepted by all of its adherents. Several members of the Board of Trustees actively opposed the broadening of CAEL beyond the assessment of experiential learning. They used terms like "protean" and "Arthurian" to describe CAEL's expanding boundaries. Several objected to Keeton's zeal, as one person put it, to "fix what is wrong in higher education" and to "recreate the world according to his values."

This was an accurate reading of Keeton's intentions. CAEL's change goals were implicit at the beginning because of the attention it gave to legitimating the assessment of prior learning, building a constituency, and gaining collective control over resources. When CAEL became an independent organization in 1977, it focused on "institutionalizing" the systematic approach to experiential learning developed in the first CAEL. In Keeton's words, this effort "would 'seed' the entire field of postsecondary education and thus. . . have a salutary effect upon the standards of good practice throughout American higher education."

This point of attack was short-lived. After that, CAEL shifted its tactics from working on institutions directly to working instead on the environments which affect them. While to some core members of CAEL and to outside sympathizers as well, these new efforts looked more like a shotgun approach than like tactics, Keeton continued to argue that CAEL was still focused on changing higher education. He wrote that CAEL's mission was "to transform the understanding and practice of collegiate and higher learning, within and outside of the academy, among adults of all ages."

CAEL's Model of Education

CAEL offered a new model of thinking about education, a "new paradigm" with a vivid populist tinge (Niebuhr, 1984).[1] CAEL framed the new model around its primary beneficiary, the "adult learner." It offered an analysis of how higher education could serve adults better, and then developed a set of procedures and practices to do so. CAEL emphasized that changes in work and family, as well as some of the recent work on life cycle development, implied that Americans needed to become lifelong learners.

Colleges and universities would have to accommodate themselves to adults more than they had in the past. Adults had full lives outside their studies. They had learned a lot from life and what they learned should be honored and recognized by colleges and universities. Some might not appear to be "college material," but thoughtful and sensitive interviewing would show that many had great potential for college work. Many, indeed, had learned things from life that could be presented and documented in portfolios and systematically assessed for academic credit.

Like all students, adults needed help in educational and life planning. They needed to get this help easily, at work sites and places near home as well as in formal educational settings. Computer-assisted guidance, carefully combined with face to face advising and information about educational programs suitable for them, was a promising tool for working with adults. Adults also needed access to courses at times and places that fit their situations—evening and weekend courses, work-site instruction, television courses. The content of these courses could be quite traditional—CAEL rarely focused on content—but colleges and universities would have to respect individual differences in learning styles and treat students as "learners."[2] Rather than being "agents of socialization," "environments for transition from puberty to adulthood," or "vehicles for transmitting from the past to the next generations a selection of the knowledge and habits of mind thought best by their faculties," as Morris Keeton put it in his frequent columns published in the CAEL newsletter, institutions of higher learning would need to "put a working priority upon the active fostering of maturation and self-development" in their students.

Focusing on colleges and universities would not be enough for this to happen. CAEL also attacked the policies of accrediting organizations and higher education associations, as well as state and federal agencies that made it difficult for adults to gain access to higher education. It worked on increasing financial support for adult learners in states and the federal government. And finally, it found new buyers of educational services among employers and labor unions.

CAEL could have set itself up as the provider of educational services directly to learners or to employers and labor unions. It could have joined the "shadow" educational system which grew up during its lifetime in the corporate sector (Eurich, 1985; Fenwick, 1983). Instead, it acted as an ambassador to the corporate sector from the nation of colleges and universities. Back home in higher education, CAEL acted as a goad and a broker.

Mobilizing for Action

CAEL needed to make its agenda a collective project. There were simply not enough resources around, despite CAEL's success in raising grant money, to change higher education without the help of many people. Even if there were enough resources, the very nature of U. S. higher education required a highly decentralized, grass-roots approach. Social movement organizations must shape their structures and strategies to the nature of their targets. CAEL faced a large set of scattered, atomized targets which operated in an extremely decentralized, if not disorganized manner. Reaching, let alone changing, such targets required enormous resources (Freeman, 1979). CAEL needed to find a way to identify and then mobilize the people who would carry out its program. This in itself takes time and money. Once mobilized, however, "people power" becomes a resource for change.

Mobilization for change is a complex process. It involves recruiting constituents, developing cadres, taking collective control over resources, and building a collective identity focused on the change agenda. Let us follow CAEL as it dealt with each of these issues.

Recruiting Constituents

Even when they have resources, social movement organizations that cannot call for dramatic events like demonstrations must put a good deal of energy into identifying their potential constituents. The original CAEL project had a tremendous advantage: it began with a core group of people who were doing things that were emblematic of many of the changes CAEL sought to bring about. Out of this group emerged the leaders who would define CAEL: Morris Keeton of Antioch, Arthur Chickering and Myrna Miller of Empire State College, George Ayers of Minnesota Metropolitan State, Urban Whitaker of San Francisco State, John Duley of Michigan State, Jane Permaul of UCLA, Sheila Gordon of LaGuardia Community College, Larraine Matusak of the University of Evansville, Diana Bamford-Rees and Joan Knapp of ETS.

Through its various activities from 1974 to 1977, CAEL drew hundreds of people from colleges and universities across the country into its orbit. How were they attracted? It is easier to recruit members through pre-existing networks than to start from scratch (Jenkins, 1983). During the early 1970s, John Valley of ETS had carried on a correspondence with hundreds of people around the country involved in innovative activities in colleges and universities. When the CAEL project began, Valley's contacts proved invaluable in identifying constituents. As some of them became involved in the CAEL projects, they recruited others from their own institutions and regions.

From the wing of non-traditional education based in programs for adults, CAEL pulled in practitioners who were either unconnected to, or uncomfortable with, existing adult and continuing education organizations and offered them excitement and a sense of being in on something new. They were faculty members, administrators and staff in the new programs and institutions for non-traditional learners, as well as people in older programs, who were beginning to look for a professional home open to new ideas about adult development and degree programs for adults. This emerging professional group in higher education was CAEL's early and constant constituency—directors and staff members in programs for adults and other non-traditional programs located at the interstices of their institutions.

Building Cadres

Some of these people were ready to do more than receive materials and attend conferences. Constituents can vary in their degree of commitment, but it is essential that highly committed members—the "core" or the "family"—share the central values of the organization. While they and less active members may receive material and social benefits from their connection to the social movement organization, a major basis for their participation must be shared values (Wilson, 1973; Fireman and Gamson, 1979). Even when members are attracted because of these values, their continuing commitment is always problematic. Social movement organizers, therefore, put much effort into building a sense of loyalty and collective identification among their constituents by using all of the means invented by human beings—rituals, symbols, emotional attachment, control over several spheres of life.

People who become involved in decision-making processes and carry out tasks and programs are the "cadres" of social movement organizations (McCarthy and Zald, 1977). The development of cadres was built into CAEL. In order to keep track of what was happening in its various projects, CAEL identified a contact person or coordinator of activities at each participating institution. This practice gave rise to the identification of unpaid "institutional liaisons" who were kept apprised of CAEL's activities.

CAEL also gathered constituents in the same region at meetings and joint projects. As time passed, a regional system became more elaborate and rationalized. The regional managers became the true cadres of CAEL, the foot soldiers who trudged through the trenches of academe. With their regional contacts, advisory committees, and conferences, the regional managers were in a position to mobilize the constituency and deploy CAEL's resources.

Building a Collective Identity Based on the Change Agenda

Americans, academics perhaps most of all, are not easily persuaded that the benefits of acting collectively are worth the costs. A key element in peoples' willingness to act collectively is trust in the others with whom they are to act, especially leaders (Fireman and Gamson, 1979; Wilson, 1973). Morris Keeton embodied the collective meaning of CAEL. Variously described as a "missionary," a "preacher," and an "evangelist," Keeton inspired great respect among people who came in contact with him. Essential to his impact was that he did not demand deference. Stories circulated among members about his penchant for tuna fish sandwiches in fancy restaurants and about his decrepit car. When Keeton sold a cherished vacation home for personal reasons, some members thought he had sacrificed it to raise money for CAEL when it fell on hard times.

Symbols, rituals, and distinctive styles are also important in building collective identity. So are incentives and frequent communication. Incentives in voluntary organizations can be material, solidary, or purposive (Wilson, 1973). CAEL relied on all three in different mixes for different kinds of members. CAEL offered rank and file members purposive incentives—the opportunity to be associated with an organization that stood for innovative ideas and respect for learners of all kinds. It held out material incentives as well, incentives based on its change agenda—the opportunity for adherents to enhance their careers in their own institutions or to move to other jobs through their connections with CAEL.

More involved members were also drawn to CAEL because of its values and for the material benefits it could confer on them. Because of their greater involvement, they were more likely to understand the implications of CAEL's new model of education. Indeed, some of them were engaged in aspects of it—education in the workplace, for example, or telecommunications. The material implications of their association with CAEL were also likely to be clearer. On the one hand, they donated much of their time to the organization, time that was often subsidized by another organization. On the other hand, many of CAEL's cadres gained visibility and contacts which they converted to career advancement. What appeared to be personal benefits often enhanced CAEL's collective agenda. When several CAEL activists became presidents of colleges and universities, for example, CAEL's influence was extended.

CAEL also held out powerful solidary incentives. While less involved members enjoyed the benefits of interacting with others in CAEL, it did not claim many aspects of their lives. Cadres and leaders, on the other hand, were connected to CAEL professionally, personally and socially. For the discernible core of perhaps a dozen people in the CAEL "family," CAEL claimed them seven days a week, year after year. Several had, in effect, "grown up" in CAEL.

CAEL also built collective identity through a unique style that conveyed the message that CAEL was innovative but... effective, responsible, trustworthy. The cream and blue stationery bespoke dignity, while its lower-case logo indicated a certain playfulness. Before long, "CAELites" began speaking "CAELish." It is difficult to keep mobilization high in any social movement organization, and leaders look for opportunities to keep their constituencies "heated up" for collective action (Lofland, 1979). The annual national assemblies—the term is itself a social movement expression—were occasions for focusing the collective identity on change goals.

The content of change, however, shifted rapidly as the central staff took on new projects. The problem was how to mobilize the constituency around the new content. The solution was to present the new content as a solution to a new problem or as an extraordinary opportunity. Social movement organizations actively shape the problems to which their programs are presented as solutions (McCarthy and Zald, 1973). CAEL's newsletter carried word of its new concerns throughout the year. Then, just before an upcoming assembly, it announced a theme which conveyed these concerns. The theme often emphasized newness—"Working at the new Frontiers," "Moving to the Next Stage." Sessions playing off the theme featured new people or CAEL veterans who were involved in new activities. A palpable excitement charged these sessions, as participants waited to see what CAEL's new offering would be.

The design of the national assemblies encouraged involvement. Waiting for participants were large name tags, with first names in large letters and color codes indicating special status. Participants could go to rooms to try out computer-assisted counseling programs, watch videos produced by various CAEL projects, and collect materials from programs across the country. They could leave notes or meet with colleagues in another room. They could go to sessions in which members of the CAEL "family" and rising stars would be featured. They would hear from Morris Keeton about CAEL's history and current status; then, they would be asked to give their reactions to options for the future.

The assemblies and newsletters were the primary means of communication between the central office and rank and file members, although many were in more direct and frequent communication with regional representatives. Constituents involved in particular projects, cadres, and staff were inundated with letters, idea papers, plans and reports from the central office. The telephone and then a computer network were other ways to keep CAEL's collective identity alive and focused on its agenda for change.

Organizational Structure

These efforts depended upon and helped elaborate CAEL as an organization. Social movement organizations must have instruments for mobilizing constituents for action, some notion of strategies and tactics for action, a program which roughly reflects strategies and tactics, and a way of coordinating constituents, strategies, tactics, and programs. An organizational structure is the main instrumentality for accomplishing these ends. Organizational structures vary according to the resources available and the environment in which a social movement organization operates. Structures can be centralized or decentralized, federated or isolated, bureaucratic or informal.

CAEL mystified people as an organization. "I can't get a hold on it," one close observer declared. "It's schizoid," said another. "It is out there like the morning fog," said a third. The first CAEL project had laid down an infrastructure for an independent organization that would be the envy of other social movement organizations: a formal transition plan; a staff and a leader; cadres who were known quantities; a mobilized constituency; a name in good standing; organizational tools like the assembly and the newsletter; relationships with key foundations and authorities—and a grant of close to $1 million.

Even so, the challenge of creating an independent organization for change in higher education was formidable. The new organization should permit the mobilization advantages of decentralization with the tactical advantages of centralization (Jenkins, 1983). It should have a broad reach into colleges and universities, associations and other non-governmental organizations, state agencies, and the federal government. It should keep its feet both in the world of non-traditional education and the mainstream of higher education. It should be able to move quickly but in a systematic and organized fashion.

As time passed, CAEL evolved into an organization that was a fitting vehicle for achieving its agenda. In their influential discussion of social movements as networks, Luther Gerlach and Virginia Hine (1970) point out that social movement organizations typically do not have a single head the way other organizations do, although they often depend on the personal charisma of a single leader. They consist of a variety of localized cells, which operate quite independently of one another. Their organizational structures are simple and the division of labor in them rudimentary (Freeman, 1979). It is often difficult to trace the reach of such a network, since the scope and nature of activities of each cell differ. What, then, holds them together? Gerlach and Hine argue that they are held together less by structures than by a complex web of personal ties and shared ideology.

This characterization fits CAEL's regional structure very well. CAEL has operated as a colonizer, either by attracting existing cells or by creating new ones. The regional cadres have some latitude to colonize within their own regions. While they differ in the complexity of their structures, most consist of one or two part-time regional managers, a part-time secretary, and an advisory committee. At the same time that they operate relatively independently of one another, they are connected to one another through personal relationships and shared beliefs.

The regional structure has been a continuing feature of CAEL. CAEL has also used more temporary forms for mobilizing new people and groups, such as ad hoc task groups and advisory committees, which also operate with much latitude. In many ways, CAEL has perfected the temporary organization, "project" or "team" approach (Bennis and Slater, 1968; McCarthy and Zald, 1977) that characterizes many innovative organizations (Kanter, 1983; Lawler, 1986).

If that were all there is to CAEL, its significance would have been limited. Its interest in state and national policies, as well as the need to present a united front to foundations and other organizations, required more control and a more complex structure. "Control" is perhaps too strong, while "coordination" is too weak. "Orchestrate" is more appropriate. While it did not possess the power of a typical hierarchical organization, CAEL functioned more proactively and held more authority than a coordinator. It required strong action to organize the movements of the regions, projects, and ad hoc groups by initiating them in the first place. Entrepreneurial effort was necessary to locate the resources and forge the relationships for them to do their work (Van de Ven and Walker, 1984).

By 1986, CAEL's basic structure had become quite complex, and Morris Keeton's multiple roles as entrepreneur, impresario and manager had still not been decoupled. Two vice presidents hired to take on the management of CAEL had not lasted long, and it was beginning to appear that this was a dynamic that had little to do with the particular people involved. Keeton's energy and charisma had built CAEL and continued to hold it together. What would happen when he was gone?

Strategies for Change

This issue focused not only on the future of CAEL as an organization, but on whether it would remain a social movement. While they benefited from Keeton's capacity to see connections among ideas and opportunities, members of the Board of Trustees, regional cadres, and staff did not always understand CAEL's larger strategies for change. In part, this was because they did not help shape them; in part, because Keeton acted intuitively and could not always articulate his strategies. When they experienced difficulties, especially in funding, CAEL activists often suggested solutions that could jeopardize the larger change agenda. It is easy to go from success to success, but it takes skill to learn from failure. When others became upset with some of CAEL's difficulties, Keeton pointed out that successes are often built on failures. "[G]ood management" is "a matter of learning from mistakes" and "above all. . .a matter of constantly trying to learn," "trying new things and analyzing the interplay of forces and circumstances as the changes played themselves out."

It is likely that Keeton was referring to his years at Antioch, when he and President Dixon lost control over efforts to change higher education by means of innovative learning centers located across the country. In many ways, CAEL was Keeton's second chance to change higher education on a national scale. With CAEL, he could try almost every point of entry into higher education—senior administrators and public officials; students, faculty, counselors, and staff; associations and accrediting bodies; government agencies and foundations.

CAEL proceeded with a mix of strategies, but followed three primary ones: the hearts and minds strategy, the top-down strategy, and the leverage strategy. The hearts and minds strategy built on the successes of the first CAEL, in particular the Faculty Development Program (FDP). An exemplar of CAEL's change goals, the FDP identified a core group of interested faculty and staff from several colleges and universities who helped design and then tried out training materials for the assessment of prior learning and related activities. They, in turn, trained others at their own and other institutions. Eventually, the faculty and staff trained in the CAEL approach would carve out a "liberated area" within their institutions, which would then serve as a launching pad for new incursions.

This strategy worked in institutions where the CAEL activist could link experiential learning to other important priorities. For example, Sister Margaret Earley, who was associate professor of religious studies at Alverno College at the time of the FDP and is now a full professor, was coordinator of the Valuing Department throughout this period. The Valuing Department is one among eight such departments, which exist alongside disciplinary departments, whose main purpose is to articulate and assess the generic abilities that an Alverno education promises to develop in its students. Along with its involvement in the Faculty Development Program, Alverno participated in other activities in the original CAEL project. This was happening at the time that Alverno was beginning to develop its unique approach to the assessment of outcomes (Ewens, 1979).

In less propitious situations, there was rarely a critical mass of CAELites at any one institution. While CAEL undoubtedly had profound effects on individuals, the hearts and minds strategy did not have much institutional pay-off. Some people moved on to other institutions and other positions for which their CAEL training may not have been relevant. Those who remained often found themselves stranded when financial austerity and conservatism took over in the 1970s. Norman Sundberg, for example, was a professor in the Wallace School of Community Service and Public Affairs at the University of Oregon when he was involved in the Faculty Development Program. The school was broken up in 1980 and, as of 1984, the university had neither accepted the assessment of prior learning nor did it have a coordinated approach to field placement.

Urban Whitaker, a staunch member of the CAEL cadre, offers another cautionary tale. While he was Dean of Undergraduate Studies at San Francisco State University, he had the support of the important senior administrators in his institution and the California State University and Colleges. As time passed, however, the interest of these people in innovative programs in general and in experiential learning in particular began to wane. By the time that Whitaker took an early retirement from San Francisco State, experiential learning had less support than when he directed the Faculty Development Program.

The Institutional Development Program (IDP), CAEL's first project as an independent organization, was designed to solve some of these problems. Instead of working from the bottom, as the FDP had, the IDP started at the top by asking senior administrators for a public commitment—an institutional plan for the introduction of experiential learning. These plans were slow in coming, if they ever did, and even less likely to stick. Agreements from senior administrators about academic practices do not mean much without support from department chairs and rank and file faculty and staff. This support was thin, despite CAEL's strenuous efforts to reach all levels in the institutions. Without constant on-campus involvement, the effects of IDP would evaporate. Yet CAEL was not in a position to become involved on campuses on a regular basis.

It was easier to go back to changing hearts and minds, but this time without assuming that individuals who came in contact with CAEL would necessarily change their own institutions. Rather, CAEL's emerging model of education would slowly begin to ripple outward. Like throwing a stone into a pond, people carrying CAEL's ideas into higher education would have effects on other people, who would have effects on others, and so on. In this view, anything CAEL did that was consistent with its agenda would add to its eventual impact. What might look like a shotgun approach could take on a certain logic when viewed in this way. It is almost impossible to catch the ripples, but eventually the new consciousness takes hold—especially if it is reinforced by external circumstances.[3]

At this point, impelled by frustration with the inertia of colleges and universities and the need to find new funding, Keeton and the CAEL cadres looked outside to groups that might affect the resource base of higher education—learners, policymakers, and non-educational institutions. The original CAEL project had published handbooks written for adult learners. A few years later, CAEL began offering services directly to learners through Learner Services, an information and advising project, and computer-assisted counseling. The regions picked up these projects and elaborated them even further. The change strategy underlying these efforts was to use adult learners' interests as leverage on colleges and universities.

CAEL attempted to exert leverage more directly, through its work on federal and state policies. Its work in the policy arena has been mediated by other organizations—the Council for Alternative Postsecondary Education at first and the Commission on Higher Education and the Adult Learner later. CAEL has been an important actor in setting the agenda for these organizations, whose primary focus has been to increase financial aid for adult learners and funding for programs for adults. Making the resources available would, in this view, be a force for change.

Tentatively, and then with increasing momentum, CAEL became involved with non-educational institutions, such as the United Automobile Workers-Ford Motor Company joint National Development and Training Center, as a broker of educational programs and services. The UAW-Ford project gave colleges and universities a strong incentive for recognizing prior learning for adults and creating services that responded to adults' needs. This incentive would be multiplied as CAEL made agreements with large companies like U. S. West Communications (formerly Mountain Bell) and the Scott Paper Company, labor unions like the Communications Workers of America, and government agencies like the Food and Drug Administration. By this time, the line between a social movement organization and a service organization was becoming blurred. As long as the focus remained on finding the levers for change in any new opportunity, CAEL would continue to be a social movement organization. When it stopped doing this, it would become a service organization.

The Significance of CAEL

Evaluating CAEL's impact was always a sore point. Viewing CAEL as a social movement organization clarifies why this was so. Looking for the effects on individual learners, faculty members or even institutions missed the point. Rather, CAEL's significance was better tested in collective terms: Did it gain acceptance from influential people in higher education as a carrier of the agenda for change? Did it win new advantages for its constituents? Did it contribute to the larger social movement for change in higher education (Gamson, 1975)? Results from a survey help to answer some of these questions. Talburtt (1986) conducted telephone interviews with 55 people from six general groupings: senior administrators in institutions, leaders of higher education associations, government representatives, foundation officers, researchers, and private sector representatives. These informants were selected because they were knowledgeable about adult learners and their needs, held a broad regional or national perspective on higher education, and were acquainted with CAEL.

Gaining Acceptance

Talburtt presented these people with a list of 17 potential changes in postsecondary education that may have occurred in the past four to five years, especially those that pertained to adult learners, and asked them to rate the extent to which they had actually occurred. Then, she asked them to rate CAEL's influence on those changes.

Among the changes in postsecondary education rated as having occurred rather extensively, CAEL was seen as having much influence. Informants rated CAEL as having a significant amount of influence even on changes which occurred less. CAEL was clearly important on any issue related to assessment and preeminent when it came to the use of prior learning assessment.

These are the judgments of the whole group of informants. There were important differences among the subgroups. Institutional leaders and government representatives saw CAEL as much more responsible for change in postsecondary education than association representatives and foundation officers; researchers and private sector representatives fell in between. In part, these differences reflect different judgments about how much higher education has changed. Institutional leaders reported more change in higher education than the other groupings; association leaders and private sector representatives saw less change.

Institutional and government representatives and, to a lesser extent, experts on higher education and private sector informants accepted CAEL as a legitimate spokesman for certain change interests in higher education. Leaders of associations and foundation officers were less willing to give such recognition to CAEL. All, however, gave CAEL its due with respect to certain issues. The assessment of prior learning was clearly CAEL's territory in the eyes of all groups. Information and advocacy services, alliances with labor organizations and businesses, information and advocacy for adults, and greater sophistication among colleges and universities about assessment were rated high.

Winning New Advantages

We have independent confirmation of the spread of prior learning assessment in colleges and universities from surveys conducted over CAEL's lifetime. In 1974, when CAEL began, there were just over 40 such programs (Willingham, Burns, and Donlon, 1975). In 1978, a survey sponsored by CAEL turned up a total of 211 (Knapp and Davis, 1978). By 1980, when the Office on Educational Credit and Credentials of the American Council on Education conducted a survey, almost 1100 of 2000 institutions said they used portfolio assessment; almost all reported awarding credit for prior learning.[4]

While it is difficult to document its impact on access to higher education, credit for prior learning must have brought more adults to colleges and universities. Certainly, some schools have found that recognizing prior learning has attracted more adults. This has been the case in the small private colleges, community colleges, and state colleges that have been CAEL's constituents. A follow-up study of 17 colleges and universities that participated in all three years of the Institutional Development Program, CAEL's first project when it became an independent organization, turned up several examples. At Baldwin-Wallace College, a small private college in Ohio, adults now comprise more than 50% of the students. The CAEL training allowed Baldwin-Wallace to offer credit for prior learning through testing and portfolio assessment. Students may take a course to help them prepare portfolios, which are assessed by a committee composed of faculty members from different fields. While these options are used by the college as a recruitment tool, the portfolio process is rigorous, and fewer than half of the 80 students in the course actually complete their portfolios and receive credit.

Another example: at East Texas State University at Texarkana, an institution with 1200 students which offers upper division and graduate programs, the student population is mostly adult. The university has a credit for experience program, in which students individually, and more recently in a course, are assessed for credit. Some 30 to 50 students receive some credit this way each year. At Clackamas Community College in Oregon, which enrolls many part-time, adult students in its student population of over 20,000, students may enroll in alternative credit programs which allow them to receive advance credit, credit by examination, credit by telecourses, and credit for prior learning through portfolio. The examination option is most popular; about 20 students use the portfolio.

These schools are constrained by the amount of money they can spend on non-traditional programs. More affluent institutions like American University and Sangamon State have incorporated prior learning assessment into ambitious programs for adults. At American University, the Apple adult re-entry program uses portfolio assessment techniques to grant up to 30 credits to older students with significant working experience and good writing skills. The 70 students in Apple take two courses when they enter, one on how to document field experience and develop a portfolio and another on composition and reading comprehension. Faculty "liaisons" from departments assess portfolios.

Sangamon State, which was created in 1969 as a non-traditional college with an experiential emphasis in all of its programs, enrolls some 3000 students, of whom half are adults. A credit for prior learning program, with between 150 and 200 students a year, requires that students who wish to develop portfolios must take an assessment course, which also serves as an orientation course. Faculty assess the portfolios and may award up to 30 hours of credit. Adults may also enroll in an individualized experiential learning program, which allows students to design their own programs.

These institutions have made a commitment to substantial efforts in prior learning assessment. They typically have strong support from senior administrators and have involved a core group of faculty and staff. But even among the institutions which participated in all three years of the Institutional Development Program, there are many which have not made this commitment. Of 17 interviewed in 1986, eight appeared to have strong prior learning or other experiential programs. The others had never been strong and had gotten weaker.

What about other items on CAEL's agenda? Sponsored experiential learning was equal to prior experiential learning when CAEL began. While there is little systematic data on the number of sponsored experiential learning programs in colleges and universities, the consensus among knowledgeable people is that internships, cooperative education, and other forms of non-classroom learning are more legitimate now than when CAEL began—though, like prior learning, they have a long way to go before the mainstream of college faculty become convinced of their value (Washington Center, 1984). CAEL has shared this territory with other organizations; it has probably brought greater legitimacy to all of their efforts.

Contributing to the Change Movement

CAEL has encountered more than its share of critics. One national figure criticized CAEL because it has not reached prestigious universities. "People in higher education are snobbish," he said. "judgments are based on who one associates with."

CAEL says they have great response because [they] have gone from 40 to 1000 institutions using prior learning assessment in four years. But, no Harvard or Ivy League or Big 10 schools are in—no Berkeley, Stanford, Northwestern or Georgetown. [All they] have are small struggling schools of middle size and state supported institutions, but these are not significant to those in the field. Get the University of Chicago, University of Michigan, Stanford, or Harvard. CAEL doesn't have that kind of base yet, to its detriment (Talburtt, 1986, p. 25).

CAEL ran into opposition at every stage in its history. In its early years, it confronted the Council on Postsecondary Accreditation and the Council of Graduate Deans. Several organizations serving adults, as well as those focused on campus based experiential education, competed with CAEL. CAEL was able to either neutralize or co-opt many of these organizations. In some cases, as with the National Society for Internships and Experiential Education and the Council for Alternative Postsecondary Education, CAEL served as a senior partner. Indeed, as long as CAEL could raise foundation money, it could be a patron of other groups which fell into its "dominant penumbra" (Zald, 1979).

CAEL could be seen as the Common Cause of the higher education reform world. McCarthy and Zald (1973) describe Common Cause as a conglomerate in the ameliorative social movement industry. It speaks and acts for reform in general, picking up and losing supporters as it moves from issue to issue, problem to problem. As one problem is solved, it moves to another. As long as it can raise foundation money, it can support its less popular causes.

As time passed, CAEL shifted from running projects of its own to orchestrating multiple efforts. The first CAEL already set the stage for this role, as "the CAEL project" became a series of projects carried out by circles of people in colleges and universities across the country. With the growth of the regional system and its growing relationships with other organizations like the Coalition of Alternative Postsecondary Education and the American Council on Education, the second CAEL extended the model further.

On all three measures of impact, then, CAEL's performance has been mixed but impressive. CAEL *gained acceptance* from some influential people and organizations inside and outside of higher education as a legitimate—in some realms, paramount—voice for the agenda it pursued. Acceptance of CAEL was quite high, especially for its work on the assessment of prior learning, among members of the national infrastructure for change in higher education. It was probably lower among representatives of elite institutions and disciplinary bodies, which operate in a very different world from the one that CAEL inhabited.

CAEL did not penetrate the academic establishment—the selective private colleges, the research universities, and the disciplinary departments in many other colleges and universities. Senior administrators, staff in special programs for adults and experiential education and maverick faculty members may have heard of CAEL. Some may have been involved in a CAEL project from time to time. Partly because of CAEL's work, but also because of the maturing of programs and the work of other organizations, experiential education became a more acceptable part of traditional higher education. But these inroads did not put adult and experiential education at the core of academia. On the contrary, institutions do not readily grant credit for learning derived from life experience and most continue to rely on traditional classrooms to educate students.

The core is not easy to penetrate. Change in higher education is much more likely to occur through the addition of parallel structures. Indeed, this is what happened during CAEL's lifetime. CAEL's base was in colleges and universities with large numbers of adult learners. Under pressure to maintain their enrollments when students of traditional age were less plentiful, these organizations received help from CAEL in reaching adults. Here CAEL played an important role in winning new advantages for adult learners. It also became involved with other organizations outside of higher education, such as large companies, government agencies and labor unions.

Not very long ago, these organizations could be dismissed as marginal to the enterprise of higher education. But as lifelong education, changes in the workplace, concerns about economic competitiveness and the sheer increase in the enrollment of adults in colleges, universities and company training programs have grown in the last decade, it is hard to call them marginal any more. They are part of a parallel framework for higher education, and CAEL was an active force in building it. CAEL has contributed ideas, strategies, know-how, money and sense of purpose to this *larger movement for change in higher education*. Indeed, CAEL has often been a ringleader.

Footnotes

1. Emily Schmeidler's work (1980) on civil rights organizations emphasizes the importance of models which guide change efforts. See also Snow et al. (1986).
2. CAEL's use of the term "learners" immediately set it off from the dominant usage among academics of "students."
3. This view of change comes close to the model associated with thinkers like Marilyn Ferguson (1980) and Erich Jantsch (1980).
4. Office on Educational Credit and Credentials, American Council on Education, Memorandum to the Committee on Educational Credit and Credentials, September 9, 1980.

References

Astin, Alexander W. *Achieving Educational Excellence.* San Francisco: Jossey-Bass, 1985.

Bennis, Warren and Philip Slater. *The Temporary Society.* New York: Harper and Row, 1968.

Eurich, Nell P. *Corporate Classrooms: The Learning Business.* Princeton, N.J.: The Carnegie Foundation for the Advancement of Teaching, 1985.

Ewens, Thomas. "Transforming a Liberal Arts Curriculum: Alverno College." In Gerald Grant (Ed.). *On Competence: A Critical Analysis of Competence-Based Reforms in Higher Education.* San Francisco: Jossey-Bass, 1979.

Fenwick, Dorothy C. *Directory of Campus-Business Linkages: Education and Business Prospering Together.* New York: Macmillan, 1983.

Ferguson, Marilyn. *The Aquarian Conspiracy: Personal and Social Transformation in the 1980's.* New York: St. Martin's, 1980.

Fireman, Bruce and William A. Gamson. "Utilitarian Logic in the Resource Mobilization Perspective." In Mayer N. Zald and John D. McCarthy (Eds.). *The Dynamics of Social Movements.* Cambridge, Mass.: Winthrop, 1979.

Freeman, Jo. "Resource Mobilization and Strategy: A Model for Analyzing Social Movement Organization Actions." In Mayer N. Zald and John D. McCarthy (Eds.). *The Dynamics of Social Movements.* Cambridge, Mass.: Winthrop, 1979.

Fund for the Improvement of Postsecondary Education. *A Decade of Improvement.* Washington, D.C.: Fund for the Improvement of Postsecondary Education, 1983.

Gamson, William A. *The Strategy of Social Protest.* Chicago: Dorsey, 1975.

Gamson, Zelda F. "Understanding the Difficulties of Implementing a Competence-Based Curriculum." In Gerald Grant (Ed.). *On Competence: A Critical Analysis of Competence-Based Reforms in Higher Education.* San Francisco: Jossey-Bass, 1979.

Gamson, Zelda F. *Higher Education and the Real World: The Story of CAEL*. Wolfeboro, N.H.: Longwood Academic, 1989.

Gerlach, Luther P. and Virginia H. Hine. *People, Power, Change: Movements of Social Transformation*. Indianapolis: Bobbs-Merrill, 1970.

Grant, Gerald and Associates. *On Competence: A Critical Analysis of Competence-Based Reforms in Higher Education*. San Francisco: Jossey-Bass, 1979.

Jantsch, Erich. *The Self-Organizing Universe: Scientific and Human Implications of the Emerging Paradigm of Evolution*. Oxford: Pergamon, 1980.

Jenkins, J. Craig. "Resource Mobilization Theory and the Study of Social Movements." *Annual Review of Sociology*. 1983, *9*, 527–553.

Kanter, Rosabeth Moss. *The Change Masters: Innovation for Productivity in the American Corporation*. New York: Simon & Schuster, 1983.

Knapp, Joan and Leta Davis. "Scope and Varieties of Experiential Learning." In Morris T. Keeton, and Pamela J. Tate, (Eds.). *Learning by Experience—What, Why, How*. New Directions in Experiential Learning No. 1. San Francisco: Jossey-Bass, 1978.

Lawler, Edward E. *High-Involvement Management*. San Francisco: Jossey-Bass, 1986.

Lofland, John. "White-Hot Mobilization Strategies of a Millenarian Movement." In Mayer N. Zald and John D. McCarthy (Eds.). *The Dynamics of Social Movements*. Cambridge, Mass.: Winthrop, 1979.

McCarthy, John D. and Mayer N. Zald. *The Trend in Social Movements in America: Professionalization and Resource Mobilization*. Morristown, N.J.: General Learning Press, 1973.

McCarthy, John D. and Mayer N. Zald. "Resource Mobilization and Social Movements." *American Journal of Sociology*, 1977, *82* (6), 1212–1214.

Niebuhr, Herman, Jr. *Revitalizing American Learning: A New Approach That Just Might Work*. Belmont, Calif.: Wadsworth, 1984.

Schmeidler, Emily. *Shaping Ideas and Actions: CORE, SCLC, and SNCC in the Struggle for Equality, 1960-1966*, unpublished doctoral dissertation, 1980.

Snow, David A., Burke E. Rockford, Jr., Steven K. Worden, and Robert D. Benford. "Frame Alignment and Mobilization." *American Sociological Review*, 1986, *51* (4), 464–481.

Talburtt, Margaret. *A Question of Transformation: Post-Secondary Education's Responses to Adult Learners and CAEL's Role in These Changes*. Ann Arbor, Mich.: Formative Evaluation Research Associates, November 1986.

U. S. Department of Education. *Involvement in Learning: Realizing the Potential of American Higher Education*. Washington, D.C.: U. S. Government Printing Office, 1984.

Van de Ven, Andrew and Gordon Walker. "The Dynamics of Interorganizational Coordination." *Administrative Science Quarterly*, 1984, *29* (4), 598–621.

Washington Center. *Preparing Humanists for Work: A National Study of Undergraduate Internships in the Humanities*. Washington, D.C.: The Washington Center, 1984.

Willingham, Warren W., Richard Burns, and Thomas Donlon. *Current Practices in the Assessment of Experiential Learning*. Working Paper No. 1. Columbia, Md.: CAEL, 1975.

Wilson, James Q. *Political Organizations*. New York: Basic Books, 1973.

Zald, Mayer N. "Macro Issues in the Theory of Social Movements." Paper delivered at the annual meeting of the American Sociological Association, Boston, Mass., 1979.

Zald, Mayer N. and Roberta Ash. "Social Movement Organizations: Growth, Decay and Change." *Social Forces*, 1966, *44* (3), 327–341.

2

The Genetics of Innovation

James W. Hall

Colleges and universities are the secular churches of America. They are in the business of changing people, if not saving souls. Their great libraries are temples of knowledge, their classrooms the place to sit at the feet of the gods. Their servants sometimes act more out of value and principle than greed and self-interest, and this lends special character to the universities' discourse and modes of action. Moreover, the secular church has its saints and its missionaries, and its zeal for outreach and access spreads its message to all who will listen.

Although closely connected historically to church and state, European prototypes for the American university did not reach out as socially inclusive institutions, limiting their mission and service to an elect clientele. American counterparts became, over three centuries, vastly different institutions. The difference is found in fundamental elements in the environment of the New World. American colleges and universities, generally independent of either national or external control, imbibed deeply in the environmental spirits of egalitarianism, pluralism and individualism. From their earliest beginnings, these institutions displayed a tendency to reach out, to convert the unwashed, to carry the word into the wilderness.

Within this missionary character may be found many of the roots of innovation in the American university. Successful leaders of innovation in the American college and university have often been individuals produced by an open, expansive social environment. As a result, such leaders have expressed in their values and commitments support for change and reform that embraces inclusiveness, opportunity, outreach, and extension. Thus, even as America built great research universities, the most consistently promoted reforms were those which expanded student access and designed curricula responsive to student and social need. More often than not the key figures in the history of American collegiate education have been individuals associated firmly with these goals.

As early as the 1820s, for example (a time of vigorous building of democratic institutions across a rapidly expanding North American landscape), George Ticknor, the first American to do advanced scholarly work at a German university, asked basic questions of traditional Harvard practices. He queried the appropriate length of the academic calendar, suggested that students be classified by talent and achievement, decried the lack of course offerings which might be directly useful to young men, and criticized the prevailing mode of learning by recitation. At about the same time, Amherst professor Jacob Abbott proposed that colleges should provide a curriculum which supported more adequately society's needs for modern languages, engineering, practical physics and history. At Nashville, Phillip Lindsley urged the creation of a European style university which would present the full humanist tradition, BUT which would offer curricula responsive to the practical needs of a highly diverse Tennessee population. By the 1830s, Charles Finney had admitted Black and Women students to Oberlin.

Ezra Cornell is remembered for founding a college "where any person can find instruction in any study." By the early 1870s, Cornell offered a full range of vocational, professional and applied science courses and enrolled 250 students in what was then the largest entering class in American collegiate history. The rise of the Land Grant universities and the belief that all citizens should have a shot, spread rapidly. By the turn of the century, state universities offered numerous extension programs for adults, mostly farmers. In 1906, President Charles Van Hise said that General Extension at Wisconsin made "the boundaries of the university campus coterminous with the boundaries of the state."

To continue this much too rapid and selective romp over three complex centuries, the explosive developments in access and extension which followed World War II were also rooted in the American Condition. The tradition of innovation, demonstrated in the success of community colleges, new school/college opportunity programs, previously unimagined financial aids arrangements, and new off-campus and adult degree programs, are all mainstream responses to the American social environment.

Perhaps more interesting is the existence of a continuum of commitment to these goals. That commitment finds focus in certain institutions at a particular time. For an intensive period a certain college or program commands the energies and loyalty of a group of persons interested in reform. Over time these people go out as missionaries. They are disciples, if you will, individuals who transmit the word to other places and people, and so become links in a chain of reform and innovation. Even though hands are not literally laid on, the fire is carried.

Innovation is usually created through a single individual responding to perceived external needs. Ralph Waldo Emerson recognized this in his Essay on Politics, observing that "everyone of [the State's] institutions. . .was once the act of a single man [sic]." He described an institution as "the lengthened shadow of one man."

But such shadow casters do not rise from nothing. Significant and lasting innovation doesn't just happen. It is built upon a strong conceptual foundation of social analysis and knowledge about how students learn. As a consequence, innovation seldom appears in a vacuum. Nothing comes from nothing. There is a pattern of genesis, incubation and diffusion for innovation. There is a linked chain of successful leaders, a clear lineage among those who have been most effective. Important families of such leadership may develop in one institution. Seminal innovators attract other creative and energetic individuals, and, after gaining experience in a kind of mentor relationship, these individuals move on to energize programs elsewhere.

One example of this kind of human idea-chain begins with Alexander Meiklejohn at Wisconsin around 1930, flows to Robert Hutchins at Chicago in the 1940s, then outward to colleges such as St. John's, Shimer, Brooklyn, and Berkeley through leaders who had wrestled deeply with the Great Books approach. Scott Buchanan worked under Robert Hutchins at Chicago before going to St. John's, and he had been a student in a Meiklejohn seminar at Amherst. Joseph Tussman worked with Hutchins before initiating Tussman college at Berkeley. Harry Gideonse, an export from the Chicago faculty and president of Brooklyn College from 1939 to 1966, did not bring the Great Books to New York, but this experience with innovation spawned a number of new and special academic programs for adults, experiments with the core curriculum, exemption from required courses through examination, and student counselling. Gideonse expressed what innovative leaders required: A president should be "an educator in his own right."[1] Goddard College under Royce Pitkin spawned a lineage that can be traced through Arthur Chickering (George Mason University) to such contemporaries as Thomas Clark (Rockland Community College), Jack Lindquist (Goddard), and Douglas Johnstone (Empire State). The New York Education Department under Algo Henderson spawned a highly innovative line reaching from James Allen to Ewald Nyquist and Donald Nolan. Thus a penchant for successful innovation recurs through a chain of reformers—individuals who have been nurtured by an older innovator, have thought deeply and philosophically about the purposes and modes of higher learning, and have made important commitments to the social environment within which that learning occurs.

Such recent centers have been Antioch College, Goddard College, Amherst and St. John's, Chicago, Empire State College (SUNY)[2] , and a national membership organization originally established to promote experiential learning and recognize non-formal academic credit, but in recent times known as the Council for Adult and Experiential Learning (CAEL). For the past 15 years, CAEL has operated both as harmony and counterpoint for innovators and reformers from across the nation who have found in this organization a source of ideas, energy and collegial support.

At the center of CAEL has been Morris T. Keeton, its founding president and intellectual and spiritual leader. While it is easier in retrospect to see the linkages, it is difficult to assess precisely how the many influences which converge upon a single person over a lifetime get translated into the ideas and actions taken by that person. Clearly, for Keeton, the most intense, extended and integrating set of experiences were those as a faculty member, and later, an administrator, at Antioch college. Keeton arrived at Antioch in 1937 as an assistant professor of Philosophy and as college pastor, the same year that Scott Buchanan initiated his reforms at St. John's College. At Antioch Keeton found a strong, nurturing tradition of faculty acculturation, especially through the "Tuesday evening group." On those evenings senior members of the faculty discussed how they taught particular courses. They infused a sensitivity among other teachers about how students actually learned, what worked and what did not. Young instructors were deeply influenced in such a setting, and modelled their own teaching in interaction with these experiences of their older mentors.

Keeton calls it the "Antioch culture." That culture had its roots far back in the nineteenth century when Antioch was founded by Horace Mann. But its more recent ethos descended from the presidency of Arthur E. Morgan who, during and after the 1920s, developed many of the programs for which Antioch has become most noted.

Algo Henderson, dean under Morgan from 1936 until 1949, saw in Antioch a training ground for democracy. Henderson later was founder of the Center for Higher Education at Michigan and a member of the Berkeley faculty. Immediately after leaving Antioch he became New York State's Commissioner of Education, thereby linking Antioch culture to the chain of important New York innovators mentioned earlier.

Henderson was succeeded as dean by W. B. Alexander, a mathematician whom Keeton describes as his administrative mentor. Alexander's tenure spanned that of four Antioch presidents, the first Henderson himself. The second was Douglas MacGregor (1948–1954), who as a psychologist known for the Theory X and Y research, encouraged the use of conscious group process and T-grouping. The third president was Samuel B. Gould (1954–1959), whom Keeton describes as a "hard-nosed but humane manager." Gould also came to New York as chancellor of the State University, bringing with him Ernest L. Boyer, another important link in the innovative lineage. Fourth was James Dixon (1959–1975). Dean Alexander was the implementer for all these presidents, providing the necessary consultation and personal attention which gained the essential faculty support for change and reform.

When President Gould obtained a Ford Foundation grant to study the Antioch educational system, Alexander asked Keeton to chair the study and the Educational Policy Committee. Through these activities Keeton became associate dean, his first administrative title. He also came to lead a four-year teaching experiment, a significant critical study of teaching and learning at Antioch. By 1965 Keeton had teased out a new Freshman year program which introduced for the first time some of the key findings from the earlier research—narrative evaluation rather than letter grades for student evaluation, and highly individualized student programs of study. With strong support from President Dixon (whom Keeton describes as willing to support "intelligence and creativity"), Antioch led the way in many of the educational reforms which were soon to become widespread in American undergraduate education.

Antioch, building upon its earlier emphasis on cooperative and experiential learning, had from the 1950s sponsored extensive year abroad work-study opportunities for students. In 1959 the college also initiated a Master of Arts in Teaching program, offered during summers for teachers. This led Keeton, in his new role as dean of faculty, to take the key decision for Antioch to absorb the Putney Graduate School of Education in Vermont (1964). This established both the principle and the practice of Antioch's distant learning centers. Shortly the concept was taken up on a truly national scale, with centers soon appearing at Los Angeles, San Francisco, Seattle, Boston, Santa Barbara, Philadelphia, and a law school in Washington, D.C. In this way one of the most important new ideas in American higher education—the development of off-campus learning centers—occurred. Antioch operated a "college in dispersion," difficult to manage given its geographic "campus," but well placed for dissemination of its experiential model. Keeton was asked to manage the network!

Although Keeton continued at Antioch until 1977, when he resigned to accept the presidency of CAEL, he shifted physically to Columbia, Maryland in 1969. Dixon and Keeton did not always see eye-to-eye on administrative strategy, and much "give and take" ensued between them. Eventually Dixon shifted Keeton out of line responsibility to a staff role as Chief Academic Officer responsible for quality control, program approval, licensing, and accreditation of the elements of this national network.

One innovative idea frequently leads to another, and the idea of an association of experimenting institutions gestated with Royce "Tim" Pitkin, founding president of Goddard College in Vermont. Since both Pitkin and Dixon were more instigators than implementers, the responsibility for promoting this new intercollegiate network fell to a protégé of Keeton and Dixon, Samuel Baskin. Baskin had directed the earlier Antioch educational study, and as director of Institutional Research became president of the Union for Experimenting Colleges and Universities in 1965. Although Pitkin remonstrates in his writings about the stealing of the new organization by Antioch[3], it was Antioch which provided the resources and staff to operate the network. After some years of affiliation, including the founding of *Change* magazine as a voice for the Union, Baskin gained a major Ford grant in 1971 to initiate a "University Without Walls." This consortium of degree-granting institutions offered open learning programs at each campus, thereby spreading the use of educational policies and precepts developed at Antioch and Goddard during the 1960s. Dissemination now occurred on a grand scale.

From this background, it is possible to see how Keeton's experiences and commitments at Antioch shaped him for leadership of CAEL. Founded as a collaborative experiment and based at the Educational Testing Service to test the awarding of college-level credit for experiential, non-collegiate learning, under Keeton CAEL rapidly established a national network of individuals and institutions committed to implementing prior learning assessment programs. Research, experiments and action became linked. That story is fully told in Zelda Gamson's history of CAEL[4]. Suffice it to say here, the human chain was linked through Morris Keeton to a whole new group of educational leaders, researchers, and practitioners, and so disseminated across a national, even international landscape.

But how did Morris Keeton combine a theorist's philosophic and educational concepts with a practitioner's capacity for dissemination and implementation? And how did he get other people to do the right things? Perhaps some hint of this unusual combination of personal qualities can be found in his early academic training.

As an undergraduate student, and later in his first teaching post at Southern Methodist University, Morris Keeton came under the intellectual influence of I. K. Stephens, chair of the Philosophy department. Stephens had been mentored at Harvard by Clarence I. Lewis, whose explorations of "Conceptualistic Pragmatism" in *Mind and the World Order*[5] offered a path between the wholly empiricist trends of the time and the ideational philosophers of the past. In that heady Harvard of Whitehead, Hocking, Lovejoy and Sheffler, Morris Keeton took his doctorate, writing about the work of the biologist/philosopher, Edmund Montgomery. The influence of these studies and of Lewis' work made Keeton somewhat critical of John Dewey's reigning theory of knowledge, more open to a pragmatic testing of the clash of purposes and ideas within actual learning situations.

Scratch still deeper and one finds in Morris Keeton's past a strong Protestant religious tradition. As a Texas Methodist, ethical and moral issues applied in the practical situations of life were more important than highly abstract theological canons. Fairness, honesty and integrity seemed to a youthful Keeton the central arbiters against which one might arrive at rational choices for behavior and action. Such commitments led Keeton away from the study of theology and preparation for the ministry (although he was later ordained as Pastor at Antioch). But this background lends insight to his extensive volunteer service as a Conscientious Objector in World War II. It helps one to understand why he accepted the appointment at Antioch, rather than in one of the developing research university philosophy departments. It illuminates his lifelong interest in learning as it affected individual, differentiated, human students. If a life often seems to consist of diversity, even random occurrences, it is nonetheless possible in retrospect to discern direction, continuity and purpose.

Who will be those most linked to Morris Keeton in the continuing passing of educational reform? So many have been touched by their association that it would be difficult to identify them all. Yet among them should be counted individuals, such as Arthur W. Chickering, John Strange, and George Pruitt, whose early work with CAEL stimulated important learning for many.

Another is the University of Michigan philosopher, Richard Meisler, Keeton's student as an Antioch undergraduate and instructor. Meisler used Keeton's *Manual of Critical Thinking Exercises* in his own teaching, and later attempted to institute an alternative learning center at State University of New York's College at Buffalo. He probably lacked some of the hardheaded practicality of his mentor, for that program was discontinued after a few years.

More recently, Keeton's work has been applied to creating new connections between higher learning and the nation's workforce through direct collaboration with corporations and labor unions. His protégés in this are Pamela Tate, president-elect of CAEL, Lois Lamdin, director of the Great Valley Business Development and Training Center, and David Justice, dean of the School of New Learning at DePaul University. Together, this generation of innovators, like their mentor, link both theory and application in what is a significant emerging direction for postsecondary education in the next decades.

So the torch is passed to another generation, and the great American democratic experiment with learning and opportunity for all is entrusted to others. Of course it is possible to understand the history and the trajectory of American higher education as an ever-widening circle, gradually encompassing more people in increasingly responsive programs and flexible curricula. But history does not just happen by itself. Rather it is persons who forge the chain, who pass the ideas and their application along from one time and place to another. Their deeds then become part of the intellectual and spiritual heritage which guides and inspires all. In that procession, Morris T. Keeton is within the legacy of forward looking American practitioners of invention and innovation—idealistic, practical, entrepreneurial, and decent. In the final analysis, perhaps the university *is* a church.

Footnotes

1. Murray M. Horowitz, *Brooklyn College: The First Half-Century* (N.Y.: Brooklyn College Press, 1981). pp. 46–50.
2. For example, no less than 13 individuals associated in the 1970s with the founding and development of Empire State College have moved to positions of primary leadership at another institution of higher education.
3. Ann Giles Benson and Frank Adams, Eds., *To Know For Real: Royce S. Pitkin and Goddard College* (Vermont: Adamant Press, 1987).
4. Zelda F. Gamson, *Higher Education and the Real World: The Story of CAEL* (Wolfeboro, N.H.: Longwood Academic, 1989).
5. Clarence I. Lewis, *Mind and the World Order.*

3

Two Heroes for Adult Learners

Malcolm S. Knowles

As we celebrate New Year's Eve in the year 1999 and reflect on the "heroes" of adult education in the twentieth century—individuals who made giant contributions to the shaping of our movement—several names will come to mind. Frederick Keppel, president of the Carnegie Corporation of New York, provided the vision of an integrated national movement and sponsored the conferences and grants that led to the founding of the American Association for Adult Education in 1926. Morse Cartwright, the Executive director of the association during its first quarter century, gave leadership in providing a coherent organizational structure to the field and laid the foundation for the establishment of adult education as a field of graduate study at Teachers College, Columbia University in 1932. Edward Thorndike, Cyril Houle, and Allen Tough gave legitimacy to adult learning as a subject for serious research in their pioneering studies published in 1928, 1961, and 1967, respectively. No doubt additional contributors to the shaping of our field will achieve "hero" status in the perspective of time.

But I would like to single out two individuals whose contributions have special significance in the context of this volume: Edward Lindeman and Morris Keeton. Interestingly, both of these "heroes" came out of the discipline of philosophy and gave the concepts of "experiential learning" and "non-traditional study" intellectual respectability.

Edward Lindeman

Edward Lindeman was the classic example of a non-traditional adult learner. Forced from childhood to work as a laborer to help support an impoverished family, his only schooling was through sporadic attendance at a Lutheran parochial school. Determined to get a college education, however, he applied for admission without a high school diploma to the Michigan Agricultural College (later Michigan State University) and was admitted as a sub-freshman in 1907 when he was twenty-two years old. After graduation four years later, he became editor of a rural journal, an assistant minister, an agricultural extension agent, and a teacher in several small colleges—all the time reading voraciously, publishing two books and many articles, and taking leadership roles in several professional societies. In 1917, at age thirty-two, he was invited to join the faculty of the New York School of Social Work to teach philosophy. He retired in 1950.

25

During his entire career Lindeman was especially intrigued with his work with adult learners, and in 1926 he published his classic book, *The Meaning of Adult Education,* in which he encapsulated the insights about adult learners he had gained both as an adult learner and as a facilitator of adult learners. When I entered the field of adult education in 1935, this book was the scriptural text by which I—and most of my age cohort—became converted to the mission of facilitating adult learning in the philosophical foundation of our field.

I should like to share a few quotations to support his "hero" status:

First, regarding individuals' goals and needs, which it is the educators' mission to serve:

> In what areas do most people appear to find life's meaning? We have only one pragmatic guide: meaning must reside in the things for which people strive, the goals they set for themselves, their wants, needs, desires, and wishes. . . .Viewed from the standpoint of adult education, such personalities seem to want among other things, intelligence, power, self-expression, freedom, creativity, appreciation, enjoyment, fellowship. . . .Briefly, they want to improve themselves; this is their realistic and primary aim. (Lindeman, pp. 13–14)

Regarding the teaching-learning process:

> I am conceiving adult education in terms of a new technique for learning, a technique as essential to the college graduate as to the unlettered manual worker. It represents a process by which the adult learns to become aware of and to evaluate his experience. To do this he cannot begin by studying "subjects" in the hope that some day this information will be useful. On the contrary, he begins by giving attention to situations in which he finds himself, to problems which include obstacles to his self-fulfillment. Facts and information from the differentiated spheres of knowledge are used, not for the purpose of accumulation, but because of need in solving problems. In this process the teacher finds a new function. He is no longer the oracle who speaks from the platform of authority, but rather the guide, the pointer-out who also participates in learning in proportion to the vitality and relevancy of his facts and experiences. In short, my conception of adult education is this: a cooperative venture in nonauthoritarian, informal learning, the chief purpose of which is to discover the meaning of experience; a quest of the mind which digs down to the roots of preconceptions which formulate our conduct; a technique of learning for adults which makes education coterminous with life and hence elevates living itself to the level of adventurous experiment. (Gessner, p. 160)

And regarding the intimate relationship between this process and democratic philosophy, Lindeman wrote:

> One of the chief distinctions between conventional and adult education is to be found in the learning process itself. None but the humble become good teachers of adults. In an adult education class the student's experience counts for as much as the teacher's knowledge. Both are exchangeable at par. Indeed, in some of the best adult classes it is sometimes difficult to discover who is learning most, the teacher or the students. This two-way learning is also reflected in the management of adult education enterprises. Shared learning is duplicated by shared authority. In conventional education the pupils adapt themselves to the curriculum offered, but in adult education the pupils aid in formulating the curricula. . .Under democratic conditions authority is of the group. This is not an easy lesson to learn, but until it is learned democracy cannot succeed. (Gessner, p. 166)

David W. Stewart, his most recent biographer, sums up Lindeman's "Agenda for Lifelong Education in America" as follows:

About the adult learner:

1. Life-centered adult learning opportunities of every type should be available and easily accessible to every citizen in a democracy.
2. All learners or prospective learners have the right to participate in determining the content and method of learning.
3. Adult education should develop, as well as serve, adult learners.
4. Ease of access to adult learning opportunities should be the right of every citizen.

About curriculum:

1. Value distinction between credit and noncredit programming should be removed.
2. Life situations should be tapped as the starting point for adult learning.
3. Societal problems should trigger associated adult education programs.
4. Adult educators should build into their programs components designed to serve the values of democracy.
5. Subject-based educational programs should be modified or adapted to better serve the needs of adults.
6. Social action programs should have adult education components.
7. Vocational education should be designed around the needs that the learner believes to be important.
8. Adult learning programs beginning with the assumption that learning should follow from life, rather than subject-matter orientation, should be instituted.
9. Process is part of curriculum.

About the teaching-learning transaction:

1. Experience-rooted learning is the essence of a teaching-learning transaction involving an adult; experience should be employed in every possible way in learning situations of adults.
2. Resources, in and out of traditional educational settings, should be identified and used to facilitate learning.
3. Good questions from a teacher are better than facile answers.
4. Programs that recognize the validity of experience-based learning should be encouraged and supported. (To which Stewart adds, "Lindeman would undoubtedly be excited by the efforts of Morris Keeton and others to develop protocols for systematically assessing and recognizing the educational value of prior experiential learning in higher education and other settings.")
5. The teaching-learning transaction should be considered democratic territory.
6. Individualized instructional arrangements should be encouraged.
7. The lecture system of instruction should be de-emphasized in favor of more interactive methods.
8. Wherever possible, arrangements should be made for adult learners to have lively interchanges with fellow learners.
9. The methods of evaluation in programs of learning toward self actualization must be internal, not externally imposed.
10. Volunteers are a valuable resource in adult education programs and should be used where possible.
11. Adult educators should use the democratic political process as a vehicle for facilitating education of the electorate.
12. Andragogical concepts should be built into existing formal systems that serve adults (Stewart, pp. 228–232).

Morris Keeton

With a more traditional background of schooling and higher education than Lindeman's, as is documented elsewhere in this volume, Keeton discovered the magic of experiential learning as a professor of philosophy and administrator at Antioch College and as a director of international seminars for the American Friends Service Committee. As executive director and then president of the Council for the Advancement of Experiential Learning (1977–1989) he earned the right to title of "hero" for adult learners by promoting (with great success) and providing tools and procedures for the granting of credit for experiential learning by even the most traditional colleges and universities.

Since this aspect of his contribution is so well covered elsewhere in this volume, I should like to put emphasis on what I view to be his great contribution to the future of education—his vision of local or regional systems that will provide access for learners to appropriate educational resources and efficient delivery of services to them:

> Imagine, for example, a region with a convenient array of counseling and diagnostic centers. . . . Such centers should have no pecuniary or other interest in where the student studies or what learning options he or she chooses. They should, however, have comprehensive knowledge and materials about these options and knowledgeable counselors who can assist a student in choosing wisely. Imagine further a region in which all of the libraries and resource banks of intellectual materials are interconnected by one catalog and reference-service system, with membership in that system being a right of citizenship in the region and with daily delivery of wanted materials by wire or by courier to anyone anywhere in the region. Imagine a regional agreement among businesses, agencies of all levels of government, schools, libraries, and other service agencies whereby space available is shared, staff time for upgrading of competence is allocated for learning as part of work, and staff competent to teach are encouraged to devote some of their time each year to the pool of teaching talent deployed among the instructional institutions. Suppose that the right to learn has been interpreted as permitting the learner to spend his or her allotment in any prudent pattern that makes possible a learning plan developed after use of one of the regional diagnostic and counseling centers. Suppose, finally, that state and federal aids to institutions of postsecondary education have been rationalized to foster efficiency in this total system and to foster competition among service deliverers in doing a good job for the resources used.
>
> In such a system for educational services, the student could enter at his or her choice any of several diagnostic and mentor-service centers (among which competition in quality of service might be fostered). With the aid of the chosen center, the student could gain access to any of the learning options for which he or she is qualified and through which he or she could most effectively and conveniently be assisted to learn. (Keeton, pp. 8–9).

Adult learners are enjoying a much richer environment for learning now and face a much richer future because of these two heroes.

References

Gessner, Robert G. *The Democratic Man: Selected Writings of Eduard C. Lindeman.* Boston: Beacon Press, 1956.

Keeton, Morris T. and Associates. *Experiential Learning: Rationale, Characteristics, and Assessment.* San Francisco: Jossey-Bass, 1976.

Lindeman, Eduard C. *The Meaning of Adult Education.* Montreal: Harvest House, 1961.

Stewart, David W. *Adult Learning in America: Eduard Lindeman and His Agenda for Lifelong Education.* Malabar, FL, 1987.

4

Irreverent Reflections on Educational Innovation

William H. Warren

This brief essay is written in tribute to Morris T. Keeton who knows a true innovation when he meets one, which is usually before anyone else.

Most of you will remember educational innovation and perhaps will have pondered, as I have, its decline. Somewhere along in the past decade or more it went out of fashion, but when it was in style it was magnetic, heady, confrontational and uncomfortable for many to have around. It survives in a few quiet corners here and there, but nowhere in the grand style of the 60s and early 70s. Perhaps that is just as well; educational institutions are limited in their tolerance for upheaval, and the seams of many institutional fabrics were showing the strain.

The innovations themselves, of course, met a variety of fates. Some, because they were good ideas, responsive to acknowledged need, well-executed or just lucky, joined the mainstream, thereby forfeiting the right to be innovations; they were among the victories, long-term and consequential. Some suffered from bad conception, bad design or bad timing and met an early and often well-deserved death. I suppose such an outcome for some of those was a victory too—for education. And there were the victims of internecine strife, fodder in the political battles for control of curricula, faculty mores and institutions. The real losses were scattered on this battleground, their quality never really tested, their potential unknown. And then some fell victim to that strange disease that sooner or later seems to afflict all movements: righteous arrogance, a.k.a. arrogant righteousness. But more on that in a moment.

Curiously, I have been a partner in educational innovation—curious because I am not by nature a rebel. But I shared the vision that there must be better ways to educate and, as a college administrator, believed that educational institutions should serve learners (in some quarters a radical notion in itself). I also was perceived as having some skill in getting things accomplished within the academy. All that served to engage me as a co-conspirator in educational innovation. Further, after a traditional undergraduate education, I was attracted to non-traditional institutions, such as the College of the University of Chicago, the invention of Robert Maynard Hutchins and his colleagues, and Antioch College, the first and primary liberal arts work-study college. The principal thing they had in common was their singularity (warning enough for someone more astute than I). For nearly three decades these anomalous institutions gave me the ground on which to be a participant-observer during the peak years of educational innovation.

"It was the best of times, it was the worst of times, it was the age of wisdom, it was the age of foolishness, it was the epoch of belief, it was the epoch of incredulity,. . .it was the spring of hope. . . ." Charles Dickens in *A Tale of Two Cities* had inadvertently described the mood of the 1960s and early 1970s. In those years critics likened educational institutions to cemeteries, full of dead bodies and monuments. Within the colleges and universities there were the anointed, who proposed to change all that, and there were the others. Wisdom and foolishness, belief and incredulity ran rampant among both the innovators and the "traditionalists," to use one of the kinder appellations. There was a regrettable lack of sound educational research on both conventions and innovations, but no lack of conviction. So we proceeded on faith—faith in technology, in experience, in common sense and in our own wisdom.

It was the best of times, rife with surprises. The Young Turks turned out to be middle-aged with tenure, usually "locals" whose futures were invested in the institution rather than in the discipline at the national level. Among the innovators, interdepartmental and cross-disciplinary cooperation flowed like water. Science and humanities professors defied C.P. Snow to find common ground. Hallway conversations fairly reeked of substance. Prolonged meetings, not always amicable, confronted fundamental educational questions. The focus shifted from teachers and teaching to learners and learning. The road to change was paved with unity and new alliances, bounded by unparalleled esprit. The idyllic community of scholars was at hand.

And it was the worst of times. Good and evil, innovation and convention were unambiguous. As the innovators evolved their arcane lexicon—"content modules, narrative evaluations, delivery modes"—the "ins" and the "outs" ceased to communicate. Lectures and other traditional teaching styles were demeaned. Innovators were determined to save their colleagues' souls for change, even without the consent of those to be saved. Grand plans for institutional renewal called for the participation of the unconverted, so they were often swept over by the tide of change, feeling they had no real choice but to acquiesce in innovations they could not endorse. Or they were simply circumvented; as one described it, "The decisions aren't made where I am anymore." Cultivation of reluctant faculty through discourse with their colleagues gave way to coercion. Uncooperative faculty were ostracized or, worse, terminated; departments ceased open discussion in their meetings, or stopped meeting. The prospect of imminent change was unbearably threatening to some faculty. To others, the proposals for change seemed intolerable nonsense and the perpetrators beneath contempt. Rational decision-making succumbed to political mischief as committees were stacked and meeting agendas unannounced. Faculties lined up to do battle on the structure and control of curricula, grading vs. evaluation, the relative status of teaching vs. learning, credit for out-of-course learning, and other issues, and the academy was split asunder. Institutions reeled, absorbing the shock of change, then assimilated some innovations and righted themselves. When the tide turned after Vietnam and the shock of Kent State had subsided (but not just because of them), convention was gradually restored on most campuses, and large scale innovation slipped into obscurity, if not disrepute.

It was "the spring of hope." This age of innovation was dominated by a vision of a different future, a view of what higher education might become that was nurtured by dissatisfaction with what it was. It offered to faculty and students alike outlets for their frustration and focus for their creativity as partners in learning. The vision drew like-minded converts from all the disciplines and tapped unknown reservoirs of energy to design and execute the changes. But within this arena of hope, the seeds of its own destruction were germinating.

Since moves for change are inherently critical of the status quo, they are usually stoutly defended against by those with even a modest stake in things as they are, and confrontation ensues. Acceptable innovations enable all the contenders to win something: gains offset losses or, at least, the changes pose a tolerable threat to the status quo. In such a context, innovations by individuals, in classrooms, or settings removed from the institutional core are at lesser risk than more comprehensive changes that challenge established policy and authority.

Educational innovation too often behaved like a movement, wrapped in its private language, convinced of its own truth, certain about the locus of evil, intolerant of the opposition, and devoted to winning. At times, change seemed an end in itself, irrespective of merit. Too often, conviction was augmented by self-righteousness and essential skepticism was abandoned for creed. In the end, the age of innovation fell victim to institutional fatigue, its own vanity and failure to honor its opposition and the cyclical swing back toward tradition. In the rising tide of reaction, the innovative spirit lost its dazzle, was consumed by irony and faded from public view.

Not that innovation came to a halt. In higher education it went underground, with new names but neither banners nor fanfare. The drive, as well as the need, for educational change has persisted but is couched in more humble terms, the work of individuals and small groups in modes more evolutionary than rebellious. Less dramatic, less intense, often apart from the institutional core, change today shuns confrontation with the establishment, seeking to live in harmony with it.

Much to the relief of college administrations everywhere, innovation has entered a gentler age, preferring to provide exemplary alternatives rather than to transform institutions overnight. The ball is clearly over, but the dance goes on.

5

Transatlantic Connections

Norman Evans

Not too many people have seen Morris Keeton being organized, directed, cajoled and generally bossed about by a four-year old girl. Nor was it his granddaughter; it was mine. The scene: a car parked on a gravel driveway outside our house in South Oxfordshire, England, next to the river Thames and in bright sunlight. The action: aircraft simulation in alternating roles as passenger, navigator, pilot, requiring instant moves from the front seat to the back seat, with instructions issued peremptorily from one small girl. Earlier, as co-workers they had picked up a spilled jarful of pumpkin seeds. (Who knows why they were there? No doubt Morris could produce an answer.) Later, hand in hand, the tall and the short of it, they walked to see riverboats passing through Culham Lock, the guide and the guided.

Passenger, navigator, pilot, co-worker and guide. Not a bad description, it occurred to me, of the many roles Morris has managed to fulfill in CAEL. And within that little scene, two of his outstanding qualities were made manifest: interest/curiosity and empathy. I suspect that people who believe they know him also feel they are known to him, but also in a subtle way, each knows a different Morris.

The very first time I "met" Morris, I did not know he was there. It was at a CAEL Regional Assembly in Boston, winter 1980. I was to take a session on "Some English Observations on Current Assessment of Prior Experiential Learning (APEL) Practice in America." John Strange had encouraged me to think about possible collaboration which could promote APEL activities in Great Britain. Morris sat in the front row, as I concluded later, to look me over. Apparently he did not disapprove. Qualified approval, let us say. For if nothing else, he can be a very cautious man. Active approval came after a gentle, firm, penetrating grilling at an airport meeting which proved to be the gateway for APEL Anglo-American collaboration.

In the spring of 1980, Morris had his first Study Tour in England, and he helped launch the idea of APEL at a day conference in the Policy Studies Institute, which became my base. Without his support, there would have been no director's grant from the W.K. Kellogg Foundation for 1980-81, which put in the foundations for APEL development in Britain. Nor would there have been the Scholar Exchange component to Project Learn II, which over a six-year period enabled 80 plus British academics and administrators on accrediting bodies, the Department of Education and Science and the Training Agency of the Department of Employment to visit colleges and universities on the East Coast of the U.S. And without that, the carefully laid plans to engage senior British figures with their hands on the levers would have come to nothing. Hence, the particular way that APEL is featuring currently in British public policy could not have happened.

There would be no Learning from Experience Trust (LET). There could have been no CAEL/LET International Seminar in England in 1988, attended by top industrialists and the director of Education Programmes at the Training Agency and convened with an eye on Joint Ventures. And so, as one of the latest developments, there could be no contract between the Trust and the Training Agency for a three-year monitoring and evaluation project of the British Ford Motor Company's version of the U.S. Ford/UAW programme to work out how the further education system could service wider replication of what British Ford calls The Employment Development and Accreditation Programme.

How else could it be that the Secretary of State for Health, a senior cabinet minister in the Thatcher government (she of the misappropriately voiced "we are a grandmother") could have included in an official letter to the chairman of the United Kingdom Central Council for Nursing Homes and Midwives explicit reference to the Trust, with clear expectations that action was expected.

APEL is up and running in Britain, and whilst, of course, it is the case that if neither Morris nor CAEL had existed, some comparable developments associated with the Trust would have taken place, the plain fact is that the APEL developments associated with the Trust came under the orders of Morris's starting pistol in 1980.

Seen from this side of the Atlantic, therefore, I wonder whether chronologically Morris's first effective Joint Venture was not the Transatlantic Connection. Remote control navigator and pilot.

That is all the short of it. The long of it is the extraordinary power for influence generated by this modest, quiet man when his scholarly mind gets engaged. I have never yet had a conversation with him (and happily, such occasions are numerous both in the U.S. and England), without being prompted into some new strand of thinking as he made connections between ideas which floated free in my mind. At a personal level he can be inspiring. Co-worker and guide.

Also in public. In December, 1986, Morris was the keynote speaker at the Annual Conference for Research in Higher Education in Great Britain. The topic was Continuing Education. Project Learn II had just finished. So the audience was treated to a review of the application of CAEL's mission and philosophy across all that range of initiatives. Questions and discussions followed. Syndicate groups followed on. A second plenary came after. So for the best part of the day, APEL held the floor. Skepticism, caution, interest, enthusiasm, were in full flood, homing on assessment, predictably, given the large number of university academics present. The general burden of their response was that it was all very subjective, wasn't it? Where was the objectivity? Morris's answer: "Objectivity is the convergence of the subjective judgments of experts with no conflict of interest in the matter."

Now how can any group of academics seriously dispute that?

And that points to the priceless quality of his intellectual leadership. He is a scholar/explorer of some of the Arctic wastes of higher education. It is the quality of seeing beyond and above, which is a Morris hallmark. Throw him an idea (he has probably thought of it before), and he is off developing, extending, deepening, so that the horizon lifts, and what was previously unimaginable becomes recognizable. Sometimes it may prove to be a chimera. No matter; it is thinking at work. And the rare quality is the facility of anchoring educational practice and theory in the honed hard mind of the philosopher. So whatever airy fairy interpretations some may try to impose on APEL, they cannot get away with it for long. The humane, respectful, optimistic view of the human race implied by APEL is rooted in secure intellectual propositions which leave no room for woolly, substandard dogoodery. Alas, we do not have such a one in Britain. Morris's empathy and interest and seeing beyond are all informed by a powerful intellect.

From time to time, Morris has been my passenger. Like all alert passengers, he takes in the scene through the windows. He has been fascinated by the differential speed of APEL developments in our two countries. Different institutional stances and practices. Different relationships between central and local government and higher education institutions. Different funding mechanisms. Different validation and accreditation procedures. Above all, different sized populations with different cultural and social traditions. They all go to explain why the seed of APEL grows and sometimes blossoms at different seasons and at different parts of the educational field in our two countries. Like all interested passengers, Morris asks the sharp question which makes the native look again.

It is usually not too difficult to find energetic actors in education whose actions are less effective than they ought to be because they are not informed by a coherent philosophy. Many visionaries have no talent for action. Morris somehow manages both. So for 10 years I have had the inestimable privilege and pleasure of having Morris as a friendly navigator, pilot, co-worker, guide and sometimes passenger, as we have tried to adapt for adoption in Great Britain the best I could glean from CAEL and the remarkable groups of men and women drawn to him, and, be it said, learning also what not to do. Neither APEL and CAEL in the U.S., nor LET in Britain, are set in gardens where roses always bloom. Sometimes it is helpful to see other people's weeds before trying to get rid of your own.

It is Morris Keeton's high vocation, drawing people to his vision. It is his high achievement to facilitate the translation of visionary idealism into action, for the benefit of countless men and women on both sides of the Atlantic.

6

The Uncompleted Task

John R. Valley

With a profound apology to Robert Frost, I take the liberty to modify his words:

Two roads diverged in a wood, and we—
We took the one less traveled by,
And that has made a difference.

In the late 1960s and early 1970s, a number of new buzz-words emerged prominently in postsecondary educational circles. Consider the following partial list of ideas and concepts that began to receive serious consideration at that time: external degree, contract learning, university without walls, satellite campus, courses-by-newspaper, open university, lifelong learning, experiential learning, experiential education, and nontraditional learning. It was an era in which proliferating commissions and task forces, both here and abroad, were reporting findings and recommendations calling for a substantial reorientation to learning and education beyond high school. The Faure report in France made the case for lifelong learning. The groundwork was being laid for the British Open University. In our country many state task forces and national study commissions advocated more options and expanded educational opportunity, particularly for adult learners.

This was the era that preceded the founding of such institutions as New York Regents College, Thomas A. Edison College in New Jersey, Empire State College, the Connecticut State Board for Academic Awards, and the Community College of Vermont. It was an era in which programs and services such as the College-Level Examination Program and the College Proficiency Examination Program had just come through their start-up phases and were showing promise for continued acceptance and growth. It was an era, too, before there was any systematic arrangement for reviewing courses taught in business and industry as potential sources of college credit.

But change was in the air. In 1970 Jack N. Arbolino (then Executive Director, Council on College-Level Examinations at the College Board) and myself (then Senior Program Director, College Board Division at Educational Testing Service) were assigned by the officers of the two organizations to examine the potential and problems associated with setting up an external degree program. While neither the College Board nor ETS seriously contemplated sponsoring an external degree program, both needed to determine how best to respond to the many and diverse developments surfacing at that time. The connection between that assignment and "a difference," namely the beginning of CAEL, is, indeed, but a thread. Nonetheless, a thread can be traced.

Our resulting report figured importantly in causing the Commission on Non-traditional Study to be formed under the chairmanship of Samuel B. Gould, Chancellor Emeritus, State University of New York. The commission's report, "Diversity by Design," was issued in 1973. It contained 57 recommendations including the following:

> #47   New devices and techniques should be perfected to measure the outcomes of many
> types of non-traditional study and to assess the educative effects of experience and community
> service.

Shortly thereafter, the Carnegie Corporation of New York invited ETS to submit a proposal to advance the intent of the recommendation.

Warren W. Willingham, assistant vice-president for program research at ETS, developed a proposal for a research and development entitled "Cooperative Assessment of Experiential Learning" which was accepted and funded by Carnegie. At the conclusion of the research, CAEL was transformed into an educational association (Council for the Advancement of Experiential Learning) under Morris Keeton. More recently, in keeping with the expanded range of concerns and interests of its institutional members and of its own activities, the association's name was changed to Council for Adult and Experiential Learning. Thus, by tracing the events detailed above, a connection can be found between the Arbolino-Valley assignment and CAEL.

Morris Keeton was the helmsman who kept CAEL, the research project, from foundering on the rocks of educational politics. And Keeton's vision and dynamic leadership has enabled CAEL, the association, to make a profound difference in expanding educational opportunities and in reducing barriers to further education for learners who, for one reason or another, are not in the educational mainstream.

The "road less traveled" refers to the fact that the Arbolino-Valley report to the officers of CEEB and ETS recommended the establishment of a National University. We assigned a dozen major functions to this agency:

1. NU could award degrees in its own name, based solely on examinations of an individual's learning, no matter where or how that learning took place.
2. NU could jointly award degrees with participating colleges. These would be degrees in which the majority of the requirements would be met by National University credits (credits earned by examination or by the procedure approved under function No. 3 below). The degrees would be awarded by the joint action of the National University and the participating college. In addition, the participating college would continue to award degrees in the traditional way as well.
3. NU could accredit college-level instruction offered outside the colleges and universities. Although the American Council of Education currently evaluates learning in industry and the armed forces, it makes "recommendations" only. The authors of the plan regard this proposed accrediting function as an important and original contribution which would make it possible to recognize individual achievement. It would not entail the accreditation of the agency offering the instruction but would focus on the adequacy of the particular instructional unit under question.

   One objective of this procedure was to make it possible for college-level achievement to be recognized without invariably resorting to the technique of validating examinations. Among the forms of instruction to be considered were correspondence, radio and television courses as well as instruction provided by government, industry, business, unions, the military, social service agencies and foreign institutions.
4. NU could award credits and certificates on the basis of programs such as the Advanced Placement Program, the College-Level Examination Program, and the New York Proficiency Examination Program, as well as on the basis of demonstrated achievement in professional and subprofessional fields.

5. NU would assist students wishing to transfer.
6. NU would encourage the development of all instructional resources, though explicitly not itself providing instruction.
7. NU would maintain records of individual educational accomplishment (a sort of credit bank, an idea which has since resurfaced in many guises).
8. NU would provide an educational counseling and referral service for individuals.
9. NU would provide an advisory and consulting service on education for employers.
10. NU would maintain a program of research and development supportive of continuing education.
11. NU would develop the examinations and other instruments and services necessary to its implementation.
12. NU would maintain an active forum, including publications devoted to the development of continuing education.

In hindsight, I now believe it was a mistake in the 1970s to propose calling the agency or service we envisioned a "National University." The term evoked strong negative and emotional reactions, particularly in the higher education community. Its connotations so fixated readers that they prevented an adequate consideration of the integrated package of needs and concerns that the plan was trying to address. Nevertheless, the work of the Commission on Non-traditional Study and the follow-up response of the educational community has resulted in a substantially different and expanded set of options and opportunities available today than was the case in the early 1970s.

Some may argue that practically all of the functions of the Arbolino-Valley proposal have had development and implementation in some form or other. Nevertheless, the task has not been completed. A more complete response to the needs of non-traditional learners will require movement along three lines:

1. Attending to the geographic maldistribution of existing services and opportunities for learners.

An important perspective was lost in the debate that followed the proposal for a National University. Non-traditional learners are not confined to particular states or geographic areas. They are to be found throughout the nation, albeit they may be concentrated in more populous cities or states. Consequently, if provision for non-traditional learners is via local or state agencies, institutions, and programs, access to services will be limited or non-existent for some learners.

When I recently moved from New Jersey to South Carolina, I was made keenly aware of the differences in services and opportunities in those two states. In this instance, it is not simply a matter of a difference in willingness or interest; New Jersey and South Carolina differ substantially in area, population, culture and economic resources.

We need to attend to the unequal distribution of services and opportunities for non-traditional learners if we are not to shut out numbers of talented adults from postsecondary education. The first unfinished task is to keep a national perspective in the mind's eye.

2. Increasing the utility and utilization of currently available services.

There is no question that non-traditional learning services and opportunities today are much more extensive than was the case twenty years ago. Entirely new programs are currently being offered. Regents College Examination, Regents College Degrees and Empire State College in New York, recognition by the American Council on Education and the New York Regents of courses taught by business, industry and labor, the programs of National Technological University which are available by cable in centers across the nation, portfolio assessment of prior learning as developed and advocated by CAEL and now carried out by hundreds of colleges and universities across the country, other opportunities for distance learning, contract learning, learning through various media, new, widely distributed competence testing mechanisms, all these are examples of promising developments of the last quarter of this century.

Yet, without exception, in every social gathering I find that a majority of those present are not aware of these new opportunities. They are not only uninformed about the kinds of available programs and services, they don't even know where people might go for advice and direction in continuing their educational development.

One reason for this situation is that each program or service attempts to inform, advertise or tout its own offerings. There is little being done to bring a composite portrayal of opportunity to the public through some neutral agency, available to the public in person or through mail, phone or computer.

3. Monitoring in systematic ways demographic, cultural, and social change in the nation and interpreting these changes in terms of new service and opportunity requirements.

It is important to recall that the findings and recommendations of the Commission on Non-traditional Study were based on inquiries and research begun close to twenty years ago. Studies of learner needs, participation patterns, barriers to learning and so on were undertaken for the Commission by the Educational Testing Service, the Center for Research and Development in Higher Education at the University of California at Berkeley, the College Entrance Examination Board, and the Response Analysis Corporation. In addition, the commission conducted open sessions to receive presentations and descriptions of new initiatives, institutions, services and programs.

However, since the commission concluded its work, there has been no comparable comprehensive monitoring of change in this country which has been linked to non-traditional learner interests and needs. From the broad perspective of our national interest, we do not really know the extent to which the plethora of new initiatives undertaken since 1970 either have made a difference or where serious gaps still remain. Of course, there have been many excellent articles and books on subjects related to these concerns, and sponsors of particular programs can and do occasionally report participation, success or experience in their own realms. But what is missing is comprehensive data that can provide a sense of how the new opportunities and easier access to more traditional educational resources are making a difference overall.

Meanwhile, we are all aware that the pace of change in our society is accelerating. The educational demographic profile of the country today is not the same as it was even twenty years ago. The economic base of the nation has shifted from production to service, and the gap between the "haves" and the "have-nots" has grown wider. While we may be conscious of these changes in general, there has not been an adequate integration of how they may interact and what they mean for problems, programs, service and opportunities for non-traditional learners and for service and program providers.

The third unfinished task, therefore, is to put into place an arrangement for systematic monitoring of demographic, cultural and social change and for interpreting these changes in terms of requirements for new programs and services and in terms of modifications required in existing learner opportunities.

It would be advantageous if the organization or agency that might sponsor this kind of activity would do so with a commitment to continue it periodically in the future. Cyclical, periodic and integrated sets of inquiries and investigations would be more efficient, more effective and less expensive than would bringing an entirely new project together on an ad hoc basis every now and then.

Having identified three unfinished tasks, the question remains as to how to proceed. I do not see that there currently exists any institution, organization, association or agency with the responsibility, capability and resources to undertake these three tasks, which, despite my brief outline, are infinitely complex. The assignment might possibly be executed through some new alliance of education, industry, business, government, professional associations and unions. It will require persons with imagination, creativity and leadership to produce an organizational structure to meet the challenge. Will Morris Keeton be available?

Part II

Experiential Learning

7

Portfolio Assessment: Ground Covered and New Frontiers

Joan Knapp

Prologue

When I was asked if I would like to contribute a chapter to this volume in commemoration of Morris' "new frontier" (which is at the same time the end of a major chapter in the history of CAEL and the beginning of a grand new chapter in his life), I was cautioned that my chapter and those of others should be a contribution to the literature of experiential learning and should not be focused solely on Morris' personal contribution to me and my colleagues or, for that matter, to higher education writ large.

In all fairness, I must say the caution was a gentle one and in the service of rewarding the reader by adding to his or her knowledge of experiential learning. We were to take care not to cloy the reader with all our stories and reminiscences about Morris and CAEL, which I am sure are legion among us.

I am not sure I can keep that promise since so much of what I have to say about portfolio assessment is inextricably married to personal and professional relationships which give rise to anecdotes and events that involve CAEL colleagues and particularly Morris. For example, the coda to the title above, "ground covered and new frontiers," aptly describes my personal and professional situation at this point in time as it relates to portfolio assessment.

Prior learning assessment and the portfolio process were so much a part of my life for five years. The CAEL efforts continued after I moved on to other things. CAEL's progress led to refinements that raised assessment standards and ultimately the credibility of the process. Now I find that I am back in this arena again. On a personal level, just as Morris, I am on the edge of a new frontier. But as the bartender said in the musical *Irma La Douce* "that's another story" and one on which I will elaborate later.

My Introduction to CAEL and Portfolio Assessment

My experience with portfolio assessment began in 1974 when, as an ETS staff member, I was "volunteered" for a project. The project was sponsored by the Carnegie Corporation, initiated under the leadership of Morris Keeton in cooperation with ETS and a small consortium of higher education institutions. It was called the Cooperative Assessment of Experiential Learning.

One thing became apparent to me when I attended the first project meeting (which, incidentally, looked like a Who's Who of innovative and non-traditional higher education). "Cooperative" is not an adjective I would have used to describe the group. Lively discussion and differing viewpoints prevailed. This was to be expected given the nature of the non-traditional movement at that time, the intense commitment to experiential learning, and the strong and vocal leadership that was present in the CAEL steering committee. It was an exciting time for me, and I knew at that very first meeting that I had made a personal commitment to the project that went beyond the realm of a typical staff assignment.

Although experiential learning covered both institution-sponsored learning opportunities and learning acquired from non-sponsored life experience, my efforts were to be focused solely on prior experiential learning. I was to target work on two major projects:

1. Defining prior learning and designing a methodology or framework for assessment that could be used by college faculty and administrators. The major purpose of the project was to create a handbook and other materials to be used by faculty and administrators to assist and guide them in student assessment.
2. Creating a faculty development program that would train the trainers of faculty who were engaged in the assessment of experiential learning. The project involved recruiting faculty for train-the-trainer workshops, developing workshop formats and training materials for faculty.

Early Beginnings

Integral to this project work was grappling with the concept of the student portfolio. In those days, portfolio was a term used by a handful of colleges which had developed this tool for evaluating prior learning for college credit. In the main, the portfolio was used in a much narrower sense than it is used today. In the early 1970s it was a file folder or notebook that contained information about a learner's past experiences and accomplishments. The learner was more often that not an adult over thirty who sought to return to college in a special program geared to the adult needs and lifestyle.

One of the first tasks I undertook was to learn more about existing programs. In my naivete, I set out on my journey assuming that my job should center on standardizing the prior learning assessment process in a way that guaranteed reliable and valid results. After all, wasn't that what educational measurement was about? Why else would ETS be involved in such a process?

Programs were visited, directors and faculty interviewed. Phone calls and letters followed with more networking. Learners were questioned about their experiences. Program literature was shared and, best of all, real student portfolios were read and reviewed.

I learned quickly that there were few similarities among the adult degree programs in terms of portfolio format, how learners were guided in developing their documents, and criteria used for evaluating this information. Each institution or program was extremely proud of its program. Each thought that it had the best system.

Other institutions were criticized for not having the appropriate philosophy, effective academic structures, or adequate resources for adult learners. Further, some interviewees candidly expressed resentment and suspicion of a testing organization being involved in this project. They feared that ETS would develop tests or highly objective methods for assessment which they felt were not relevant to the nonacademic learning resulting from adult experiences. In addition to my "experiential learning" about portfolio assessment, I did a review of the literature. There were few hints as to how the assessment of prior learning could be done in a reliable and valid manner, with or without portfolios.

It was not surprising that the majority of faculty in post-secondary institutions criticized such processes openly and, at times, bitterly. These critics forcefully pointed out their grave concerns to adult degree program faculty, who were very often colleagues at their own institutions. These centered on academic standards and value of the degree awarded to all graduates of the institution, receiving graduate institutions, and third parties who employed the graduates of the institutions under question.

The debate was underscored by the probing of the postsecondary accrediting agencies about these matters. The controversy that I had uncovered for myself had long before come to their attention, and they began to question these practices, albeit in a constructive way.

In summary, adult degree programs and portfolio assessment had established a place in higher education. However, the context for this assessment was highly charged. The majority of the academic community was opposed to assessing prior learning and, in turn, found portfolios an inappropriate vehicle for the evaluation of learning. The minority (we estimated some 80 institutions) were proprietary about their programs, reluctant to make changes, affronted by and defensive toward collegial criticism, anxious about the CAEL project, suspicious of ETS involvement. Clearly, there was much work to do.

There was no doubt that our efforts needed to be focused on resolving issues concerning the new student—the adult learner, credibility, ownership, and rigor of prior learning assessment programs. It was critical that any process or methodology developed needed to address these issues during the design phase as well as the implementation phase in that order of importance. This was an unusual strategy for a person who had a Ph.D. in educational measurement and was on the staff of the oldest and largest testing agency in the United States—credibility and ownership before reliability and validity?

I knew from my introductory experiences with CAEL and member and non-member institutions that developing a rigorous methodology without scrupulous attention to the context, politics, and emerging new directions of higher education would ultimately be unsuccessful. I was painfully aware that failure to account for the context could jeopardize the dearly won status of adult degree programs and ultimately affect the opportunity for future adult learners to have access to degree programs that would meet their needs. True, I knew there was a problem and I should proceed carefully, but how to implement my strategy was not readily apparent to me.

Looking back to what actually happened (I sometimes think that we learn more from retrospection than when we are in the heat of experience), I gained guidance and advice for the job ahead of me from those front line educators whom I met in my travels. I'd like to give credit to all of them, but I fear I would leave someone out if I did so. Warren Willingham at ETS helped me to put what I learned into a rational structure and urged me on as the assessment methodology began to take shape.

While my ETS and CAEL colleagues were my learning resources and support, Morris was my mentor, coach, and model. By observing him in action, it was clear that I had to learn how to listen, suspend coming to any quick conclusions, set aside firmly held beliefs about educational assessment, sample a variety of opinions (i.e., accreditation teams and staff, administrators, educational leaders, educators, program directors, learners). In other words, I should use what I learned from my experience to put strategy into action.

The New Student—The Adult Learner

The adult learner was the new student of the 1970s. It was predicted that within a decade nearly 40 percent of the learners in higher education would be over 25 years of age. Prior learning assessment was the way adults could gain admittance to higher education and obtain credentials in a cost effective manner and in a way that affirmed the academic worth of rich life experiences. At the same time, prior learning assessment was not to "rip off" these students and diminish the degree they sought. It was essential that this process take into account the special needs of adults—a marketing requirement—and the nature of adult learning—a pedagogical requirement.

Credibility

Portfolio assessment could not focus on the portfolio as a product; process should be the target. This process needed to have its roots in sound educational concepts which linked the process with traditional higher education outcomes.

Sound educational theory and pedagogical principles needed to be included in the design of the assessment process. Some innovators would accuse their opponents of condoning a double standard for prior learning programs, since such demands were rarely put on traditional higher education offerings.

Many ground breaking program directors felt that sound pedagogy had never entered the minds of most of their fellow faculty members. Nevertheless, the deep roots of experiential learning in the history and development of scholarship and advanced study needed to be uncovered.

Ownership

There is a close relationship between ownership and credibility. We knew that if we failed to enlist reputable and visible institutions and faculty in the development of portfolio assessment models, credibility could not be achieved no matter how scholarly and logical our argument.

Before enlisting new converts, we needed to acknowledge the contribution made by the front runners of experiential learning. After all, portfolios did exist before ETS and CAEL thought it was a good idea. How could we even begin our development work if we did not use the best of what was already available?

Surveying the state of the art was important, but choosing a strong and knowledgeable implementation group was crucial. Participation needed to be more than committee work. A consortium model was needed; that is, groups of institutions would come together to work on faculty development, research, and design and implementation of portfolio assessment programs.

Rigor

Although prior learning options/programs were well underway at a number of institutions, portfolio approaches varied dramatically in degrees of standardization, faculty training and participation, student involvement and preparation, and the reliability of faculty judgments.

In many institutions, portfolios were merely repositories for student information and learning products. In far fewer institutions, students took a course in portfolio assessment and received credits for undergoing the process. There needed to be some assurance that learners were being treated fairly, faculty were making reliable judgments about credit awards, and the process was not diluting academic standards.

Designing an assessment process that results in reliable and valid judgments implies a prescriptive and objective methodology. We knew early on in our investigations that such an approach would not allow for the flexibility that diverse institutions needed to fulfill the goals of their programs and to meet the special needs of the populations that they served.

Ground Covered in Portfolio Assessment

Our fourfold strategy, which took into consideration adult learners, credibility, ownership, and rigor, was put into action and miracles occurred in the process of building our model, thanks to the volunteer administrators, program directors and faculty who joined the consortium-based implementation effort:

— State-of-the-art papers were written to glean the best available knowledge from practice in the field so that others could stand on the shoulders of the program innovation already implemented.

— Assessment procedures were developed and modeled from these efforts. We created nothing new; we merely embellished the best of what higher education had to offer.

— Prior learning assessment handbooks were created for students and faculty to guide them in the portfolio process. Additional materials were created as needed.

— Research was conducted with some 50 institutions in conjunction with students, faculty and administrators. The results revealed that, in the main, faculty made fair decisions about college awards, and, thank goodness, made these awards on the basis of the learning from the experience, not the experiences themselves.

— Faculty were trained in prior learning assessment by a cadre of trainers who were colleagues and, further, who developed the materials, agenda, and approach used in the training sessions for this particular brand of adult learners. We trained some 300 faculty in the first wave. Our commitment to the Lilly Endowment, which funded the program, was for 200. The program continued, and it is estimated that possibly three times as many were trained in the two years that followed.

As a culminating activity to CAEL's development phase, Alden Dunham, the project officer at the Carnegie Corporation whose vision was instrumental in bringing CAEL into existence, urged Warren Willingham to craft *The Principles of Good Practice in the Assessment of Experiential Learning*. This was to embrace all of CAEL's accomplishments and pull together what we had learned about experiential learning in all its forms into a document that could be disseminated to all the players in higher education—accrediting agencies, presidents, administrators, faculty and program directors.

Three years after its inception, as the number of institutions with prior learning assessment options grew, CAEL was no longer a project on experiential learning and an interesting new wave phenomenon in higher education. CAEL had become a bona fide educational organization, and portfolio assessment was an established procedure for adult learners.

In the decade that has followed, more ground has been laid in establishing higher standards and more explicit procedures on the part of institutions—almost as an industry would regulate itself. As this "self-regulation" has increased, the accrediting agencies have become more comfortable with program innovation, and their role is much easier. Site visit teams are infused with administrators and faculty from prior learning programs.

Portfolio assessment has shifted from being product focused to being process focused. It is no longer good enough to collect all the learner's products and memorabilia from on the job, volunteer and other experiences. Faculty are not confused by a barrage of experiential stimuli. They do not have to root around for the kernels of learning resulting from the experience. Guidelines, procedures and actual courses have been developed to reduce the dross rate of experiential trivia and to set the learning in clear bas-relief.

The learner is assisted in a responsible way by counselors, faculty and program directors in the successful completion of the portfolio process. The "bleeding hearts" of the 1970s who welcomed the adult learner with open arms and often evaluated portfolios too leniently by filling in the gaps between experience and learning have applied muscle to their assessments by using CAEL guidance and materials. Those who are weak in this area no longer assess. Another quality control step—qualified people are doing the assessment.

Another interesting change in portfolio assessment is that portfolios are no longer labeled as prior learning assessment tools. In fact, the term "prior learning" is very nearly passe. Distinctions are no longer being made about types of experiential learning. The portfolios are being used to plan and document all sorts of learning, whether prior, recent, or taking place in "real" time. Also, the distinction between portfolio as assessment and portfolio as a learning tool has been blurred so that portfolio construction, assessment and feedback have become a powerful learning process and one in which portfolios are a continuing lifelong educational activity.

New Frontiers—The Best Is Yet To Be

Yes, through Morris' vision and CAEL's organizational strategies, portfolio assessment became a credible and legitimate option for adult learners. The process as it has been refined since 1974 is sound. Thanks to Warren Willingham, and now Urban Whitaker in his revision to Warren's earlier work, principles of good practice in assessment can be used and adapted by a variety of groups not limited to postsecondary experiential education. CAEL is "the source."

It is perhaps not evident to many CAELites working in the vineyards that portfolio assessment and the principles of good practice have been transformed to serve a variety of publics for purposes not envisioned by the CAEL change masters of the 1970s. Portfolio assessment is no longer focused just on the adult learner and prior learning.

Portfolio assessment has been initiated as part of the exit requirements for students in secondary education. In the United Kingdom, this assessment tool is called "records of achievement." These records are developed as part of a negotiating process on the part of students and teachers. Parents get involved as the documents grow in the students' portfolios. Feedback is given so that ongoing evaluation is encouraged rather than a summative evaluation at the end of the student's secondary school experience. Students then leave school with a dossier of achievement that can be presented to employers rather than a grade report.

In this country, Vermont high school students will be required to prepare a portfolio of work samples from their courses to be judged against criteria as part of their graduation requirements. The Department of Education wants to know not only what high school graduates know but what they can do.

By far the most remarkable frontier for portfolio assessment is the use of portfolios in teacher evaluation. Recently, I have become involved in helping to develop techniques and processes in this area. This has created a wonderful opportunity for me to renew my relationship with CAEL, Morris and my colleagues with whom I have not worked for a number of years. Thus my reference in the Prologue about the personal implications of the title of this chapter.

The impetus for the use of portfolios in the evaluation of teachers has come from three different streams: the Teacher Assessment Project at Stanford University; changes in the state licensing programs; and the recent formation of the National Board of Professional Teaching Standards, formed with the assistance of the Carnegie Corporation in response to the public concern for quality education. Teachers, regulators, parents and the public in general, all want to know what teachers can do and how they perform on the job. The Board is concerned with advancing teaching and developing standards of excellence against which the experienced teacher will be assessed.

It is not surprising that portfolio assessment is being considered as one of the most relevant assessment tools and that all the problems encountered in developing a portfolio model have surfaced once more. I and others working on this project are fortunate to have had available to us the legacy of the CAEL experience and strategy as we attempt to develop effective portfolio procedures. Perhaps the next time I am asked to make a contribution to the topic of portfolio assessment, the use of the portfolio to assess teacher competence will be the "ground covered." Would anyone care to predict what will be the "new frontier?"

8

Experiential Learning and the Liberal Arts

John H. Strange

As I reflect on the many experiences and challenges that working closely with Morris Keeton over a number of years have brought to my life, and as I think about what I should write to capture the quality of the instruction and encouragement he has given me, several things stand out. Morris is deeply committed to a liberal arts education, and he encouraged me to explore how experiential learning and liberal arts intertwine. Morris sent me "on the road" to encourage experiential learning among liberal arts professors, who, it seems to me, are the most resistant of any to experiential learning. Morris generated an increased desire to help shape the future, to change the world.

So, in preparing my article for this book, I have tried to combine these goals: to link experiential learning and the liberal arts; to provide a document that might help "sell" experiential learning to liberal arts professors not yet convinced; and to identify some tools that will, perhaps, help shape the future.

Since my comments are most likely to be read by those already convinced of the importance of experiential learning, I hope they will evoke some of the great times we have experienced together in CAEL, and that they will provide some tools to carry on Morris's missionary efforts.

Terminology

Caelic, the language of CAEL. (It seemed no one understood us. And Morris insisted that we be understood. So CAELIC, a language characterized by irony, emerged.)

Experiential Learning. The educational community has determined that experiential learning is a subset of learning, particularly that learning which occurs outside the classroom. Classroom (or laboratory) learning is real learning! Everything else is experiential learning.

Sponsored learning is experiential learning that is under the purview, or control, of an educational institution but which takes place outside the classroom. Internships, work-study assignments, independent projects are all examples of sponsored learning.

Prior learning is experiential learning that is not sponsored or supervised by an educational institution. Supposedly it is that learning acquired by a student before he or she enters college, which is acquired as a result of career or life experiences. But we all know that learning never ends. Thus "prior learning" could also be "during learning" and "after learning" (during and after enrollment in a college or university). Morris tried to get "non-sponsored learning" to be used as a replacement for "prior learning." He has not yet succeeded.

The Growth of Assessment of Experiential Learning

In the years since 1972, the number of colleges and universities in the United States which evaluate experiential learning, and more particularly prior learning, has grown exponentially. In 1972 fewer than a dozen institutions of higher education recognized the legitimacy of prior learning. By 1987, according to a recent survey by the Council for Adult and Experiential Learning, almost half of the postsecondary degree granting institutions in the United States had implemented procedures to evaluate prior learning. Admittedly, many of these programs are small, and many are well hidden from the student population, but they do exist. In addition, it is generally believed that on virtually every campus there is at least an informal mechanism, or some professor, that will evaluate and give advanced standing for what a person knows, or can do, that has been learned outside normal academic classrooms.

Some Explanations

A Demand for Accountability

There are many explanations for this growth in the recognition of experiential learning. Perhaps the most important is the dramatic increase in demands for accountability. Funding agencies, politicians, foundation executives and the public at large have demanded to know what is being taught—and learned—at all educational levels of the academic world in our country. As these demands are made and grow, educational institutions are forced to be more precise about their educational goals and objectives—outcomes if you will. And as the outcomes are specified more precisely and more clearly, it is evident that many of the objectives can be, and are being, attained outside normal classroom experiences. This has led to a demand, at some institutions, that techniques be developed to evaluate and certify this learning in order to conserve resources. If students already know, or can do, something that is being taught by an educational institution, why waste resources having the student sit through the instruction again?

To Recruit Adults

Experiential learning, its recognition and encouragement, has also grown because educational institutions have increasingly begun to recruit adults. Adults are being recruited, in part, to maintain enrollments seriously affected by the drop in graduating high school seniors that started several years ago and will continue for at least eight more years. Many schools would be unable to stay open or maintain their current faculties without a large number of adult students. These adult students do not want to repeat the learning which they have already acquired. They are demanding programs which evaluate, and honor, their prior learning—and educational institutions are responding.

Career Emphasis in Curriculum

The career orientation of current students has increased the use of field and other sponsored learning activities as well as the use of procedures to evaluate prior learning. This is especially true where adult students are encouraged by their employers to return for additional education. Often the employers have provided extensive and expensive educational and training programs in-house. Both the employee and the employer want some way to "count" that learning. This has resulted in a large number of educational contracts between educational institutions and employers to evaluate, and give credit for, the learning acquired in corporate training programs and work experiences.

Ideology

Finally, a few institutions have adopted experiential learning because of an ideological commitment to the proposition that the degree should be linked to what one knows and is able to do rather than be associated with "seat time," i.e., the time spent in a classroom or the amount of tuition paid. (Of course there are some institutions, especially the Veterans Administration, that seem uninterested in what people learn. They just want to be sure that students have put in a specific number of hours in a classroom.) A college degree is seen as a method for allocating rewards in society. It is recognized that degrees help people get jobs and get higher pay. It is also observed that many people, doing exactly the same job with the same skill, get paid considerably different amounts for the same work—only because one has a degree and one does not. Therefore it is believed that there should be a technique for evaluating what a person needs to know, be able to do, have experienced to do a job successfully. When these are identified they should "count" toward a degree which will bring about a more equitable distribution of the rewards and benefits of society. This ideological argument is not the basis for much of the experiential learning movement. But it was a major factor in the early days of the movement and in some of the institutions that are current leaders in the evaluation of experiential learning.

Opposition to Experiential Learning

Despite the growth in the number of colleges and universities evaluating and honoring experiential learning, especially prior learning, there has been considerable opposition among faculty members, often those in the liberal arts, and even in some traditionally minded state departments of education and accrediting bodies. The complaints offered by these people and groups are many. They are often stridently made.

Experiential Learning Will Cheapen the Degree

One of the most frequent charges is that the evaluation of experiential learning, especially prior learning, will cheapen the degree. The argument is made that the content required of students will be changed, that the standards will drop, that non-academic evaluators will sully the purity of academic decisions. A separate charge is that emphasis on theory will be replaced by the honoring of practical skills to the detriment of academic tradition.

In response, I contend that a program which evaluates and credits experiential learning need not lower academic standards at all. In fact, the faculty, in a properly organized and run experiential learning program, must be specific about the standards to be employed. The faculty set the standards, and presumably enforce them. If standards are lowered, it is because the faculty has lowered them, failed to specify them, or failed to insist upon them. There is certainly nothing inherent in the evaluation of experiential learning that will lead to a lowering of standards!

The Content Will Be Changed

Now the charge that the content will change is most likely true. Again that is controlled by the faculty, but the specific content covered by a faculty member in a given course may not match the content known by the adult student. If specific content (the faculty member's) remains as the required outcome, the content does not change but the adult student often does not get credit for what he or she knows. So there must be flexibility on content. Later in this paper I will suggest that content, as an outcome, should probably be limited in favor of the mastery of generic capabilities and the development of the habits, interests and values of the life of learning. Nevertheless, content is now the major outcome demanded of postsecondary students.

Theoretical Knowledge Will Be Replaced By Practical Skills

The relative weight of the theoretical and the practical is also a troubling one to faculty. It is quite clear that adult students most often acquire practical skills through experiential learning rather than knowledge of a theoretical nature. I argue that educational institutions have failed, for the most part, to teach anything but the theory. And I also suggest later in this article that a combination of the practical and theoretical is more appropriate than either by itself. The faculty of an institution can decide what mix they wish to include in their curriculum. But the failure of a faculty to honor and recognize the practical skills of their adult students is, in my opinion, shortsighted, unfair, and demeaning of a proper educational approach. But if a faculty member only knows theory, it is often hard to honor the practical. One thing is certain: The failure to address the need for practical skill building is serious if effective liaisons are to be established and maintained between the worlds of academia and work.

Faculty Will Lose Their Jobs

An argument often offered by faculty against the formal recognition of experiential learning is that assessment of experiential learning programs reduce the need for faculty. If we recognize the learning that students acquire elsewhere, the argument goes, they will need less from us. There is an appropriate response to this job protection fear. Every institution which has wholeheartedly recognized the validity of experiential learning, and developed an effective program for implementing its evaluation, has significantly increased its enrollment and the demand for faculty. Rather than reducing the need for faculty, the need for faculty has grown. Why? Because the recognition and evaluation of experiential learning increases enrollments, which creates a greater need for teachers and evaluators!

Learning Outcomes Cannot Be Disclosed

Another argument against assessment and recognition of experiential learning is that the outcomes of an educational program cannot or should not be disclosed. I will address the cannot argument first. The argument is made that an educational program, especially a bachelors degree program, involves certain experiences, certain objectives, that cannot be made explicit. Most often this complaint is offered by faculty teaching traditional undergraduates in a traditional residential environment. It is almost as if there is a "magic" which occurs in the hallowed, ivy covered halls that cannot be described.

Perhaps these faculty are referring to the "growing up" or "maturing" of their students. Certainly the students at an educational institution change while they are there, often not as a result of the educational program they receive, but because they are older, have had many more significant interpersonal experiences than when they arrived, and have encountered a diverse student body. All of that is true and important. Certainly educational institutions do not give credit for such happenings, but they are important to their students and to the institution. But we are not talking about what happens to 18–21 year olds. Experiential learning and its evaluation are directed to adults who have "grown up" in the real world. Their growing up may not be the same as that of the 18 year old in an ivy league establishment, but it is no less real or honorable!

Learning Outcomes Should Not Be Disclosed

And now the should not argument. This was made by a professor of sociology in one of the southern states. I will respect his wishes and he will remain anonymous. The professor stated to me that he objected to the requirement inherent in the evaluation of experiential learning that the objectives of the learning be stated explicitly. He said his objective in the criminology class that he taught was to present his students with evidence that would overwhelmingly lead to their disgust with the existing penal system in his state and lead to effective efforts on their part to replace that system with a different one. In other words, the professor's objective was to modify the students' entering value systems by replacing theirs with his. And he believed that if it were known that his objective was to get students to adopt his value system, he would be fired from his position at a major state university.

There are several responses. As will be elaborated upon later, I believe it is vital for an educational institution to address the question of values. Students should certainly know what their value systems are, where they come from, under what conditions they can and are altered, and what other options are open to them. And it is probably appropriate, especially if we are open about it, to warn students that we have certain value systems, as institutions or individuals, which we will attempt to get them to acquire. But I disagree with the professor with whom I had this discussion on two counts. I certainly think it totally inappropriate not to be open and explicit about our own value systems, even if that does cost us our jobs! And second, I am totally opposed to any requirement that a student believe the way I do in order to get credit for my course or to be acknowledged as a learner. The argument that we should not disclose our objectives, as teachers or educational institutions, is totally incompatible with my value system. But each institution and individual must ultimately make its own choice in this matter!

Faculty Must Be Retrained...And That Is Expensive Or Impossible

Another argument is that the adoption of an experiential learning program necessitates faculty retraining—and that faculty retraining is impossible. Certainly the first part of this argument is correct. The introduction of an effective assessment of experiential learning program cannot be done without extensive faculty retraining. That takes time, money, and a willingness on the part of the faculty to participate. One president of a well-known liberal arts college in Massachusetts commented recently in a meeting of university and business executives that "Faculty cannot be retrained. The only thing we can do is wait until they retire or die." Now I am not familiar with any data to support this conclusion. In fact I am wont to doubt it. But that president is convinced, and as long as he acts on his conviction, it is a certainty that his faculty will not be retrained—for anything. The shortsightedness of that approach should be evident immediately!

Experiential Learning Costs Too Much

Experiential learning and its evaluation are also challenged on the grounds that it costs too much. Several responses are possible. First, you can charge what it costs to evaluate experiential learning. People are willing to pay for saving time and tuition dollars! Second, the evidence I have had at the University of Massachusetts/Boston, and the evidence that has been shared with me from many other programs around the country, is that experiential learning programs can make money for an institution. To do this the programs must not be entirely individualized (although at least one program has developed a cost effective program that is totally individualized!). Students must be taught in groups how to gather evidence and how to submit that evidence for evaluation. Done properly this is no more expensive than any other instructional offering.

Credit Is Given For Experience, Not Learning

A common argument is the complaint that experiential learning programs give credit for experiences, not learning. We have all read newspaper exposés which reveal that some institution has given a mother 15 hours credit in sociology for rearing two children, or a police officer 6 hours of criminal justice for having been promoted to sergeant. This does happen. But it happens not because of the nature of the experiential learning process, but because individuals and institutions lower their standards below that which I find acceptable. This also happens in traditional programs. I have encountered many transfer students who have great difficulty in reading or writing, for example. But their transcripts reveal B's in English 101 and 102. Why? Perhaps they came to class regularly, and "tried hard." The point is that standards are standards. They exist in all programs. There is nothing inherent in experiential learning programs that necessitates a lower set of standards.

I must add one warning however. In most institutions faculty are not responsible for recruiting students and often are not aware of the techniques used to increase enrollments. I have known many institutions which advertise that they have programs which give credit for life experience. It is often difficult for faculty to know about, or to control, such practices. And if they do occur they can cause problems. If students are admitted and believe, because of advertisements, admissions counselors, or for any reason, that credit is given for the experience, not the learning, then the students will undoubtedly be shocked when they are forced to prove they know, or can do something, rather than prove only that they have experienced something. That is why it is essential, especially in experiential learning programs, for all involved to be clear that *experiential learning credit is awarded for the learning acquired through life and work experiences, not for the experiences themselves.*

Credit Already Awarded For Experiences By Educational Institutions

Having said the above let me back off a bit. First, having warned vigilance on the part of academic institutions and faculty to the necessity of awarding credit for learning only, not experiences, let me point out that educational institutions regularly award credit for experiences. There are most often two ways that this happens. First, transfer credit. Transfer credit is awarded without a direct examination, or even knowledge of, what a student knows, can do or has experienced. We know that a student has had the experience of taking a class and completing it, but we do not know what he or she has learned as a result of that experience. We nevertheless give credit for that experience. It would be politically difficult not to do so in the vast majority of cases. Of course there are exceptions. Sometimes institutions do not count certain transfer credits toward major requirements, or they do not accept transfers from "weak" institutions, or they refuse to accept work done before a certain date. But accepting transfer credit is a common practice; and yet the experience, not the learning, is what is being accredited.

This is also true when an educational institution accepts the recommendation of the American Council on Education (ACE) for credit awards for military and business courses. The credit recommendations are based on an examination of the course content and structure, not an evaluation of the learning acquired by the students in these programs. Again we are accepting experience, not learning.

Perhaps this is appropriate. Perhaps we can tell, after a large number of cases, that students entering with say PS 212 from Bluegrass Community College, regularly perform well in PS 517 at Metro U. Or that former military personnel who completed a specific military course in psychology can usually perform well in advanced psychology courses at our institution. Then our acceptance of the experiential evidence seems appropriate. Two comments are necessary. This is all well and good, but I dare say that most institutions have not really documented whether or not this is correct (and maybe they should!). Moreover, if we can reach such conclusions about ACE recommendations, and transfer credits, with appropriate evidence collected over time, we can certainly do the same with job experiences, especially when a college commonly recruits large numbers of students with similar job experiences. So perhaps there is a place for granting credit based on a knowledge of what experiences someone has had—if we have good reason to believe, after collecting sufficient evidence, that most, if not all students with that experience have specific knowledge or skills.

Experience May Be A Desired Outcome

Another comment is to be made about experience. Sometimes an experience is the outcome desired by an educational institution. Earlier I commented about the "magic" that some believe is a part of the educational experience. Although what I am talking about is related to that argument, it is not the same. To make my point clear, let me call attention to courses in art appreciation or music appreciation offered in most liberal arts programs. The final exam does not evaluate an experience. It is factual. In most such courses slides are flashed on a screen every 15 seconds or a needle is dropped on a record (the more advanced institutions now use tapes or CD players controlled by computers), and the student must answer a series of true/false or multiple choice questions about the artist, the period, the nature of the work seen or heard. Now I really do not believe that the desired outcome of such courses is the ability to identify the artist of a work of art within 15 seconds! Rather the course is a set of experiences to acquaint a student with art or music, to increase the likelihood that in later life students will "appreciate," will incorporate art or music into their life, will be more likely to visit the National Gallery in Washington D.C. But we cannot test for behavior we hope will result in the future, so we substitute facts instead. Since we believe, and probably rightly so, that the experiences of such a class are likely to increase the odds for the desired behavior in the future, why not be honest and say it is the experience that counts! And if the experience really counts, then similar experiences of adults (or better yet an evaluation of the behavior: incorporation of art into one's life) become appropriate and possible.

It Wasn't Learned Here!

My offering of the above argument on experience, during a presentation I made to the Program Planning Committee of the Academic Senate at the University of Oregon some years ago, led to the discovery of another widespread objection to experiential learning. I was introduced to the assembled committee by the chair, a distinguished professor of English. In introducing me he noted that I was then vice president of the Council for the Advancement of Experiential Learning (CAEL's name at that time), and that I was to address the committee on experiential learning. But he immediately reassured the committee that his unyielding opposition to experiential learning was still intact despite my presence at the committee meeting. I had been invited by the provost! Needless to say I was less than thrilled by my introduction. But after having made the argument cited above about the appropriateness, in specific instances, of specifying experiences as desired outcomes of an academic program, the committee chair, who was also the English professor and undying opponent to experiential learning, suddenly said: "Dr. Strange, we do agree! Now I understand what a B.A. degree really is." Shocked, I turned to the professor and asked in what way we agreed. "Well," he said, "a B.A. program is the experience of working with scholars." "And how much work with scholars is required for a B.A. degree?," I asked. "Four years!" was the instant reply.

I went on to suggest that I did, indeed, think it appropriate for an educational institution to establish an objective of close interaction with scholars as part of the requirements for a degree. And this could certainly be specified in terms of an experience. But four years, really! It seemed to me that most schools had very well established routes whereby students could avoid any effective interactions with scholars of the type obviously desired by the English professor. Whereupon someone in the back of the room said that just that week one of his advisees had proudly proclaimed that she was about to complete her fourth undergraduate year without having taken any examination other than a true/false or multiple choice examination. The English professor was rightly appalled. But I asked his indulgence for a bit more conversation before the committee directed its attention to how to solve the problem raised by the report of the student's academic experience (or lack of it) at the University of Oregon.

To make my point I recited the story of a "composite" student, a combination of the experience of several of my students at UMass/Boston. Gail was 36. She worked for Bell Laboratories. She had gone to work immediately after high school when she was married. Her husband went to college and she helped support him. She was successful at Bell Laboratories, being promoted to a senior researcher. She had published over 20 articles in her specialty area, and her book, written with two other members of her research team, was in press. Her husband was moving to a state where there was no Bell Lab facility, and Gail was worried that without a degree she would be unable to get a job, or one that paid as well and was as interesting as her current position. She wanted a B.A. degree!

Turning to the English professor, I reminded him that he had suggested that a B.A. was really four years of interacting with scholars. Accepting that, I proposed that we award Gail with the B.A. degree. The English professor was appalled. "Surely," I responded, "it is not a question of interacting with scholars. And even if we throw out several years while Gail was merely a secretary, or a lab assistant, we have 18 to play with." "No," replied the professor after some thought, "it is that she has not acquired sufficient breadth in her education." Accepting that, I proposed then that we merely award the credit equivalent to her major. Still the English professor objected. "Why not?", I demanded. And in a moment of total candor and honesty he replied: "She didn't do it here!"

"She didn't do it here!" That is, in fact, the most difficult problem that experiential learning has to overcome. It wasn't learned from me (or someone like me). And until we recognize that we all learn in a great variety of ways, and from a large number of sources, we will never be able to overcome the "She didn't do it here!" argument of the English professor at the University of Oregon and his countless colleagues throughout academia.

Types of Experiential Learning Programs

The Suitcase Method

Despite the objections to experiential learning and its assessment, the number of assessment programs has grown tremendously. But implementation has taken several different forms. The earliest form I describe as the suitcase method. This method was the first approach used for the evaluation of experiential learning. It was the product of the group of 10 colleges and universities, working closely with the Educational Testing Service and funded by the Carnegie Foundation, the Fund for the Improvement of Postsecondary Education, the Ford Foundation, and the Kellogg Foundation, that Morris Keeton chaired in 1972–73. This was the first CAEL, the Cooperative Assessment of Experiential Learning, a research project to determine valid and reliable ways for evaluating experiential learning.

From that research, and the related activities of the participating colleges and universities, came the suitcase method. Students applying for the evaluation of experiential learning credit were encouraged to gather all evidence available to them to demonstrate learning that had been acquired through their life experiences. In one instance that I observed, a 55-year old mother (who obviously was a pack rat) wheeled in a dolly loaded with boxes while being accompanied by her two grown sons, each carrying mammoth suitcases filled with the evidence of Mother's learning. Hence the "suitcase" name. Marching into the Director of Assessment, the mother proudly said: "Here's my evidence. When can I find out what it's worth?"

The director of Assessment did not faint, probably because this was an exceptional event, but it points out the process. The student would gather his or her evidence and bring it to the educational institutions. The educational institution would then constitute a panel, representative of the faculty. The panel organized and arranged the evidence. Based on their understanding of the general objectives of the courses offered at that institution (or elsewhere if that was a part of their practice), they awarded a block of credit. In rare cases credit was awarded for specific courses. The CAEL/ETS study documented the reliability and validity of this approach. And for some time this was the primary approach to the evaluation of experiential learning.

The Petition Approach

The suitcase method was soon joined by what I call the "petition approach." (There is a third method, "competency programs" which I will not discuss here. These programs define the degree in terms of outcomes that must be attained and demonstrated by a student rather than in terms of the courses offered by an institution or a program.)

Specialized Evaluation Possible

The petition approach differs in several ways from the suitcase method. First, more efficient and specialized evaluation is one of the most important outcomes of the petition method. Students organize their own evidence around course descriptions and outcome statements. Evidence is submitted challenging a specific course (or in some cases a set of related courses or even a modularly defined set of competencies). This evidence is then submitted to a faculty member in a specialty area, rather than a panel, for evaluation.

Organizing And Argument Skills Learned

There are other impacts that the petition method brought to the experiential learning evaluation process. Schools adopting the petition method, as opposed to the "suitcase" method, have found that one of the most significant differences is that in the petition method students have to develop skills for organizing and presenting a claim or case. This resulted in the necessity for classes in which students are provided career counseling in order to determine what areas of their previous experience they wish to probe in order to address a program of learning that will meet their current career goals and objectives. In addition, these portfolio, or assessment courses as they have been called in various places, acquaint the students with a very different model than that with which they are familiar.

Lack Of Self-Confidence Revealed As Major Student Problem

These portfolio courses also clearly identify one of the central issues related to an adult's entry into or return to college: lack of self-confidence. At the University of Massachusetts at Boston's College of Public and Community Service (CPCS), which has every entering student prepare a portfolio of evidence of prior learning, the faculty were originally concerned that all the entering students would want massive amounts of credit without being willing to provide the evidence to support that claim. They believed everyone would be what I called a "worldsaver," someone who would offer these comments: "I'm distressed that I am asked to come in and talk to you about all the wonderful things I have done in my community. Everyone knows my skills and abilities. Now if I could just get my degree by 5:00 p.m., or noon would be even better, I could get back to my community and continue my good works."

Our experience at CPCS was not this at all. Rather the major problem we have had is that students (as well as many educational institutions) do not value their learning from experience. The students' major problem is a lack of self-confidence as I noted earlier. I call it the "I'm just a housewife and don't have any competence" syndrome. This is in part due to the socialization of students to the belief that education only results from a series of 55-minute courses taken three times per week for 14 weeks. The educational jargon of the educational establishment also contributes to their lack of self-confidence, as does the emphasis by faculty on theory and theoretical knowledge to the detriment of practical skills, about which I will say more later.

Students Believe In Their Learning

The petition method encourages students to believe in themselves, to value their learning. The suitcase method returned a number (credits awarded), a number for which the students were thankful, but the reasons for which were not at all clear. It seemed like magic, or a gift. The petition method, in contrast, provides students with an opportunity to gather the evidence and prove to themselves that they have learned something of value. This is important in overcoming the low self-esteem of which I spoke earlier.

But it also raises another two other issues and needs. First, the need for some method for appealing decisions in which the student and faculty are in disagreement. If a student truly believes he or she has gathered and submitted evidence of college-level learning and the faculty evaluator disagrees, the presence of a safety valve, a method for resolving the dispute, helps diffuse any possible difficulties. In the 16 years of the operation of the appeals process at CPCS, we have seen it used very infrequently. The fact that an appeals process exists is important, however.

Second, the need is created to teach students how to gather evidence and organize that evidence into a petition, a claim for credit. The ability to organize and make an argument is central to the academic process. This is not needed by all students, but it is an essential ingredient of the petition method.

The Educational Institution Must Specify Learning Objectives Or Outcomes

Finally, and most importantly, the petition method forces colleges and universities to be specific about the outcomes of their educational programs. In the suitcase method outcomes do not have to be specified. Students gather any and all evidence which they feel might be worth something and the faculty, in committee, sort it out and attach credit to it. But if the student must generate a claim on the curriculum, the student has to know what he or she is supposed to know, be able to do, or have experienced in order to gather appropriate evidence that might lead to an award of credit for prior learning.

Addressing Educational Outcomes

Facts vs. Skills

There are three main issues that arise when colleges and universities begin to face the question of outcomes. First, what is the relative weight given to knowing specific factual information, as opposed to demonstrating certain skills that can be applied in a variety of factual settings? Now on the surface this seems not really to be an issue. The general claim is made by faculty that even though their courses may cover specific factual material, the real objective goes beyond acquisition of factual material. (However the recent insistence on cultural literacy seems to undermine this argument.) There is one serious problem with this claim: research done by the Educational Testing Service has shown that over 70% of a college student's grade is determined by the ability to regurgitate specific factual information on a test. Grades are given on the basis of what specific information students know. Some 20% of grades are the result of evaluating cognitive skills, albeit indirectly, primarily through questions requiring essay answers, which in some cases offer and test hypotheses or produce generalizations. Another 5% is reported to be an evaluation of written communication skills, and another 5% is a fudge factor which includes rewarding initiative, completion, decision-making, creativity and other affective behaviors.

This same research at ETS goes on to show that faculty, when writing letters of recommendation for their students, do not rely on factual knowledge to differentiate among their better and weaker students. They discuss intellectual problem-solving skills, communication skills, interpersonal skills and affective behaviors. These affective behaviors or skills include: creativity, going beyond the assigned task, challenging accepted theories and explanations, motivation, decision-making, meeting deadlines, judgment, honesty, integrity, ability to handle ambiguity, self-confidence as a learner, ability and a desire to engage in lifelong learning, being able to adapt.

Another example of a devotion to facts by faculty was quite evident when I visited a prestigious liberal arts college in Virginia some years ago. Under pressure from the state legislature, they were introducing a program to evaluate experiential learning. A subgroup of the faculty was meeting to decide how to proceed. Meetings had been held and it had been decided to use CLEP exams. Entering adults were to be given subject oriented CLEP exams to test their factual knowledge in a specific discipline. I attended a meeting in which there was a debate over what level of performance on the CLEP tests would lead to an award of credit for prior learning. Needless to say I was appalled by this approach since research has clearly shown that people forget facts about as fast as they learn them unless they use them. And here was a plan to award credit to adults only for the facts they currently knew!

Fortunately I was never called upon to discuss this issue with the faculty. The leader of the effort to institute a realistic program for evaluating prior learning had come armed—with CLEP tests! In the middle of a vigorous debate on whether acceptance of an 80 would demean the academic standing of this outstanding college, the group leader pulled out the CLEP tests and said "Well, let's see how well we do. Let's take some CLEP tests ourselves." You can imagine the conflicting meetings that were suddenly remembered as the faculty fled the room! The point was well made. Factual tests are inappropriate unless the student has been continually using those facts and has retained them.

So where do we turn?

Well, I believe that the evaluation of prior learning will force teachers to be specific about what students should know, or be able to do, after taking a particular course. In other instances we may be interested in what experiences a student has had, as I will explain later. When students ask how they can find out what they should know, be able to do, or have experienced to get credit, they are often told to look up the course in the college's catalog. It is often claimed that catalog course descriptions are sufficient. Thirty words (what is allowed in the computer) is all that is needed to describe the outcomes of a course? Not in my catalog! Well, syllabi are then offered as a source of this information. In some cases that may be accurate, but most syllabi describe topics to be covered and material to be read, not what you should know, be able to do, or have experienced as a result of having taken the course. And for a program that evaluates experiential learning to work well, this topic must be engaged; students must know what outcome objectives they will be evaluated against.

Now I believe that this is a healthy process for an academic institution to undertake. I even have my own list of some of the things that should be attended to by an educational institution at the undergraduate level. First, content cannot be totally dismissed. It is the route to the development of the intellectual skills that I advocate. But a particular content, "my facts, my specialty," as an outcome is not, in my opinion, a particularly desirable objective except perhaps in a career area. And even there it must be acknowledged by the student that the facts he or she has learned are not at all permanent. They are highly transitory!

Some Suggested Outcomes

What then should we have as desired outcomes for an undergraduate degree? Here is my short list:

Communication Skills: reading, writing, speaking, listening skills; the ability to communicate using new technologies including word processing, data communication, and video;

Intellectual/Problem Solving Skills: the ability to observe, describe; compare and contrast; analyze and generalize. Put another way we can call for an ability to understand complexity—to see many sides of an issue; the ability to process information—to learn, recall, relearn; the skill of conceptualizing—analyzing, synthesizing; the ability to learn from experience—to be able to translate observations from experience into a theory that can be used to generate behavioral alternatives;

Affective Behaviors: initiative, honesty; integrity; curiosity; judgment; motivation; challenging accepted ways of doing things; ability to handle ambiguity; being able to adapt quickly; self-confidence as a learner; a commitment to lifelong learning; ability to experiment; timing; management; decision-making;

Interpersonal Skills

Values: to have values and to recognize values and their source; to recognize the values of others and their source; to demonstrate the ability to modify and adopt new values when it is felt appropriate by the student;

Computational Skills: at least the ability to add, subtract, and multiply. Dare we hope for more from the general student population? (I suggested at one point in the development of CPCS that our minimum computational skills be pegged at the level at which all faculty members could demonstrate competence. The math instructors were appalled!)

Experiences: I like the notion of an experience of interacting with scholars suggested by the English professor at the University of Oregon whom I discussed earlier. I would encourage at least one such semester experience with at least one faculty member—perhaps a group research effort, or a directed internship. Adult programs, commuter schools, and even many of our residential colleges do not offer any intensive, small group interaction with the faculty even once in a student's experience. I would like to see that change. And it is the experience that counts, not the specific outcome, the facts learned or skills acquired.

Of course these objectives are presented in the most condensed format possible. But genuine attention to the outcomes of a liberal education will force us to grapple with these issues. And the evaluation of experiential learning forces us, ultimately, to deal with outcomes.

Practical Skills As Well As Theoretical Knowledge

One other issue that I raised earlier must also be addressed—the relative merit of theoretical knowledge versus practical skills. Visiting in western Michigan several years ago, I was asked to assist a college as it made final its plans for the evaluation of experiential learning. This particular institution had decided to let an entering student petition any course from any accredited institution in the world. The motives were honorable: the institution did not provide courses in a variety of fields; it was expected that students would have skills and knowledge that went beyond the offerings of the institution. To be fair, some mechanism must be devised to provide an opportunity for those students to demonstrate their skills and knowledge.

Now it was my belief that the college would have its hands full with the courses in its own catalog. To demonstrate that I opened the catalog to a course in psychology which was called something like Psychology 333—Hot Line Counseling. I cannot recall the specific description of the course but it went something like this: "This course will prepare you to work in a community based or hot line counseling facility. Topics include crisis identification and intervention; support techniques; community resource identification; interviewing and report writing. This course follows a seminar format and is restricted to majors." (The instructor must have gotten special permission to exceed the 30-word limit imposed by the catalog!)

I decided it would be useful to engage in a little role playing with the faculty deliberating so earnestly the guidelines they were writing for their new experiential learning program. "Well," I said, "I am a Hot Line Counselor Grade 4 in Our City. I have worked there eight years. I have gotten excellent reviews for my work. I have taken six courses offered by the Michigan Department of Human Services in counseling and have 18 CEU's. If you want to observe my counseling you may do so by arrangement. I will supply you with the evaluations done of my work, or you can contact and interview my supervisor. I will tape my sessions if you wish, if I can be assured that there are no violations of confidentiality or privacy for my clients. Can I have credit for Sociology 333?"

"No!" was the immediate response from one of the faculty. It seems that I had inadvertently selected a course taught by one of the committee members.

"Why not?" I asked.

"Well, you have offered only evidence of practical counseling skills. That is not what I cover in my course. I insist that my students be familiar with the latest theoretical knowledge that relates to counseling" the instructor replied.

"What? I read the catalog and it doesn't say anything about theory. I can do everything it talks about!"

"Well, I'm sorry. I expect you to understand the theory of counseling. Not just be able to do it. In fact, you probably aren't doing a good job of counseling if you do not understand the theories behind what you do!"

"Now wait a minute! Here I am a Hot Line Counselor. I am a good one. You can look at any evidence you want. Now you say I can't get credit for the course. . .that I must know theory. Why didn't you say that? What are you trying to do? Change the rules on me? If I have to know theory, why didn't you say that? And why can't you give me credit for being a good counselor?"

You can imagine the rest of the role play. The faculty member admitted that the central element in the course was theory and that she didn't even address practical skills. She went on to say that she had discovered that if she mentioned "theory" or "theoretical" in her course descriptions, she did not get as many students as when she made the description career oriented. Further discussion revealed that very little attention was paid to practical skills at that institution. And that is true of many liberal arts colleges! But we should remember that adults enter college with a great deal of practical experience, and very little theory. If we fail to honor those practical skills, or demean or dishonor them unless the theory is learned first, we do our institutions and our students a disservice. We would be well advised to clearly identify practical skill objectives as well as theoretical knowledge among the outcomes we specify for our programs. And we should be honest about our catalog descriptions.

Faculty Development

Introducing the evaluation of experiential learning into a college or university requires faculty development efforts. As I discussed earlier, the objections that can be raised to a program for evaluating experiential learning are many. I am convinced that not only is the evaluation of experiential learning the correct thing to do, it is also a healthy thing to do—to get the faculty to think about and clarify what they really are about, what they really want to accomplish as teachers and educators.

Examinations And Letters Of Recommendation

But to do that they need some assistance. We need to offer them some faculty development programs. I would like to share three suggestions with you which I have found to be very successful in my work in experiential learning.

First, the facts versus other outcomes issue. I would suggest having two meetings. At the first meeting ask faculty to bring copies of several of their last examinations. Analyze these exams together. Do they test primarily for facts as I have predicted? What else is tested for? Generate a discussion of *why* facts should be required of students. Try to reach agreement among the faculty of what factual knowledge should be required. Avoid the tendency to avoid the issue by carving up the question into turf: You decide on the facts from your discipline; I'll decide on mine.

At the next meeting have the faculty bring to the meeting the last six letters of recommendation they have written. See if my prediction is correct that a command over a particular set of facts will not be prominent on the list of skills and characteristics that faculty use to differentiate students in the letters of recommendation. Lead the discussion toward an examination of how these affective and intellectual skills can be identified, how evidence can be gathered for their evaluation through a variety of content areas. Engage in some brainstorming about how cognitive skills and affective behaviors can be taught!

Four Strange Questions—An Exercise

The second exercise I invented while listening to Art Chickering speak at a CAEL meeting in Augusta, Maine. I have used this exercise hundreds of times throughout the country, and it has been used by many others, in a variety of forms: CAEL, Joint Ventures: Caterpillar Tractor Company; Royal Oak Public Schools; Birmingham Michigan Public Schools; Association for Supervision and Curriculum Development workshops, and in many other places. I have never known it to fail.

Subdivide the faculty, or whatever group you are working with, into four groups. Each group works on a question for 10 minutes. The four questions are:

What Have You Learned Recently? Where? How?

> *Group 1*: What have you learned (a new counseling technique, how to use a new piece of software, new budget information, how to fix a leaky toilet, anything) in the last day, week, or month? How did you learn it?

What Do You Need to Know to Do Your Job? Where Learned? How Learned?

> *Group 2*: What do you need to know, be able to do, have experienced for your current job? How did you learn it?

What Are The Desired Learning Outcomes?

> *Group 3*: You are in a room of 200 people. Half have the degree offered by your school, half do not. How can you identify who has the degree and who does not. You cannot ask the people there whether or not they have the degree. You cannot make inferences from SES data or from appearances. In other words you must identify what your degree requires: what one should know, have experienced, be able to do in order to be awarded the degree? (Acknowledge 10 minutes may not be quite enough time to complete this, but get started.)

What Proof Is Necessary?

> *Group 4*: You have a degree. All records of that degree are lost. I have a job opening. You want that job which requires that degree or equivalent skills and abilities. The job pays a lot of money! How are you going to prove you have the degree or equivalent skills and abilities?

What will happen?

Group 1 will report that they learned a lot of different things, most of which we would not readily link to college work but some of which we might. The way in which the learning occurred is what is important. That will include talking to experts, trial and error, watching a television show, doing it, consulting with a specialist, redoing, etc. All experiential learning! It is unlikely that traditional classroom work will be mentioned at all.

Group 2 will produce the same results except most will be at the college level. Added to the techniques will also be observation, or some form of internship or mentoring. Faculty may claim a knowledge base in the discipline which they teach and identify graduate school classes as a source of their learning. If this happens, I ask where and how they acquired their teaching skills, interpersonal skills, other skills and knowledge they use daily. The point again is that most have been learned experientially.

Group 3: You will either get specific content requirements, where compromises have been made quickly by the group; a dispute over content; or a discussion of some or all of the outcomes I identified in my list above. Whatever the response, the discussion can lead to a more complete examination of the outcome approach to learning.

Group 4: This group will identify all of the techniques that we *should* use in evaluating portfolios, in assessing experiential learning. Unfortunately, we usually insist on written work or tests. The faculty in group four will have many more suggestions: tests; oral presentations; written material (old and new); direct observations; reported observations; video or audio presentations; awards, citations; products (publications, art work, plays produced, etc.); letters from the teachers, employers, others who have evaluated them; simulations. The point to be made here is that this whole range of evidence should be encouraged and used in the evaluation of experiential learning. Unfortunately the portfolio approach, especially the petition variation, almost always is implemented in such a way that new written material is the primary type of evidence submitted for evaluation. We should not let that happen. But we have to work hard to avoid it.

Turn Every Classroom Into A Kindergarten

Finally, I offer another focus for a faculty development effort. We could suggest that we turn every classroom into a kindergarten. Why kindergartens? Well, in kindergarten you learn experientially (and you said that is how you learned what you need to know to do your current job). The emphasis is on cognitive and affective skill development, not memorization of facts. Practical skills are emphasized rather than theoretical.

Group learning and evaluation is encouraged and rewarded. The importance of self-directed learning is introduced. Questions are emphasized rather than answers. Sounds like my model curriculum, doesn't it? Unfortunately, as you move to middle school, high school and college, you move further away from the ideal I have suggested.

To generate a discussion of the central issues that are involved, I present six Strange Graphs. These graphs report some of the findings of my research supported in part by the Strange Foundation. Feel free to use, or adapt them, if you like. They work!

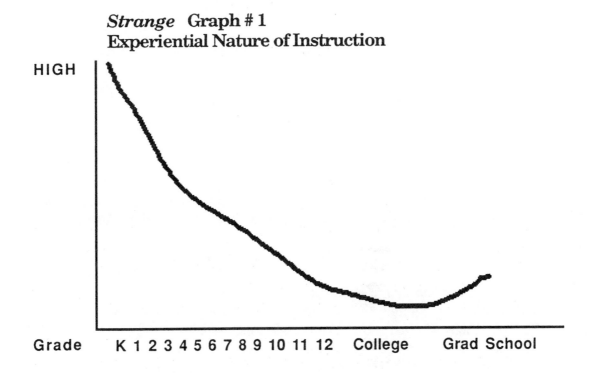

Strange Graph #1
Experiential Nature of Instruction

HIGH

Grade   K 1 2 3 4 5 6 7 8 9 10 11 12   College   Grad School

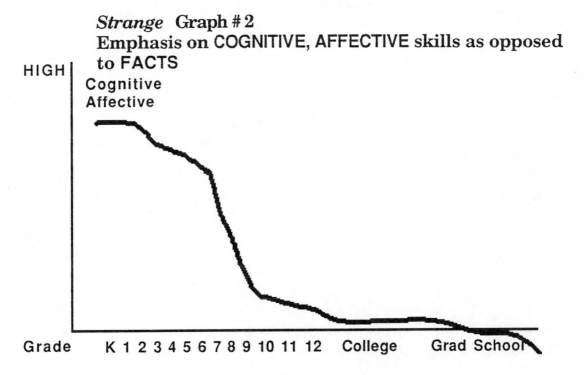

Strange Graph #2
Emphasis on COGNITIVE, AFFECTIVE skills as opposed to FACTS

HIGH
Cognitive
Affective

Grade   K 1 2 3 4 5 6 7 8 9 10 11 12   College   Grad School

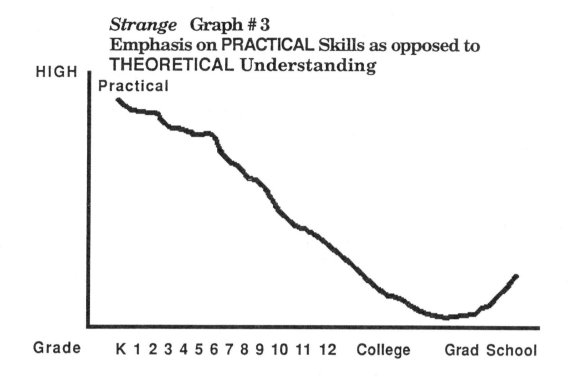

Strange Graph # 3
Emphasis on PRACTICAL Skills as opposed to
THEORETICAL Understanding

HIGH

Practical

Grade   K 1 2 3 4 5 6 7 8 9 10 11 12   College   Grad School

Strange Graph # 4
Encouragement of Group Learning and Evaluation

HIGH

Grade   K 1 2 3 4 5 6 7 8 9 10 11 12   College   Grad School

Strange Graph # 5
Importance of Self Directed Learning

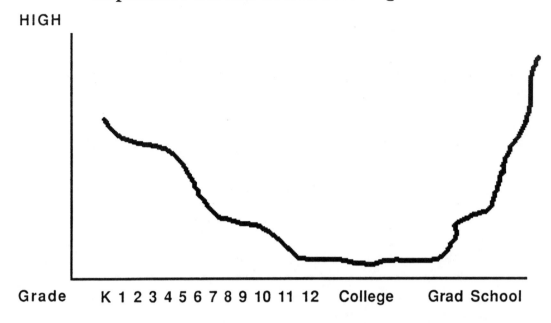

Strange Graph # 6
Importance of QUESTIONS as Opposed to ANSWERS

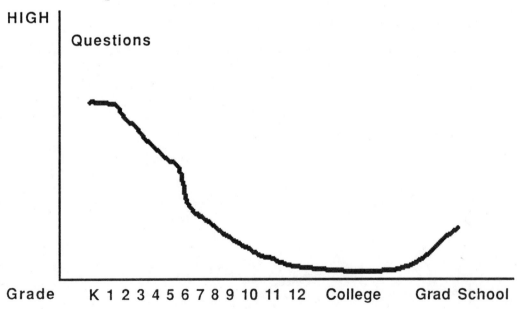

Conclusion

I hope this personal account of the implications for liberal arts of the evaluation of experiential learning will stimulate your thinking and your action. Morris started us down a long and important road. Thanks, Morris! I hope my comments will make the trip somewhat easier and more enjoyable for all of us.

9

The Power and Problematics of Experience-Based Curriculum Methods

Jackson Kytle

Preface

Experiential education, as the word is used today, is inseparable from the life work of Morris Keeton. Keeton, who came to Antioch College in 1947 as college pastor, both helped shape—and was shaped by—that institution, known since the 1920s for its "co-op program," which made on-the-job experience an essential part of undergraduate education in the arts and sciences. When Keeton, now Acting President, left Antioch thirty years later to found CAEL, Antioch College had become Antioch University, and the role of first-hand experience in the curriculum was now more complex than an alternation of on-campus study and off-campus work.

I write here about experiential education with a debt to Morris Keeton and to Antioch. I, too, was shaped by Antioch over fifteen years. In that period, I learned with—and from—him, and from the ferment about the nature of learning that is an ongoing, necessary part of Antioch—and of Goddard College, where I am now President.

Introduction

Experiential methods are varied and powerful. Using such methods will make student and faculty experience a legitimate, if not always equal, partner with academic study. This paper reviews the most common methods, underlying concepts and values, and addresses their problematics (in the sense that the choice of method assures certain problems). Students and faculty alike are asked to test their ideas through experience or to derive their theories from experience. Other terms speak to the same dynamic: the integration of theory and experience, of theory and practice, of work and study, or more simply, experiential learning or cooperative education. As a class of strategies, experience-based methods offer distinct advantages; they begin with the same good motive: to make learning more vital and democratic. When these approaches work, the result is involved students who, one hopes, become involved citizens.

Experience-based curriculum methods make use of student experience. The methods vary, more so than is generally acknowledged: use of practica, internships, co-op placements, clinical supervision, using

67

the portfolio method to assess prior learning, use of outward-bound settings, use of experiential methods in groups or classes including role plays, psychodrama and the like. At some colleges, one just refers to the "co-op program" which includes procedures and faculty for overseeing students when they take jobs off-campus. Experiential learning as a topic will take us into adult education generally and other topics such as self-directed learning, collaborative learning, and andragogical learning.[1]

The variety of methods is underestimated; so, too, is the number of theoretical puzzles, partly because there is so much discussion about one or another method. The methods are potent, and theory and experience interact in wonderfully complex ways. At first, the basic model appears simple, containing only three variables: theory, experience, and implicit or explicit values contained in that theory or experience. But three assumptions about this model will suggest the complexity ahead: First, learning is most probable when all three are interacting. Second, theory and experience are not static categories. The emerging concepts are shaped by their application and vice versa. In concert with values, they usually transform each other in complex iterations across different settings or over time, much as Alfred North Whitehead conceived of the alternation of romance and precision in learning.[2] Third, one can improve the power in this triad by entering the nested relationships from any direction: by improving emergent concepts, by searching for better experience, or by clarifying implicit values.

Beyond an abstract, three-variable model, the puzzles and problems multiply. If we want to know more about the best ways to incorporate student and faculty experience in the curriculum, the domain of inquiry must be expanded beyond looking at one or the other method, as I will suggest shortly. There are many reasons for advancing experiential methods and theory.

First of all, experience is the dominant force in informal learning (that is, learning not sanctioned by the faculty of a school or college) throughout the life span. Adults, for example, typically spend about six hundred hours yearly in self-directed learning, as Stephen Brookfield suggests. It is only in the most traditional academies—governed by hundreds of years of tradition—where the potency of experience outside of the classroom and its fundamental legitimacy is suspect.

One's own imperfect educational practice can be improved if we study the theory-experience dialectic, taking seriously the many questions about learning from experience. In this regard, I want to distinguish between the theory and methods of one's specialization (say, social psychology) and one's pedagogy, which usually lags far behind. While it is never easy to stay current in one's primary discipline, the second discipline— the presumed discipline—expects educators to have an up-to-date, self-reflective theory of learning. Master teachers may learn this discipline on their own by trial and error, but it is rarely taught in one's career. While most colleges have faculty development programs, teaching skills and learning-about-learning remain undeveloped.

Non-traditional educators have an added burden because they have had to learn experiential methods after completing a traditional graduate education that emphasizes theory and research methods, not pedagogy or reflective teaching. Too many teachers, for example, simply do not know how to use student internships effectively or how to use experiential methods in class. If faculty know these methods, they may not know how to use them well or to prevent their abuse.

How these new alternative models are titled is worth noting because the modifiers cooperative, experiential or self-directed suggest, correctly, that traditional learning theory does not give enough weight to these factors. All teachers, to some degree, use student experience in their teaching, and the importance of experience in learning is hardly a new topic; after all, it has preoccupied philosophers and educators of every generation. The importance of experience is acknowledged at many institutions, of course, and experiential educators should neither exaggerate their own strengths nor castigate the practices of traditional colleges. Many colleges have internships or practica, especially in engineering and in the human services like nursing, social work, medicine, education or clinical psychology.[3]

Where experiential educators differ is in the extent to which experience is made welcome and legitimate, and in the extent to which experience-based methods are included in the mission of the institution, thus leading to the self-selection of certain types of faculty and students.

Other things being equal, experiential methods have many strengths although some of these strengths, seen dialectically, foreshadow problems. Experiential learning is not a well-ordered topic.[4] There are many methods, but few theories, and fewer empirical studies of claimed effects.

There is another reason to pursue this research: a better understanding of experience-based methods will provide clues to improving traditional schools and colleges. Traditional education is, once again, in crisis, even though the complaints about standards, discipline, and access are not new.[5] But the putative crisis comes and goes; few of the reforms appear to work. The need for, and interest in, "free" and "community" schools and other experiments during the late 1960s—as well as the reaction to the excesses of this movement—is similar, for example, to the rise and fall of Progressive Education beginning in the 1920s.[6] The critical study of non-traditional methods and theory may help us to break the cycle and to improve the quality of education in all schools and colleges.

The Evolution of Experience-based Education at Antioch

The imperative that practical experience extends and enriches human learning is at the center of Antioch's mission. Even though Arthur Morgan deserves the credit for introducing experiential learning to Antioch in 1920, we could begin with Horace Mann. Before Mann became the first President of Antioch, he wrote a defense of what was, then, a reform in educational circles in the East, namely the introduction of theory to what had been a vocational, practical curriculum. Mann characterized the two poles in the debate vividly:

> The blind mole, as he runs along his covered furrow in the earth, is a perfect prototype
> of the merely practical man; the miller that flies a second time into the candle's blaze, after
> having his legs and wings once scorched there, is a perfect prototype of the merely theoretic man.[7]

He argued, in that era, for moderation, and the use of practice *and* theory:

> ...there is no such thing as intelligent practice which does not originate in theory;
> and no such thing as established or credible theory, which has not been ratified by practice.
> All intelligent action includes both theory and practice.

Mann also argued for two related concepts, that learning should be for the "whole person" (not just the mind), and that education should be for social change.

Arthur Morgan, in 1919–20, introduced the idea of a co-op program, modeling his ideas on the University of Cincinnati that had a co-op program at its engineering college. (The cooperative in co-op refers to the fact that two or more students must "cooperate" to provide coverage of one position in a company.) Antiochians, at least, believe that Cincinnati was the first to have a co-op program, whereas Antioch College was the first to apply this concept to all students in a liberal arts program. Today, some 1,100 colleges and universities have co-op programs, although they vary considerably in scope and intention. But Antioch College's use of a co-op program remains unique in two ways: first, its centrality in the curriculum, and second, the co-op program is not tied to a prospective vocation because students typically experiment with different co-op jobs. Antioch's co-op program is demanding because it requires students to hold at least six different jobs before they graduate, usually off-campus in different cities, in what is a sharp test of maturity and motivation.

Morgan, not Mann, laid the curricular foundations of modern-day Antioch. In addition to cooperative learning, he argued that education should further the development of small communities, and he wrote extensively about their future. In addition to the co-op concept, Morgan introduced the notion of community participation within the College before he left, at President Roosevelt's request, to lead the Tennessee Valley Authority.

That students should participate in college governance was institutionalized into formal committees with student participation by Algo Henderson, who followed Morgan, serving as President during the 1930s and 1940s. The exact connections between first, the fundamental legitimacy given to student experience and then, the legitimacy of their participation in college governance (in the l940s!) is not straightforward, but there is a certain kinship.

In the 1950s, President Douglas McGregor, a social scientist who was fascinated by communication in groups, organized the campus into "buzz groups," thus presaging "T-groups" and later, encounter groups in what became, outside of Antioch, an entire movement in group dynamics. Eventually, a whole class of methods using groups was developed by applied social scientists, and these methods continue to be potent, if neglected, technologies for advancing learning and participation (as sponsored by the National Training Labs or in Tavistock training).[8]

The College developed education abroad following the experience of alumni abroad during the 1940s who, in the later 1950s, asked President Samuel Gould to develop a program consistent with the value given to learning from experience.

Experience-based learning took another form at Antioch in the late 1960s. Morris Keeton, as Vice President for Academic Affairs, sponsored many programs that applied experiential learning to what was, then, a largely invisible sector in higher education, namely working adults. His pioneering work, using the portfolio method to document prior learning by adults, led to the establishment of several nationwide associations and the use of prior learning assessment in hundreds of colleges and universities. Under Keeton's leadership, Antioch created more than thirty-five adult learning centers nationwide—the exact number is still debated!—and these centers initially used experiential learning in two ways: first, through the evaluation of prior learning for adults and second, through the academic evaluation of the adult student's paid or volunteer work rather than an alternating co-op plan. Gradually, a third form emerged as faculty introduced experiential methods used in anthropology, counseling, or social psychology to their classrooms.

Experience-based Curriculum Methods

Having an understanding of the many types of experiential learning, the intermarriage of key concepts, and some of the recent history inside one institution which draws upon these ideas, let us turn now to the strengths and weaknesses of experiential models in higher education. What follows is, itself, an attempt to integrate theory and experience because I try to make sense of my personal experience using these methods.

The Power and Problematics of Experiential Methods

The great strength of an experiential approach to learning is that, done well, both the teacher and student are engaged as active learners. Experiential learning strategies also hold promise because the basic theory generates many new strategies by which to involve bored students or weary faculty, and many theoretical puzzles about human learning are surfaced. But there are problems, small and large. Consider the following example.

Adult students in a non-traditional management program are interested in the problem of bureaucracy. They read one popular critique of the problem before going off campus to a Saturday retreat. Various group methods are used to "break the ice," involving students in different assignments. They are given lists and asked to interview each other about the problem; they write their own notes and then exchange lists. Members of sub-groups report on the work of their groups at several plenary sessions throughout the day. The gentle group leader rarely intervenes except to structure a group activity. At day's end, there are lists of perceived problems and solutions on newsprint which now cover every wall. Group members are tired, yet satisfied, by what has been an involving day.

This true example poses troubling questions. Where, we must ask, was the intellectual content or coverage of the formal literature on bureaucracy? Who read Weber, Blau or Habermas? The group was not asked to encounter or apply current theories on bureaucracy, especially those European works that challenge the American reader because of the intellectual preparation presumed or the use of dialectical reasoning. Indeed, no formal sources, Western or Eastern, were used other than student experience. Students were not asked to derive, inductively, formal theory from their experiences. Neither did the instructor, a natural group facilitator, model intellectual values nor bring his own research to bear on the problem.

As motivated as the students became, we must ask: What happens to their sense of individuality when students let themselves be put, however gently, into a group? Can they really say "no" in front of peers and a "mentor" when it is "for your own good?" When will students learn to struggle with difficult conceptual material on their own? How will this personal discipline be learned, and when will students learn the special joy of mastering difficult arguments?

These are not easy questions, of course, and similar challenges could be put to the methods used in the most traditional classroom, one which depends upon the lecture method, closed-book testing, and grades. Used well, I have found experiential methods to be effective; they do involve students in real ways, learning can be fun, and students can be motivated to take on difficult, once- feared subjects. But if the consequences are reduced coverage of a field, the avoiding of difficult texts, inadequate experience with the "terror" and exhilaration of solitary scholarship, and the masking of potent authority relations, the question must be: To what end?

Experiential methods, student empowerment, faculty morale and authority, democracy in the schools, community involvement, and educational quality and access—these are important topics that, however, are as entangled as a snarled fishing line. Where does one begin? Indeed, perhaps the greatest single contribution of experiential methods is the way this imperative to use experience, when introduced to the curriculum, simply complicates everything. Assumptions about what should be studied, how it should be studied, and what is the role-set linking teacher and student—all conventional assumptions about learning can be questioned. The legitimacy of student experience in the academy functions, in essence, as an opening wedge that then legitimizes student participation in governance and work on campus, and encourages students to find their experience, to test their ideas, in community projects. In so doing, the introduction of student experience unfreezes the learning situation and raises the possibility of students (and faculty) becoming motivated which, in turn, extends the ways in which experience can be introduced, and so on, as a dynamic of proactive, cooperative, engaged problem solving begins.

To focus the discussion, let us next consider a series of crude propositions about the use of experiential methods. With each proposition, I will focus on the dilemmas presented when using such methods.

Proposition 1: Experiential methods increase student and faculty motivation to engage one another and the material.

Students and faculty are more likely to become involved in learning as they try to apply what they learn in class (or while reading) to past or present experience. The introduction of the "messy world" shakes things up, reframing the expectations of both students and faculty. Astin and his colleagues have reported a cluster of reinforcing attributes: involved college students are more satisfied, more persistent in learning, do more homework, are more active on campus, interact with more people, and continue their education after college.[9] For faculty bored with the traditional lecture format, their anecdotal reports suggest that their own alienation is reduced if they use experiential methods.

Experience-based methods enhance motivation, but there are potential problems. The most serious threat with process-based education is a certain casual attitude about intellectual matters reflected in the neglect of traditional literatures, especially formal theory and research. Where formal theory or methods are introduced, the coverage may use secondary rather than primary sources, may be limited (as in an "exposure" course), or may neglect non-Western literatures. Process-based educators, adept at involving students in learning, are less interested in, and skilled at, theory and research methods. Experiential educators may not be well read or current in the literature of an academic discipline, some totally rejecting academic discourse.

The use of theory in non-traditional courses and practica is the weakest leg of our three-legged stool: theory, values, and experience. Theory is sometimes rejected because it is too abstract, presumes skills in logic or math, or is simply difficult. Sometimes social theory is criticized, correctly so, because it imports conservative social biases without acknowledgment or reflects the narrow domain assumptions of European civilization.

But there are benefits to the formal study of competing theories: first, it gives students concepts they can use to pass on to others, one hallmark of a college education; second, having to struggle with abstract theory may, in time, advance cognitive complexity and the development of a differentiated view of self and society; third and most important, some of that theory should have a critical side to it, reflecting on contemporary mores and institutions. The study of critical theory, in particular, will help counter the seductive pull of the "okay, everyday world." Thus theory, in the social and administrative sciences, should have an emancipative motive, as Theodor Adorno suggests:

> The call for the unity of theory and practice has irresistibly degraded theory to the servant's role, removing the very traits it should have brought to that unity. The visa stamp of practice which we demand of all theory became a censor's place. Yet whereas theory succumbed in the vaunted mixture, practice became nonconceptual, a piece of the politics it was supposed to lead out of; it became the prey of power. (Adorno, 1973, cited by Giroux, 1983).[10]

There is a second problem. It takes discipline and training for a teacher to move a discussion, back and forth, from personal experience to college-level, conceptual learning. Many experiential educators have difficulty getting their students to go beyond deeply felt experience, to derive (or apply) theory from (or to) that experience.

Proposition 2: Traditional authority relations between student and teacher are more easily challenged when student experience is made legitimate.

The nature of authority in relations between students and faculty is not well understood; few theories of learning, traditional or otherwise, try to account for how authority shapes the enactment of the roles of teacher or student or the expectations and fantasies brought to these roles. (Theories of psychotherapy like psychoanalysis do consider this topic.) A crack may appear in the formal, hierarchical role set of traditional education in which the teacher teaches and the student is there to learn from the teacher.

Experience-based methods thus tend to diminish authority based on ascribed status and to embolden students who might otherwise be intimidated. This is especially important, of course, for adult students: first, many return to college with rigid, frightened perceptions of academic authority. Second, they are the same age as their teachers (or older) and their prior life experience makes them formidable competitors on many topics.

At the same time, by softening the boundary between the roles of student and teacher, the nature of authority may be mystified. A too-narrow commitment to experiential methods (and student-centered learning) leads, in the extreme, to anti-intellectualism and a jejune rejection of all authority, textual or personal. Also, the deep power of authority in social relations is not grasped and that means, according to psychoanalytic theory, that the authority can never be transcended, then to be incorporated into the self. In the worst case, the "soft" forms of leadership used in group dynamics mask and further mystify underlying authority, while appearing democratic.

Proposition 3: The use of experiential methods increases the possibility of dialogues about basic values.

When students move into the community or draw upon their personal experience, especially if they are involved in social action, personal values are highlighted. In personal dialogues, values are challenged and made legitimate. If experiential learning tends to legitimate the student as a collaborator in what can now be a jointly constructed learning situation, it also introduces values, directly or otherwise, into class exchanges and student-faculty discourse. Of course, one should not exaggerate this difference because values surface in the most traditional lecture. Indeed, values are at the center of Allan Bloom's conservative jeremiad or Henry Giroux's radical critique of education. But the extent and intensity of the engagement—the personal involvement in discussions—will be intense.

Increased dialogues between students and faculty (and among students) about values can advance, over time, the level of student moral or ethical reasoning. Substantive changes in a student's developmental stage do not come easily, but there is the possibility, at least, that he or she will be encouraged to use universalistic rather than particularlistic criteria to make moral judgments.[11]

When values are permitted, if not encouraged, in a discussion or paper, the teacher will need special skills to manage conflict in class (as in a discussion about abortion). It is not easy to develop a common search for the facts and higher order principles while also encouraging diverse, honest expression.

Proposition 4: The use of personal experience in papers and class discussion increases the depth and extension of learning, thus increasing motivation.

Students will be motivated to learn if they are asked to integrate a topic with their values, fears and hopes, providing that conceptualization is expected.

Many adults return to college fearful, usually because of prior failures in school, real or imagined. Few returning adults are self-confident in class and one must deal with deep-seated feelings and attitudes, often before the subject matter can be considered. In Carol Gilligan's terms, students—particularly women—have learned not to ask certain questions and there is "an underground" which holds these muted voices.[12]

Experiential methods, well chosen, can surface these feelings and unasked questions. While this is a dynamic approach to learning—witness the progress of good psychotherapy—the possibility of abuse is much greater than in a traditional classroom where strict limits are set on the use of personal experience. While there are, of course, limits on what can be safely discussed in any group setting, those limits are not usually approached. And most faculty either know, or can be taught to recognize, when the discussion takes a destructive turn. By forcing students to separate their deeply held, although partially explored, experience from formal education is to miss the power of learning tied to personal values.

But the power of group methods comes from the pressure to conform brought to bear on one person. Sometimes, students are put into groups, without much real choice, which then raise sensitive, personal topics. In addition to the invasive nature of such social technologies (invasive because they threaten one's right to psychological privacy), these groups are sometimes led by untrained faculty who appear to enjoy, not always consciously, the power of being a group leader with such potent methods.

These dangers point to the need for careful selection of faculty, appropriate supervision, and ongoing training. In this sense, the demands made of faculty using experiential methods are greater than would be the case with a traditional format.

Proposition 5: The proper use of experiential methods promotes individuation in students.

By individuation, I mean the development of a distinctive, well-organized personality, a true individual who can adapt to most circumstances. The relationship is not straightforward, but the proper use of experiential methods can motivate shy or passive students to become involved and to take risks. Many students find themselves quite lost in the herd of a large school, especially when they attend for the first time. A well-run orientation to college that uses experiential methods can help such students become proactive.

At the same time, true individuation and personal autonomy are not promoted if students do not learn about authority relations and the limits of all groups. First, individual students may not learn to question the "soft" authority of a group facilitator, and they may not really become differentiated from the group. Second, this diffusion of personal identity is particularly important at experimental colleges like Antioch, Prescott, or Evergreen that emphasize community building. The ethos in many non-traditional colleges puts so much value on being a good group or community member, that it may work to the detriment, one fears, of individual initiative and self-understanding. (New students at Antioch College can be recognized by the gingerly steps they take while learning to go barefoot.) Thus the very methods used to promote individual involvement in learning may limit the emergence of individual character.

Individuation should proceed on emotional, intellectual, and moral lines. Graduates of experiential curricula often are comfortable dealing with people and groups. But we should ask them to also understand themselves as individuals, true individuals in modern times, who must make sense of rapid social change, great poverty and great affluence, and the intrusion of consumerism into virtually all facets of life. That is, how will the curriculum prepare them for an unsentimental analysis of contemporary civilization?

Proposition 6: Experiential methods increase the possibility that students and faculty will work on real problems in daily life, thus increasing motivation.

Real problems (the low self-esteem one feels, for example, from a demeaning job) in contrast to scholastic problems (whether there are four or six types of alienation and what Marx might have said about the matter) are intrinsically motivating, once broached in class. There are no end of important problems which students (and faculty) face, now and in their futures—sexuality and intimacy, being a leader and a follower, finding meaningful work, contributing to the community—but traditional classrooms are not always hospitable to frank discussion.

This is another difficult boundary in which traditional education, in my opinion, has drawn the lines too conservatively. Students should be able to talk about their problems at work and have the opportunity to apply academic concepts to advance that understanding. Sometimes, if a student's requests to talk about these issues are too intense, he or she is sent to the specialist, the school psychologist or a psychotherapist. That is not to say that there should not be limits on disclosure, or that intense personal problems are appropriately discussed in class. But there is much vitality and learning possible when one relaxes the boundary between the personal and the public or between what can be discussed in school, now, or with a counselor, later.

Proposition 7: Because most adult students work or have volunteer interests, there is the possibility of immediate help for local institutions, the community, and other people.

Students who are working "on co-op" at a counseling center or devising a business plan as part of a course will try to improve conditions in their institutions. Also, because academic ideas are often put immediately into practice, methods and basic theory can be tested. Many adult students already hold important jobs and can put their knowledge to immediate use.

The risk, of course, is that things will be made worse, or that ambitious students will find themselves in trouble at work if they challenge an institutional practice or company authority. Faculty who supervise student co-ops or practica should be alert to this responsibility.

Proposition 8: Experiential methods increase the amount of interaction among all participants in a learning setting, thus increasing the opportunities for learning.

The direct channel, so to speak, from the teacher to the student is augmented by many different interactions. Peer interaction, as it occurs in cooperative learning groups, is greatly increased. The broader network of social interactions brought by most experiential methods means that, other things being equal, there will be more opportunities to rehearse difficult concepts, thus strengthening what is learned.

By increasing the amount and breadth of interaction, experiential methods allow the possibility of a major step in student development: the comparing of "my" experience to that of "their" experience and the experience of other peoples, ages and cultures, thus to reduce ethnocentrism. Asking students to evaluate their experience compared to other cultures and ages also opens the door for theory-based study of culture, history, creativity, and the like.

Proposition 9: In-class experiential learning strategies promote the learning of group dynamics.

Students tend to learn good "group skills;" they learn about group processes, how to manage a group, leadership and "followership," and how to find their own way in a group. Indeed, knowing how to work in a group may be more important than the manifest content of the course. Corporations and community institutions, not to mention the family, need these skills, especially in an era when many problems require the expanded resources that only a group can muster.

While these methods can be abused—consider how they are used in various cults—many classrooms could be made interesting and effective if the faculty knew these methods and could apply them judiciously.

Proposition 10: Because experiential methods are intrinsically powerful, they are easily reified.

Faculty and students can become caught up with one or another method, thus neglecting the purposes for using the technique as well as theory construction. One form of the portfolio method, which is used to document prior learning for adults, asks students to force their personal life experience into the existing courses and theory taught by a particular faculty. The problem is that too many student portfolios focus on trivial procedures and documentation while neglecting evidence of college-level conceptual learning. Worse, these products do not satisfy even the sympathetic critic that there has been college-level learning. Too many portfolios I have seen are long on documentation of experience and short on its analysis.

This reliance upon the correct "papering" of experience via a clumsy portfolio, three inches thick, seems to say that, as academics or intellectuals, we respect paper more than learning itself, or the engagement of student and faculty. The real value in the portfolio method is not captured by forcing the inchoate learning of students into specialized courses found in the catalog. Most important are the subtle changes in self-assessment which occur when students are asked to assess what they may have learned before, or outside of, college. Done well, this is not just an academic or intellectual exercise designed to assure conservative faculty that credits are not being given away. Rather, the task has a psychotherapeutic dynamic to it that is more important over the long run than documenting that the student has covered the content of Introductory Psychology 101. Indeed, the course-based portfolio system has always had a defensive quality to it which, in my opinion, has led it towards bureaucratic procedures and away from the original motive and excitement.

The point is this: the portfolio is a technical intervention into complex human affairs. Role-playing techniques, too, can be just a gimmick; when this happens, they are misapplied in the same way that the multiple choice test, as a technical solution, is misapplied inside the traditional college. As technology, the unintended consequences of these purposive interventions in social affairs are not well understood or applied.[13]

Proposition 11: The use of experiential methods provokes discussion about learning and teaching.

Students and faculty will be forced to examine the pedagogical assumptions governing their encounters and exchanges. It becomes legitimate, even expected, to challenge the professor's authority and the way the class is organized. Students may ask to negotiate parts of a syllabus. As a result, faculty find that they have to articulate a theory of education, if only to defend what they want to do. Students, too, argue more about pedagogy, and in this fashion, both students and faculty tend to be conscious of, and articulate about, educational theory. If this were the only advantage, it would be worth many failed experiments.

A practical suggestion follows: students should learn about learning *early* in their course of study (typical learning and teaching styles, experiential learning theory, how to evaluate theory, their personal needs and strengths). At Antioch's weekend college in Yellow Springs, for example, a semester-long course called Applied Learning Theory covers these topics, asking students to better understand themselves as learners (students and teachers). All college graduates, regardless of their major, should be highly literate about learning and the optimal design of learning environments.

More Questions and More Problems

There are many interesting questions and problems which can only be suggested. Because learning from experience is multi-dimensional, it is not easy to isolate the essential variables; there are dimensions that I have not discussed, notably the choice of subjects or content for the curriculum, an omission that may perpetuate the fiction that content and process can be separated in human learning.

I have advanced these crude propositions to provide a way into the theoretical puzzles that must be addressed. Much more should be known about how to optimize both student involvement and student mastery of difficult topics—a challenging task under the best conditions. What are the best ways to sequence the iterations of romance and precision, in Whitehead's terms, in a class or over the course of the semester?

Much more should be known, too, about the complex interplay of personal autonomy and the "ebb and flow" of authority in learning. How can one empower students, and empower faculty—at the *same* time—without having the process degrade into rhetoric or diminish the other's involvement, integrity, and learning? Part of the problem for the researcher is that most "theories" of learning are silent about authority relations. The classical liberal tradition does not have much of a role for experience-based methods, and authority is given only to the professor. The humanistic tradition supports student experience, of course, but gives primacy to affective states and feelings rather than to intellectual development. The Progressive tradition of the 1930s and 1940s emphasized practicality, if not vocational preparation, so that immigrants could participate in the democracy. Radical traditions, finally, tend either to be idealistic in giving the authority to students or careless about the role of authority in interactions with students. What we need is an integrative effort that makes realistic, searching assumptions about authority relations in learning, especially in non-traditional schools and colleges where the boundaries are blurred.

Empirical research is needed to explore or test the kind of claims which this paper has asserted. We need creative methods, empirical and phenomenological, which somehow balance the need for precise measures with the reality that most of the constructs are poorly defined and the real power comes from their interaction.

Experiential learning would be made stronger by improvements in its basic theory, specifying the elements to be combined and postulating the calculus that would coordinate those elements. At a different level of analysis, however, we might worry about the intellectual narrowness of non-traditional strategies. Too many discussions do not use more than one intellectual tradition. This is curious, indeed, because few topics have so engaged intellectuals of all cultures as the proper mix of theory and experience, a pre-eminent dichotomy that humans use to understand their nature. The vocabulary varies as do the methods; but this is most certainly not a subject discovered or exhausted by John Dewey or Malcolm Knowles.

The technicist bias—the fetishism of certain methods—in the sprawling field of experiential learning can be managed by applying the methods inside the moral and intellectual contexts built, over many years, by earlier generations of scholars and activists. Most contemporary discussions of experiential learning neglect continental intellectual traditions and are the poorer for this fact. Consider just two philosophical traditions, each rather extensive, but neither commonly used in adult programs: that of Existentialism and of Marxism.

The most interesting book I have found to use with returning adult students is Maxine Greene's *Landscapes of Learning*.[14] She writes beautifully about being wide awake in the world, a concept that she borrowed from the social philosopher Alfred Schutz. She writes about being alone with one's experience—and one's choices—in an impersonal, amoral world. Adult students in a post-modern era identify with Existentialist ideas, perhaps because many came of age in the late 1940s and early 1950s.

As discredited as its political forms may be, Marxist theory, too, is a mine of ideas about the tangled relationship between theory, practice and values. Indeed, the Marxist category of praxis is, itself, an attempt to fuse theory, values and social action.[15] Neo-marxist criticism is important for a full understanding of the social and administrative sciences which many adult students want to study (that is, the critical theory of the Frankfurt School: Theodor Adorno, Herbert Marcuse, Walter Benjamin and in the present, Jurgen Habermas).[16] This largely theoretical work—which is not easily read by students because the arguments are abstract—would point to the ways in which student experience and the social theories students might try to apply to their experience, for example, are shaped by a popular culture rooted in commodity fetishism. Critical theory also asks what has happened to the possibility of real individuality in modern times, a strong sense of self as an intellectual with values and social commitments, not a self based on consuming endless "new" products and services.

Indeed, the tendency not to seek the intellectual roots of what then appear, falsely, to be modern or innovative ideas is, itself, a sign of a far more serious problem than a dispute about pedagogy. The abuse or ineffective use of one or another experiential method is not as important, in my opinion, as the anti-intellectualism in American culture and institutions, a topic with which I will close the paper.[17]

An anti-intellectual attitude can be found in the inattention to formal theory, to not requiring the coverage of certain difficult topics like math or science in the curriculum, and in the relaxed, "flexible" standards which are sometimes applied to a non-traditional curriculum. A "here-and-now," ahistorical mentality might lead one to forget the contributions of a Thomas Jefferson or a Henry David Thoreau, America's own intellectuals.

One fears unintended sexist assumptions, if not patriarchy. There is, after all, a nasty political side to this discussion when one realizes that many adult students are women or minorities who already face enough discrimination because of their age, race, sex or a late start up a career ladder. Who benefits if they graduate as involved learners who are, nonetheless, unprepared to be leaders in a technological, global economy? To what extent does progressive rhetoric like "empowerment" mask what is really a retreat from the dilemmas of mass society and complex, demanding skills? By focusing too much on "process" and joining that to a facile critique of Western civilization, the unintended consequence may be that we only perpetuate and extend the subordination of women and minorities.

Like the questions raised about the example I began with, this query, too, could be put to traditional education. Although some of the discussion above may seem impatient or tendentious, I am writing in strong support of non-traditional education, in general, and experiential education, in particular. The power of experiential methods needs to be tempered and extended by critical research about the contexts in which these methods are applied.

More than just a balance of content and process, I am asking for a certain critical spirit within experiential education, a restlessness comparable to Albert Camus' definition of an intellectual: "A mind that watches itself."[18] This has been an argument against sleeping on one's hobbyhorse.

Footnotes

1. S. Brookfield, *Self-directed Learning: From Theory to Practice* San Francisco: Jossey-Bass, 1985); M. Knowles & Associates, *Andragogy in Action: Applying Modern Principles of Adult Learning* (San Francisco: Jossey-Bass, 1985).
2. A.N. Whitehead, *The Aims of Education* (New York: The Free Press, 1929).
3. D. Shoen, *Educating the Reflective Practitioner* (San Francisco, Jossey-Bass, 1987).
4. D. Kolb's *Experiential Learning* (Englewood Cliffs, NJ: Prentice-Hall, 1984) is the best single book available even though many educators only use his scaling method, neglecting his discussion of theory.
5. A. Bloom, *The Closing of the American Mind* (New York: Simon and Schuster, 1987); cf. S. Aronowitz and H. Giroux's biting critique, "Schooling, Culture and Literacy in the Age of Broken Dreams: A Review of Bloom and Hirsch" (Harvard Educational Review, Vol. 578, No. 2, May, 1988); T. Sizer, *Horace's Compromise: The Dilemmas of the American High School* (Boston: Houghton Mifflin, 1985).
6. See L.A. Cremin, *The Transformation of the School*, (New York: Vintage Books, 1964).
7. H. Mann, *The Common School Journal*, Vol. X, No. 5, page 67 (Boston, MA: March 1, 1848).
8. E.B. Klein, "An Overview of Recent Tavistock Work in the United States," in C.L. Cooper and C. Alderfer (Eds.), *Advances in Experiential Social Processes* (New York: John Wiley and Sons, 1978).
9. A. Astin, *et al.*, *Involvement in Learning* (Washington, DC: National Institute of Education, 1984).
10. H. Giroux, *Theory and Resistance in Education* (South Hadley, MA: Bergin and Garvey Publishers, Inc., 1983); T. Adorno, *Negative Dialectics* (New York, Seabury Press, 1973).
11. A. Erdynast, *Field Experience and Stage Theories of Development*, (a monograph by NSIEE, 3509 Haworth Drive, Suite 207, Raleigh, NC 27609; see also J. Kendall *et al.*, *Strengthening Experiential Education within Your Institution*, same address, 1986.
12. C. Gilligan, *In A Different Voice* (Cambridge: Harvard University Press, 1982); also, her 1988 address to the AAHE National Conference on Higher Education; M.B. Belenky *et al.*, *Women's Ways of Knowing* (New York: Basic Books, 1986).
13. See J. Ellul's critique of the use of technology in all spheres of life, *The Technological Society* (New York, Knopf, 1964).
14. M. Greene, *Landscapes of Learning* (New York: Teachers College Press, 1978).
15. See Paulo Freire, *Pedagogy of the Oppressed* (New York: Seabury Press, 1973).
16. M. Jay, *The Dialectical Imagination* (Boston, MA: Beacon Press, 1975); Peter Dews; (Ed.) *Habermas: Autonomy & Solidarity* (London: Verso, 1986).
17. R. Hofstadter, *Anti-intellectualism in American Life* (New York: Vintage Books, 1963).
18. Giroux asks that teachers be "transformative intellectuals" in S. Aronowitz and H. Giroux, *Education Under Siege* (South Hadley, MA: Bergin & Garvey, 1985).

10

Among the Talmudists and Missionaries: Cross-Cultural Perspectives on Prior Learning Assessment

Elana Michelson

For many of us who have been inspired by the work of Morris Keeton, the advancement of prior learning assessment has been at the center of a cluster of important concerns. In addition to its primary function, that of facilitating degree completion for returning adult students, PLA has also provided a focus for the range of adult educational issues: institutional structure, academic culture, curriculum.

Yet there is no easy agreement as to the function and limits of prior learning assessment; rather, there is an ongoing implicit debate as to the relationship of prior learning assessment to traditional academic disciplines. One model of PLA practice says, this is what academic subject matter is—to the degree you've got it (and can package it to look like ours), we'll give you college credit. The subject matter of academia is fixed, or determined unilaterally by academe itself; what changes is the student's ability to relate to academic subject matter, to follow its set lines of inquiry and discourse, to adjust to its assumptions. PLA in that context is an academic match game scored with numbers, one that all too often provides non-traditional students with one more standard to fail by, one more way to be judged and found lacking.

Those of us who have been privileged to work with Morris Keeton have come to look at PLA in another, more interactive way. Learning, Morris taught us, must begin with the learner. Prior learning assessment and other adult learner services err when they see themselves exclusively as bridges, put there solely to get bright but "limited" students situated comfortably within academic norms. Under his leadership, we have sought a framework for adult learners in which access is defined as broader than entry into a pre-determined curriculum. Together, we have advocated for student-centered learning, in which students have, not only access to the curriculum, but visibility within it.

Seen in this regard, PLA goes beyond the systematizing of equivalencies and correspondences, in which we discover and rediscover the overlap between experiential learning and academic disciplines. That aspect is important, to be sure. But by making the experiential learning of students part of the regular discourse of the academy, PLA engages us in a re-examination of just what "knowledge" means. In its broadest sense, PLA is the process through which the academic community opens itself up to qualities of knowledge it may have closed itself off from, placing our own, and not just our students' knowledge within a multiplicity of perspectives.

It is this characteristic of prior learning assessment, this requirement that we interact among differing cultures of knowledge, that makes PLA so enriching to academic life. Yet the fit among those cultures and the way we render them mutually visible is never fully delineated. We renegotiate the boundaries every time we encounter a new population of students, and occasionally those new populations require that we begin at the beginning again.

During the 1988–1989 academic year, I served as director of the Empire State College program in Jerusalem. My students, predominantly Americans, were in Israel for a variety of reasons: to study, to live, to work with synagogue or church organizations. They came to Empire State College both for the opportunity to study in English and out of a desire to combine a variety of learning modalities into an individualized degree.

For many students, in Jerusalem as elsewhere, the availability of prior learning assessment was part of the attraction. In particular, students from religious Jewish or Christian backgrounds (given the current political situation, it was unfortunate but not surprising that we had no Moslem students) brought with them extensive prior learning from seminaries, yeshivot, and other religious institutions of learning. Having spent years in serious but non-college-accredited study, they were eager to apply this prior learning towards their college degrees.

The translating, so to speak, of religious education into the matrix of an Empire State degree program was one of the challenges of the director's job. Empire State is a liberal arts college within American public higher education, proud, to be sure, of its individualized approach to students' needs, but equally proud of its values steeped in a broad, secular humanist tradition. The question of how to make religious studies a viable part of an Empire State degree allowed me—perhaps forced is a better word—to reexamine my own most dearly held convictions about prior learning assessment, convictions by which I most centrally define myself as an educator.

One example can serve for many. I am in conference with a new student whom I will call Jeremy, a young man just beginning the assessment process. The first draft of his prior learning portfolio includes, in addition to a good deal of Judaica, an essay on holistic medicine. In our ensuing conversation about his knowledge in this field, he reaches into his pocket and retrieves a book on the subject. As he flips through it, I notice that each chapter contains paragraphs, at times whole pages, that are crossed out in heavy black ink. These paragraphs, he replies to my question, treat the theoretical foundations of holistic medicine in Eastern religious philosophies, which he is not willing to read.

I am appalled, as one might imagine. "Jeremy," I gulp, "it's only Buddhism. It's not an infectious disease."

Jeremy does not agree. "Of course ideas are infectious," he replies. "Most books are written to convince someone of something. Why else do people go to the trouble to write them?" Jeremy shrugs. "So the easiest way not to be convinced is not to read them in the first place."

I sit gaping at him, as open-mouthed with insight into myself as with astonishment at Jeremy. I have always campaigned against the notion that, to be accreditable, students' accumulated knowledge has to look like that of academics, not only coming programmed into courses and disciplines, but surrounded by the glow of secular humanist values. I have been proud that my career as an academic has let me work, not only with adults in general, but with specific populations whose experience and ways of knowing have been insufficiently visible within academia: women, people of color, workers. I have sought to educate other academics about the intellectual and analytical sophistication, the social and moral intelligence that goes into the paid and unpaid activity through which humanity perpetuates the world. Above all, this has entailed asking academics to relativize their own value systems, to acknowledge the validity, including the college-equivalency, of other constructs of knowledge.

Now, in my little office, within blocks of the holy sites of the three major religions of the West, I am hoisted on my own petard, as it were. I have become the enemy. I am overcome with the irony that literate, verbal Jeremy can make me believe what I have always despised others for believing, namely, that liberal arts education will somehow save our students' souls, make them see a more enlightened perspective, make them broader, better people, somehow. I smile grimly to myself, wanting nothing so much as to rise from my chair and start pounding Jeremy over the head with *The New York Review of Books.* . . .

In a number of important ways, Jeremy and his crossed-out paragraphs pose a different challenge to that which has typified our experience of PLA. Our initial challenge was to formulate procedures that remained true to the culture and standards of academia while being even-handed to our students. The populations we have served were often adults whose practical expertise was more sophisticated than their theoretical perspective, individuals with more college-level learning than college-level language skills.

Such is hardly Jeremy's problem. It is not for nothing that "Talmudic" has entered the parlance of secular education to mean a rigorous grasp of the particulars of evidence and the construction of theoretical argumentation out of an extensive familiarity with primary and secondary texts. My students in Jerusalem, both Jewish and Christian, revealed a staggering array of "book-learning" and finely honed analytical and verbal skills. Moreover, their knowledge was seemingly the easiest kind to accredit: it was based on a major text within the Western intellectual tradition; it was best demonstrated in verbal form; because it was often legalistic in approach, it was built on an explicit relationship between theory and practice and on the notion of alternative interpretation.

Nor were these students, I quickly learned, the anti-intellectual Bible-thumpers secular humanists love to hate. Their essays revealed a deep appreciation of the nuances of language and rhetoric, a grasp of multiple meanings, a taste for fine distinctions, wit. Students with Jeremy's narrowness of focus were a distinct minority within this population; most were eager for the interplay of ideas and were glad to accept the challenge of other points of view.

Yet the minority Jeremy represented was unsettling, and I could not simply shrug back at him and submit his various portfolio essays for evaluation. His insistence on not exposing himself to Eastern religious traditions made me question the accrediting, not only of his knowledge of holistic medicine, but his far more extensive knowledge of Jewish religious lore. Nor was I convinced that this was simply my own prejudices, those of a proudly secular Jew and epistemological skeptic. But the implications frightened me. If I were suddenly reluctant to accredit erudite, textually-trained scholars, what would become of the skilled auto workers, human service administrators, and telecommunications technicians who have become a new constituency for prior learning assessment? What about those whose learning is workplace and community based and yet, we argue, academically accreditable?

And what would become, moreover, of the vision of student-centered learning, the commitment to "start where the student is at," in that ungrammatical but useful phrase? What of my opposition to PLA as a kind of cultural imperialism? What of my insistence that we academics have not cornered the market on the examined life?

Prior learning assessment rests, at least in part, on a belief in the liberating effect of student-centered learning.

> [In education] the individual is central; an individual in the deepest sense, is the culture,
> not the institution. His culture resides in him, in experience and memory, and what is needed
> is an education that has at its base the sanctity of the individual's experience and leaves it intact.

So what, then, is wrong with assessing the wealth of Jeremy's knowledge and building a degree program around the culture that, indeed, resides in Jeremy, in the sanctity of how and what he has learned?

I don't know.

But there is a tension, it seems to me, between beginning with the students' experience and ending there. We must resist the tendency to make the academic perspective the only one that is visible, but in so doing we argue for the democratization of perspectives, not for their elimination. As Samuel Bowles and Herbert Gintis say of the above quote in another context, "education can recognize the sanctity of the individual's experience, but it cannot leave it intact."[1]

Thus, student-centered education is liberating to the degree that it situates individual experience within a broadening of perspectives. It presupposes that we are empowered by an inquiry of the broadest possible breadth, that we draw our best conclusions from a range of ideas and methodologies. What is liberating about knowledge, according to this model, is not that it takes us beyond ourselves, but that it frees us into choice.

Michael Polanyi characterizes closed logical systems and the thinking patterns of their adherents as revealing what he calls circularity, self-expansion, and suppressed nucleation. Closed systems survive in the face of falsifying evidence, first, by linking that evidence to other notions within the same system and, second, by treating it as a "special case" around which to posit further elaborations. Thirdly, and most importantly for this discussion, adherents retain the seeming stability of closed systems by denying the validity of any rival framework; thus, kernels of evidence or insight cannot take root owing to a lack of alternative conceptions through which to view their significance.

Most people, including most academics, think this way to some degree, and in raising these points, I emphatically do not mean to characterize the lore and wisdom of the Jewish or Christian religious tradition. There is nothing closed about the concerns that typify the religious tradition at its best. My interactions with this community taught me that the breadth of subject matter spans the human experience: the nature of the world and of human beings, the centrality of human responsibility, the vicissitudes of courage, of love.

But if the concerns of students such as Jeremy were not closed, the ways in which they legitimated knowledge often were. All religious fundamentalism is self-authenticating, that is, self-referenced in procedure if not in subject matter. The pieces out of which the system of thought is built—ideas, texts and references, sages and scholars—are allowed to reflect on each other in ways that encourage infinite subtlety and insight within the system but posit no way out of it, even to allow it to interact with alternative systems of thought.

Thus, the very process that allows us to accredit the knowledge of experiential learners, namely, the dialogue between what they have learned and what academia posits, is not possible here. The connection between students' prior learning and the curriculum is thereby broken, not by the lack of resemblance between them, but by the lack of dialogue, the refusal of relationship.[4]

Let us take as an alternate example a student more typical of returning adults, say, a competent, experientially-taught office manager. The skills and theoretical understanding she has developed may be articulated, documented and assessed. Her knowledge may not yet have all the theories of management and office systems that are organized within academic constructs. But the assessment process and the planning of her degree program can introduce a broader perspective on how her knowledge fits with other knowledge like itself, exposing her both to the disciplines and interdisciplines of academic inquiry and to the practical arts and sciences of management. For those skills to then be translated into part of an academically defensible degree program—accredited, in other words—she cannot merely maintain that hers is the only way to do things; the assessment must have initiated a dialogue in which she becomes aware of the relationships among what she knows, the experience of other practitioners, and the academic fields of inquiry that address the stuff of her experience.

What ensures that this exposure is not an exercise in academic arrogance—(OK, now that you've limped along on your own, we're going to give you the real stuff)—is that the exposure be reciprocal, that students not simply be required to judge their own knowledge in the light of academic theory, but that academic theories themselves be held up to the test of alternative scholarship and the scrutiny of the practitioner. It seems to me that the point of secular humanist inquiry is to take us beyond any and all self-authenticating, self-referenced frameworks, out of self-enclosure, so to speak. The great contribution of PLA is the requirement that this integration among cultures of knowing be interactive, that it afford an opportunity for all of us, student and faculty alike, to engage each other in dialogue.

And it is a dialogue, which means that both student and faculty are responsible for coming to it with good will and open hands. To a great degree, the onus is on us, to treat what students know with respect, to be willing to allow our knowledge to be tested by that of others, to be, as my colleague Lee Herman has put it, prepared to be surprised. But students, too, have a responsibility to the dialogue through which their knowledge becomes recognized within academic discourse. Without that dialogue, the process of assessment is incomplete; students' knowledge, even after it is assessed, remains institutionally disembodied.

To be sure, students can refuse the invitation; in my year in Jerusalem, some did. Secular humanist liberal arts education is not for everyone, and it should not try to be. But there is a vision of education to which we, at least, must be faithful, because, ultimately, Jeremy is right. Ideas are communicable. Knowledge is, and should be, dangerous to one's smug convictions about what one already knows. And if we engage in this process with integrity, it is dangerous to us as well, for it is not only our students who are challenged by alternative frameworks for knowing, or changed by them.

I will always be grateful to those of my religious students who engaged in that dialogue with me; I can only hope they profited from the exchange half as much as I. I felt privileged to peer into the depths of learning that these students wore so gracefully, so wisely. For the liberating function of student-centered education—and this is the crux of the matter—rests on the growing understanding of choices: about how to manage an office, how to interpret the Bible, how to know the world.

Footnotes

1. Peter Marin, quoted in Samuel Bowles and Herbert Gintis, *Schooling in Capitalist America* (New York: Basic Books, 1976), page 273.
2. *Ibid.*
3. For a full discussion, see Joseph Weizenbaum, *Computer Power and Human Reason* (New York: W.H. Freeman, 1976), pp. 121–126.
4. That the point is not the system of thought itself but the need for multiple perspectives is made clearer if we view one way in which the same framework of religious studies was used to broaden and relativize other frameworks. Many of my ultra-Orthodox Jewish students came to secular education for purposes of professional preparation, often choosing fields such as computer studies because they seem to promise a value-free way of earning a living in the secular world.

   In helping such students design degree programs, we often used their backgrounds in Jewish philosophy to broaden the context through which they viewed their studies, utilizing the enormous moral strength and subtlety of the Jewish tradition to bring other conceptual frameworks to bear on issues raised by twentieth-century technology. Students read such works on computers as Sherry Turkle's *The Second Self*, Robert Howard's *Brave New Workplace*, and Joseph Weizenbaum's *Computer Power and Human Reason* in order to identify the social and ethical questions raised by computers. They then worked with a mentor in Judaic Studies to discover what insights and constructs are offered by Jewish philosophy concerning the nature and uniqueness of human intelligence, will, the morality of social choices, privacy, creativity and craftsmanship, etc. As one of these students wrote in the essay that accompanied her degree program,

   > Had I been asked last year to name an area of study that involves almost no ethical or moral problems, I would have chosen the field of computers. After all, what could be wrong with the processing, assembling, and record-keeping that computers do? . . . I have come to see that, in fact, computer technology has some moral consequences and ethical decisions that need to be dealt with. . . . The Biblical commandment to master and rule the world has inherent in it a responsibility. . . .

Part III

Adult Development Theory:
Implications for Teaching and
Professional Development

11

Classroom Teaching, Personal Development and Professional Competence

Arthur W. Chickering

It was toward the end of May in the year 10 B.C. (Before CAEL), 1963 according to the traditional calendar. I was sitting in my office staring at twelve different complimentary introductory psychology text-books stacked ponderously on my desk. The fall semester lay ahead. So did Intro. Psych. 101. With a mixture of anguish and despair I wondered whether there was any way the students and I might somehow get through the intro course more productively and happily. Probably there are few freshman or sophomore courses where the gap between student motives and course content, between what they want and what they get, is so great. In the very area where students hope to glean some insights useful to their lives, we traditionally provide content distant from their most pressing curiosities.

For four years I had struggled with this course the way most of my colleagues did. I picked out what I thought was the most lively and pertinent text, selected provocative examples and exercises which I hoped connected with student concerns, and worked my way through perception, learning, motivation and human development. I used pre- and post-multiple choice tests, which I constructed simply by lifting items from the ubiquitous workbooks and teacher's guides which customarily accompany examination copies of introductory texts.

Some students became interested in the ensuing course. For most it was something to survive so they could get to personality theory and abnormal psychology.

In that fateful year of 1963, I spread the texts across the desk as I always had and started perusing their tables of contents, checking out relative areas of emphasis, what was asserted as known, what questions "needed further research." And of course, as always, I wanted to make sure that those key topics, which in my wisdom I knew were absolutely essential to understanding psychology, were covered. Then I had what students in my second lecture and demonstration on perception learn to call an "Aha!" experience. I suddenly asked myself, "Why shouldn't the students be addressing these questions of emphasis and differences among these textbook authorities, why shouldn't they be asking what is known and what is still in need of further research?"

I began to think about what it would be like for them to examine these different texts, ascertain the differences among the authors, identify what is called fact and what is still open to question. Further, why not provide a chance for students to take particular personal concerns or professional aspirations and search out pertinent concepts, principles, hypotheses, or experimental paradigms?

I figured I had little to lose. I knew it would be more interesting for me. Perhaps it would work better for the students as well. So I rethought the course. I put my twelve examination copies on reserve in the library and had the bookstore order eight copies of each (not without some bureaucratic hassles, naturally). Then I wrote a brief piece entitled "How to Select Your Own Text" and made copies available to all enrollees together with a new course description. The "How To" piece was nothing special. It simply suggested that they think about their own interests and motives for enrolling, check the tables of contents and indexes in the various texts to see what the authors emphasized, leaf through each volume to get a general impression and read a few sections at random to sample the writing styles. By the time of the second three hour class meeting, each student was to have selected a text.

That fall 55 students enrolled. All twelve textbooks were selected, though two were especially popular. As far as I could tell, one was popular because it had a creative format with many inserts, exercises, diagrams and so forth. The other was popular because it was thin; it also had a strong physiological orientation which made it distinctive for pre-meds and others with special interests of that kind.

The first class meeting started, just as always, with a pre-test. I briefly described the major concept areas the course would cover: perception, learning, motivation and human development. Then we discussed four different ways students could pursue the course:

1. An individual could simply work along on his or her text and answer three basic questions for each major concept area:
   a. what are the major concepts or principles given as fact, as known?
   b. what are the issues, concepts or principles still under scrutiny, the areas of active or needed research?
   c. what major findings have been reported in pertinent journals during the last five years for one of the issues needing further research when the text was published?
2. Two or more students who had selected the same text could form a group to tackle these questions together. For those selecting this option, each would have to do the journal search on a different issue.
3. Two or more students could form a multi-text group. These groups would deal with the same three questions, except that their responses would also identify differences among the authors in assertions about what was known and about the issues requiring future research. In these groups each student would also select one of those issues for a journal search and report.
4. Individual students, in consultation with me, could identify a personal concern, social problem or professional interest and develop a learning contract. In this learning contract they would: (a) define their objectives; (b) examine one or more texts for pertinent principles or concepts; (c) search journals during the previous five years for information relevant to their organizing questions; (d) carry out other small research projects, field studies, interviews and the like as a basis for a final report; and (e) specify the methods and criteria for evaluation.

Class meeting time was used to create summary answers to the questions concerning what was known and the areas for further research. We also identified differences among the authors, listed the topics individual students would be studying, and shared their written reports. Thus the outcome for the three weeks devoted to perception, for example, was a list of the major concepts agreed on by all 12 authors, a list of areas where they differed, a list of major research questions and brief summaries of recent findings based on the student reports. That cycle was repeated for learning, motivation and human development.

Formative evaluation by myself and the students occurred during the semester based on the group and individual reports. The final grade was based on these evaluations and on the final multiple choice exam taken by all students regardless of the study option they chose. Those undertaking learning contracts were free to attend class or not, as they saw fit. The final exam counted 50 percent for these students and the contract 50 percent.

Four persons chose to work alone. There were two same-text groups, one of two persons and one of four. There were six multi-text groups varying in size from five to eight. Five students pursued individual contracts: two focused on issues concerning sexual behavior and sexual identification, one on aggression and hostility, one on civil liberties and one on causes of academic under-performance.

Pre-post test gains on the multiple choice exams differed from previous years in two ways: the average gain was about half a standard deviation higher, and the range and standard deviation on the final was smaller. But three other outcomes were perhaps more important. Student satisfaction, perceived benefit to themselves, and perceived sense of psychology as a living discipline dealing with complex issues were much more positive. Furthermore, I had a lot more fun and learned a good bit myself in the process. The following year, with a class of 43, I had basically the same results.

I share this course description in some detail so we can examine issues concerning personal development and professional competence in addition to the more specific outcomes in understanding basic psychology. Let's take human development first and then turn to issues concerning professional competence.

Loevinger's conceptions concerning ego development provide a useful framework for thinking about human development. This conceptual framework, though more complex than most, is powerful because ego development is a "master trait" whose different structures influence other areas of human development. One could, for example, take a more narrow focus using Kohlberg's theories concerning cognitive/moral development or Perry's scheme concerning intellectual/ethical development. The numbers of persons applying these theories to educational practice is increasing, and I commend that growing body of research and application to anyone who wants to pursue those ideas more explicitly. I choose to tackle the broader perspectives offered by ego development because they provide multiple handles for application and a wider range of implications.

Table 1 (see following page) gives Loevinger's basic sequence of successive developmental structures, each comprising "an interwoven fabric" of impulse control and character development, interpersonal style, conscious preoccupations and cognitive style (p. 26). There is not time for detailed discussion of this theory, but five key principles are critical:

1. Ego development does not consist of four separate dimensions; there is just one dimension, and the four columns describe the elements of a single coherent process.
2. Beyond the Conscientious stage, the others are additive. They are structural transformations of the earlier stages.
3. Movement along this hierarchy results in an expanded repertoire of behavioral alternatives; a person at the conformist stage cannot function autonomously, but one at the autonomous stage can choose to conform.
4. "Ego development is at once a developmental sequence and a dimension of individual differences in any age cohort" (Loevinger, p. 13). Age and stage are not highly correlated. Stage differences are pertinent descriptors of individual differences among typical college age students as well as among diverse adults throughout the life cycle.
5. Developmental stage is not necessarily associated with increased happiness, adjustment or mental health.

> There is a temptation. . .to assume that the best adjusted people are those at the highest stages. This is a distortion. There are probably well adjusted people at all stages. . . Probably those who remain below the conformist level beyond childhood can be called maladjusted. . . Some self-protective, opportunistic persons, on the other hand, become very successful. . . Certainly it is a conformist's world, and many conformists are very happy with it though they are not all immune to mental illness. Probably to be faithful to the realities of the case one should see the sequence as one of coping with increasingly deeper problems rather than as the successful negotiation of solutions (Loevinger, p. 7).

Table 1. Some Milestones of Ego Development

Stage	Impulses, Control, Character, Development	Interpersonal Style	Conscious Preoccupations	Cognitive Style
Presocial Symbiotic		Autistic Symbiotic	Self *vs.* non-self	
Impulsive	Impulsive fear of retaliation	Receiving, dependent, exploitative	Bodily feelings, especially sexual and aggressive	Stereotyping, conceptual confusion
Self-Protective	Fear of being caught, externalizing blame, opportunistic	Wary, manipulative, exploitative	Self-protection, trouble, wishes, things, advantage, control	
Conformist	Conformity to external rules, shame, guilt for breaking rules	Belonging, superficial niceness	Appearance, social acceptability, banal feelings, behavior	Conceptual simplicity, stereotypes, cliches
Conscientious Conformist	Differentiation of norms, goals	Aware of self in relation to group, helping	Adjustment, problems, reasons, opportunities (vague)	Multiplicity
Conscientious	Self-evaluated standard self-criticism, guilt for consequences, long-term goals and ideals	Intensive, responsible, mutual, concern for communication	Differentiated feelings, motives for behavior, self-respect, achievements, traits, expression	Conceptual complexity, idea of patterning
Individualistic	Add: Respect for individuality	Add: Dependence as an emotional problem	Add: Development, social problems, differentiation of inner life from outer	Add: Distinction of process and outcome
Autonomous	Add: Coping with conflicting inner needs, toleration	Add: Respect for autonomy, interdependence	Vividly conveyed feelings, integration of physiological and psychological, psychological causation of behavior, role conception, self-fulfillment, self in social context	Increased conceptual complexity, complex patterns, toleration for ambiguity, broad scope, objectivity
Integrated	Add: Reconciling inner conflicts, renunciation of unattainable	Add: Cherishing of individuality	Add: Identity	

Note: "Add" means in addition to the description applying to the previous level. Loevinger, Jane, *Ego Development*, Jossey-Bass Publishers, San Francisco, 1976, pp. 24–25.

Figures 1 and 2 (following pages) suggest some of the implications of ego development theory. The basic points made by these figures are that different motives for learning, orientations toward knowledge, educational practices, student-faculty relationships and methods of evaluation are systematically linked to different levels of ego development.

Although in 1963 I was not nearly as sophisticated about the implications of developmental stage theories for teaching and learning as I am now, in retrospect it's quite easy to see how the four major options for learning coincided rather nicely with the self-protective, conformist, conscientious and autonomous stages. Working alone with one's own text, coming to class and taking good notes, selecting safe, straightforward research topics for journal searches and reporting, was clearly the least challenging, simplest approach to meeting course requirements. The same-text groups allowed students to function in conceptually simple fashion, relying on a single authority, addressing required questions, and obtaining necessary information with a minimum of uncertainty and ambiguity. Class sessions provided them with added reinforcement concerning the concepts and issues they identified and also supplied handy lists of additional concepts to add to their notebooks. For those same-text groups there was not much occasion for critical reactions or probing questions. Any differences were rather easily resolved by going to their common text and identifying the right answer. Feedback and evaluation from peers was minimal because the amount of contribution one student could make to another was fairly limited, assuming that the basic reading had been done.

The multi-text groups had a more complex challenge. Each participant not only had to identify the major points for his or her text but had to explain those points with sufficient clarity to ascertain the points of agreement or disagreement with students using other texts. There were no right answers here. Recognizing shades of gray, tolerating ambiguity, defining the shifting boundaries between what was known and what needed further research, all required more sophisticated skills of analysis, synthesis and evaluation. Feedback and evaluation from peers within groups were substantial and continuous because each person in each group had a stake in understanding the reports of others so the group report would be sound and complete. Feedback and evaluation occurred across groups during class sessions where the strengths and weaknesses of various group reports quickly became apparent.

The five students pursuing individual learning contracts had the opportunity: (a) to define their own purposes; (b) to specify in more detail the readings, writings and experiential learning activities they would pursue; and (c) to negotiate with me the methods and criteria by which their work would be evaluated. Peer evaluation was more limited, but self-evaluation concerning progress and outcomes from the learning activities was more important. These students had to come to terms with trade-offs concerning less comprehensive coverage of course materials and the potential for a lower final exam score versus more heavy investment in their own objectives and a resulting strong evaluation of the contract. With these students I was much more a resource person and in a more collegial relationship than with students pursuing the other options.

In my judgment the improved outcomes in learning psychology, in satisfaction, in perceived benefit to themselves and in perception of psychology as a living discipline resulted from two dynamics. Some students chose the approach and the content emphases with which they were most comfortable, with which they could pursue the course requirements in ways which fit their motivation, orientation toward knowledge, student-faculty relationships and evaluational frameworks. Other students made choices which represented approaches to learning to which they aspired or for which they wanted to test their readiness and emphasized content important to their own needs or interests. These students were supported by the process, by their peers and by the teacher in this self-testing, and discovered new motives, orientations and ways of learning.

Did this way of teaching Psych 101 encourage student development? Did it result in any movement toward stage changes in ego development? I have no evidence. My pre-post testing for content mastery and my questionnaire concerning satisfaction, perceived benefits and perceptions of psychology did not give me any hints. Moreover, at that time I was not, in any conceptually explicit way, trying to encourage "stage change." I was just trying to teach better a course in which I had experienced mediocre success before. And I was

Figure 1. Ego Development and Orientations Toward Knowledge

Ego Development	Motive for Education	What is Knowledge?	What Use is Knowledge?	Where Does Knowledge Come From?
Self-Protective Opportunistic	Instrumental; satisfy immediate needs	A possession which helps one get desired ends; ritualistic actions which yield solutions	Education to get: means to concrete ends; used by self to obtain effects in World	From external authority; from asking how to get things
Conformist	Impress significant others, gain social acceptance; obtain credentials and recognition	General information required for social roles; objective truth given by authority	Education to be: social approval, appearance, status used by self to achieve according to expectations and standards of significant others	From external authority; from asking what others expect and how to do it
Conscientious	Achieve competence regarding competitive or normative standards. Increase capacity to meet social responsibilities	Know how: Personal skills in problem solving; divergent views resolved by rational processes	Education to do: competence in work and social role; used to achieve internalized standards of excellence and to serve society	Personal integration of information based on rational inquiry; from setting goals; from asking what is needed, how things work, and why
Autonomous	Deepen understanding of self, world, and life cycle; develop increasing capacity to manage own destiny	Personally generated insight about self and nature of life; subjective and dialectical; paradox appreciated	Education to become: self-knowledge; self-development; used to transform self and the world	Personal experience and reflection; personally generated paradigms, insights, judgments
Integrated				

Note: Just as each developmental stage incorporates and transforms earlier stages, so also each subsequent learning process and institutional function incorporates and transforms earlier levels.

Source: Personal communication; adapted from materials developed by Harry Lasker and Cynthia DeWindt, Harvard Graduate School of Education.

Ego Development	Learning Processes	Institutional Function	Teaching Practice	Student-Faculty Relationships	Evaluation
Self-Protective Opportunistic	Imitation: acquire information, competence, as given by authority	Arouse attention and maintain interest to show how things should be done	Lecture-exam	Teacher is authority transmitter, judge; student is receiver, judged	By teacher only
Conformist		Provide predetermined information and training programs; certify skills and knowledge	Teacher-led; dialogue or discussion Open "leaderless" "learner centered" discussion		By teacher only By teacher and peers
				Teacher is a "model" for student identification	
Conscientious	Discover correct answers through scientific method and logical analyses; multiple views are recognized but congruence and simplicity are sought	Provided structured programs which offer concrete skills and information, opportunities for rational analysis and practice, which can be evaluated and certified	Programmed learning; correspondence study; televised instruction	"Teacher" is an abstraction behind system. Student a recipient	By system
Autonomous	Seek new experiences; recognize past conception on the basis of new experiences; develop new paradigms; create new dialectics	Ask key questions; pose key dilemmas; confront significant discontinuities and paradoxes; foster personal experience and personally generated insights	Contract learning: 1. Time, objectives, activities, evaluation negotiated between student and teacher at the outset and held throughout	Student defines purposes in collegial relationship with teacher; teacher is resource, contributes to planning and evaluation	By teacher, peers, system, self; teacher final judge
Integrated			Contract learning: 2. Time, objectives, activities, evaluation defined generally by student		By teacher, peers, system, self; self judge

Note: Just as each developmental stage incorporates and transforms earlier stages, so also each subsequent learning process and institutional function incorporates and transforms earlier levels.

Source: Personal communications adapted from materials developed by Harry Lasker and Cynthia DeWindt, Harvard Graduate School of Education.

trying to teach it in ways which responded to differences among the students which I had experienced in my prior years of teaching. But at least it can be said that there was an opportunity. For those students ready to test themselves in new ways of learning, to experience and grapple with differences with other students in information and interpretation, to take more responsibility for identifying what they wanted to learn and how they wanted to learn it, to think through methods and criteria for evaluation, the chance was there to do so.

There is an important point here. Good teachers reflect on the differences in backgrounds and approaches to learning among their students and try to teach in ways which reach and challenge all those different students, not just the minority who suit the teacher's style. Such teachers probably make significant contributions not just to improved content learning but to student development as well.

If I were to teach this course again I would be more explicit with the students about the possibilities for personal development, for "ego development." First, as part of the initial course description, I would share the ideas presented earlier in this paper concerning interactions among ego development, motivation, orientations toward knowledge and educational practices. I would ask them to think about how they wanted to pursue their studies in the light of those ideas and discuss some of the trade offs which might occur when trying new approaches which did not suit them. I would encourage them to think about how they could emphasize content and identify processes which would create manageable developmental challenges and provide the kinds of supports from peers and teacher which they might need. I would encourage them to negotiate with me, individually or in groups, other options which might be more productive developmentally while also achieving the basic content objectives which were important to me. Then, at the end of the course, I would ask for a retrospective essay concerning the interactions between their learning and personal development. As part of that essay, I would ask them to consider whatever implications they might see for future content and learning activities which might serve their own continued development. I have been using devices similar to these in my current doctoral seminars, and I see no reason why they would not work equally well with undergraduates whose basic verbal skills are equal to the task.

Now, let me turn to the issue of professional competence. Today and for the foreseeable future, the workforce will be primarily service workers and knowledge workers. In the last hundred and fifty years we have gone from an agrarian through an industrial, post-industrial and technological society to the age of information and service. Each of the changes has generated increased need for more wide ranging education and professional skills. The current changes have dramatically accelerated those needs. Achieving high quality performance in an information and service society is much more complicated than producing high quality goods. Producing high quality television sets is simpler than producing high quality programming. It's easier to design high-powered automobiles and supersonic airplanes than to design transportation systems and environments that serve humans well. What kinds of competence and personal characteristics are required for quality performance in today's world of work? Here is what one well recognized group of researchers found by studying the most effective workers in a variety of settings: small businesses, military services, sales, police work, civil service, industrial management, counseling, consulting.

> Our most consistent—though unexpected—finding is that the amount of knowledge one acquires of a content area is generally unrelated to superior performance in an occupation and is often unrelated even to marginally acceptable performance. . . In fact, it is neither the acquisition of knowledge nor the use of knowledge that distinguishes the outstanding performer, but rather the cognitive skills that are developed and exercised in the process of acquiring and using knowledge. These cognitive skills constitute the first factor of occupational success (Klemp, p. 103).

What were these cognitive skills? They included the ability to synthesize information from prior analyses and diverse sources; the ability to understand many sides of a controversial issue; the ability to learn from experience.

Interpersonal skills were the second major factor in top notch performance: communication skills, especially with reference to the importance of non-verbal communication; "accurate empathy," the ability to both understand a human concern and to respond appropriately so others recognize that they have been understood; the ability to be helpful to others in ways which strengthen their capacity to do better; the ability to control one's own hostility so that it is not unleashed on others in ways which diminish them.

The third critical factor was motivation, the ability to initiate action which overcomes barriers, to see oneself as an effective agent in a chain of events, to invest oneself in something larger than one's own self-interest.

These areas of generic competence, critical for professional success in our knowledge and service society, must underlie the special knowledge and skills associated with particular occupations. They have much in common with the characteristics associated with the higher stages of ego development described above.

Do I have any direct empirical evidence that my approach to teaching Psych 101 created such generic competencies? No, I do not. But I can say that students were asked to engage in behaviors which encourage such outcomes. They were asked to exercise their analytic skills, to synthesize information from diverse sources, to prepare reports and contribute to group reports which called for such critical thinking skills. They were also required to function as members of the larger class and make contributions to it.

Those students participating in the same-text and multi-text subgroups experienced additional tests of their interpersonal competence. They had to understand and reconcile differences in points of view presented by their peers based on the authorities who wrote the different texts. They had to arrive at agreements about how best to share their joint positions. During the class meetings, they not only had to help represent the views of their subgroup but also had to help arrive at common understandings across the subgroups. In all these activities, they were investing in and contributing to the common good, the common collaborative class effort to arrive at shared understandings concerning what was known, what was under research and what recent research added to those understandings.

So the least that can be said is that they were being asked to engage in behaviors consistent with those required for high level professional performance. How much this experience of a single semester contributed to enduring learning that transfers to actual professional performance remains unknown. I do believe, however, that we would be on safe ground in suggesting that if all their learning throughout their college career were characterized by such behaviors, the competence thus gained would carry over to the world of work.

There is really no reason why such behaviors cannot characterize most teaching and learning in higher education. There is nothing special about this teaching. Any thoughtful and motivated faculty member could do likewise.

A recent statement of "Principles of Good Practice in Undergraduate Education" applies to this particular example:

Good Practice Encourages Student Faculty Contact

Frequent student-faculty contact in and out of classes is the most important factor in student motivation and involvement. Faculty concern helps students get through rough times and keep on working. Knowing a few faculty members well enhances students' intellectual commitment and encourages them to think about their own values and future plans.

Good Practice Encourages Cooperation Among Students

Learning is enhanced when it is more like a team effort than a solo race. Good learning, like good work, is collaborative and social, not competitive and isolated. Working with others often increases involvement in learning. Sharing one's own ideas and responding to others' reactions improves thinking and deepens understanding.

Good Practice Encourages Active Learning

Learning is not a spectator sport. Students do not learn much just sitting in classes listening to teachers, memorizing pre-packaged assignments, and spitting out answers. They must talk about what they are learning, write about it, relate it to past experiences, and apply it to their daily lives. They must make what they learn part of themselves.

Good Practice Gives Prompt Feedback

Knowing what you know and don't know focuses learning. Students need appropriate feedback on performance to benefit from courses. In getting started, students need help in assessing existing knowledge and competence. In classes, students need frequent opportunities to perform and receive suggestions for improvement. At various points during college, and at the end, students need chances to reflect on what they have learned, what they still need to know, and how to assess themselves.

Good Practice Emphasizes Time on Task

Time plus energy equals learning. There is no substitute for time on task. Learning to use one's time well is critical for students and professionals alike. Students need help in learning effective time management. Allocating realistic amounts of time means effective learning for students and effective teaching for faculty. How an institutions defines time expectations for students, faculty, administrators, and other professional staff can establish the basis for high performance for all.

Good Practice Communicates High Expectations

Expect more and you will get it. High expectations are important for everyone—for the poorly prepared, for those unwilling to exert themselves, and for the bright and well motivated. Expecting students to perform well becomes a self-fulfilling prophecy when teachers and institutions hold high expectations for themselves and make extra efforts.

Good Practice Respects Diverse Talents and Ways of Learning

There are many roads to learning. People bring different talents and styles of learning to college. Brilliant students in the seminar room may be all thumbs in the lab or art studio. Students rich in hands-on experience may not do so well with theory. Students need the opportunity to show their talents and learn in ways that work for them. Then they can be pushed to learning in new ways that do not come so easily (Chickering and Gamson, 1987).

I submit that these practices are well within the grasp of faculty members throughout the two and four year colleges in this country.

In closing, I want to address one final issue, the issue of human engineering and social control. I am suggesting that classroom teaching be carried out in ways which explicitly encourage developmental outcomes and generic areas of professional competence. Is this a thinly veiled argument, fancied up with psychological theory, for serving the current establishment, cooling out hot sources of social transformation, developing more subtle categories of social classification which reinforce class and ethnic prejudices? I have no clear cut answers to these critical issues. But I urge we push ahead in spite of these dangers.

The basic reason to push ahead is that there really is no choice. For better or worse, education is not, and never has been, value free. Laurance Veysey, in the *Emergence of the American University*, puts the issue this way:

The university in the United States has become largely an agency for social control. . . .The custodianship of popular values comprised the primary responsibility of the American university. It was to teach its students to think constructively rather than with an imprudent and disintegrative independence. It was to make its degrees into syndicated emblems of social and economic arrival. It was to promise, with repetitious care, that the investigations of its learned men were dedicated to the practical furtherance of the common welfare. It was to organize its own affairs in such a businesslike fashion as to reassure any stray industrialist or legislator who chanced onto its campus. It was to become a place prominently devoted to non-abstractive good fun: to singing and cheering, to the rituals of club life and "appropriate" oratory; it was to be the place where the easy, infectious harmonies of brass band and stamping feet found few toes [un]willing at least faintly to tap in time. The university also tolerated its minority of insistently vocal malcontents, unless they threatened flagrantly to harm its public name. The unhappy faculty "idealist" survived. . . . Pockets of strenuous dedication to goals that were absurdly unpopular (for instance, too insistently democratic to be widely shared by the American people) persisted in odd places within the institution (pp. 440, 441, 442).

There is not much question as to whether the academic system, in our two and four year colleges and universities, public or private, church-related or not, are in the business of social control and shaping human lives. They are. It is the bedrock basis for state support, federal incentives and tax exempt status.

Given these conditions, where am I left with my argument for intentional devotion to human development and generic areas of professional competence? John Wilson, lecturer at Oxford, addresses one key dimension of the issue this way:

Performance in the moral area is surely not wholly arbitrary. For instance, it seems clear that principles like "face facts" or "get to know yourself and other people" are required by anybody who is going to evolve his own moral beliefs in a serious and sensible way. Similarly, qualities we may call "self-control" or "being able to act on one's own decisions" seem to be required by any person, whatever his particular moral values. If someone abandoned such general principles as these, we should say—not that we disagreed with his particular moral values, but that he was not taking morality seriously at all. . . . .   This is a matter of logic. . . . It does not rest upon any particular creed, or faith or axiom. Such principles as "facing facts," "not contradicting oneself," "gaining understanding" and so forth. . .are part of what it means to be a thinking human being, as opposed to an animal or a psychopath. Understanding and following such principles is part of what we mean. . .by "being educated" in morality and in other areas of life. They are an expansion of the concept of education itself, not a set of particular moral values. I repeat this because it is just as important that students. . .grasp this as educators should. They, and we, would rightly resent any attempt to foist a particular morality or faith on them, but no one can sensibly object to clarification of what it means to be educated. . .(Collier, Wilson and Tomlinson, 1974, pp. 7, 8).

Wilson's views, and my own, bring me directly to questions like these. What consequences will follow if there is greater awareness of interactions between self and system? Consequences for individuals? Consequences for society? If increasing numbers of persons become more aware of developmental differences and take a more active part in creating their own development and in helping others, what then? If men and women throughout society become more aware of the opportunistic, conformist, conscientious and autonomous dimensions of ego development, of the dominant structures organizing their existence; if they better understand their dualistic thinking, or unfettered relativism in the context of larger conceptions of moral and ethical development, how will their frameworks for judgment and action change? If they understand better the experiences which work for and against their own development, what conditions will they establish for themselves and to what ends? If they see more clearly the forces steering their own professional or vocational development, recognize more fully the path on which they are set, contemplate the pros and cons of alternative directions, what will result? If they develop increased critical thinking skills and cognitive complexity, increased interpersonal competence, will that development be turned toward manipulation and exploitation of others, or will it not? If they acquire more clear purposes, through better grasp of the complex interactions among individual goals, institutional objectives and societal needs, what form will these purposes take?

It is my conviction that the answers to these questions come down on the positive side. I make no claim for definitive evidence. Surely the news is full of self-centeredness, self-protection, self-interest and exploitation, world wide. But the evidence from research on human development, and from larger perspectives on social change, suggests cause for cautious optimism. The direction of change in ego development is toward integrity, not opportunism.

Change in moral and ethical development is toward commitment in relativism which places human welfare as the highest value. Human development occurs in the direction of increased intellectual competence and complexity, toward increased concern for collaborative inquiry, toward increased capacity for intimacy and the expansion of caring. Individual purposes and identities do become more clear and strong, more often identified with outcomes larger than one's own narrowly defined self-interest. The "Evolving Self" culminates in the "interindividual" stage which "acknowledges and cultures capacity for interdependence, for self-surrender and intimacy, for interdependent self-definition" (Kegan, p. 227). Change in "Women's Ways of Knowing" is toward "constructed knowledge, a position in which women view all knowledge as contextual, experience themselves as creators of knowledge, and value both subjective and objective strategies for knowing" (Belenky et al., p. 15). Persons *do* learn how to learn and how to take charge of their own continued development.

Given the social forces and cultural context at play with all of us, we seldom reach those developmental goals we value. Our becoming typically falls short of that which we would become. But the striving is there in most of us. Thus it is that I argue for increased attention to those strivings, increased opportunities for each person to define more clearly those issues of human development and professional competence significant for him or her, increased devotion of institutional resources and expertise in the service of such purposes.

References

Belenky, M.F., Clinchy, B.M., Goldberger, N.R., Tarule, J.M. *Women's Ways of Knowing*, Basic Books, N.Y., 1986.

Chickering, A.W. and Gamson, Z. *Seven Principles of Good Practice in Undergraduate Education*, the Wingspread Journal, Johnson Foundation, Racine, 1987.

Kegan, R. *The Evolving Self*, Harvard University Press, 1982.

Klemp, G.O. "Three Factors of Success," in *Relating Work and Education*, D.W. Vermilye (Ed.) Jossey-Bass, Inc., San Francisco, 1977.

Loevinger, J. *Ego Development*, Jossey-Bass Inc., San Francisco, 1976.

Perry, W.G., Jr. *Forms of Intellectual and Ethical Development in the College Years: A Scheme*, Holt, Rhinehart & Winston, N.Y., 1971.

Veysey, L.R. *The Emergence of the American University*, University of Chicago Press, Chicago, 1974.

12

Experiential Learning: A Key to Adult Development

Barry G. Sheckley and George J. Allen

The relationship between experiential learning and adult development needs to be explicated in more detail. Current discussions of adult learning (e.g., Chickering, 1981, Sheckley, 1987) encourage educational institutions to design learning programs which appropriately match the developmental phase or stage of their adult clients. Research provides limited guidance to educators who want to use learning strategies to advance development of adult students.

We discussed this issue one evening with a group of older students. To stimulate further reflection on the topic, we encouraged individuals to conduct imaginary conversations with themselves as high school sophomores. Each person was to counsel their former self about ways to avoid pitfalls along the road to adulthood. Their responses provided insightful commentaries on the relationship between learning and adult development.

First, they affirmed that learning from experience was central to their development.

> Quite frankly, as a sophomore, I couldn't understand my adult self. When I tried to discuss the many faces of love, commitment and morality encountered on the road to adulthood, I didn't make any sense to that youngster. I guess she had to learn these lessons as I did—by living them.

Secondly, these older students emphasized that learning about levels of complexity accompanied their development.

> I realized how naive I was in high school. My sophomore self knew the meaning of words like "values," "ethics" and "intimacy," but he didn't understand them. It was like talking to my own kids. We can talk about the same things—but it's on two different levels.

Finally, learning how to make relevant applications of knowledge played an important role in their development.

> Why was I so different from that charming teenager? I felt so much wiser than she had been. I know that if we had taken a multiple choice test on almost any subject, she would

have gotten a better grade. But I knew that wasn't important. Over the years I learned how to make what I knew work for me. She didn't know how to do that yet.

The conversations throughout the evening suggested that a fundamental relationship existed between adult learning and adult development. Student reflections indicated that learning from experience and learning how to make relevant applications of knowledge promoted their development. Their comments also implied that advancing development led to greater appreciation of complexity which, in turn, enabled new learning.

A Developmental Model of Adult Learning

Figure 1 (following page) illustrates the relationship between adult learning and development. The boundaries of the model are established by an individual's level of current and potential development. One student in the seminar provided a graphic validation of the model.

> This summer I purchased a new sailboat. My level of potential development was evident in the smooth voyages I took when experienced sailors were aboard to guide my every move. Their assistance indicated that I clearly had the potential to sail my new boat. When I tried it alone, however, my level of current development—rather, ineptitude—was readily apparent. I capsized the boat so many times even my son refused to sail with me.

Learning promotes development by enabling a person to reduce the gap between levels of current and potential development. Unfortunately for our sailor's fortunes, theoretical models do not describe the exact nature of the learning process which promotes development. This omission occurs throughout the field of psychology. Many elegant depictions of the zone of potential development exist (e.g., Loevinger, 1976; Maslow, 1954; Perry, 1970), but few explicate the learning process which best advances development.

The lack of attention to this important topic might be attributed to the seemingly chaotic nature of movement across the zone of learning (Figure 1). As one participant at our adult development seminar noted, turbulence always accompanied development.

> During these times I felt like a grey squirrel trying to run across a road to avoid an oncoming car. Everything was all right until I started out for new horizons on the far side of the road. Then I would get confused about what I wanted and run back to where I started. Then I would change my mind and head for the new horizons again. I ran one way, then the other. Finally I managed to avoid the car and get to the other side. . . Development never involved just running straight across the road. I always had to run around for a while.

Recent research on chaos (Gleick, 1988) suggests that a structured process may be associated with this apparently aimless "running around." Lewin (1951), for example, described the turbulent process using a "freezing—unfreezing—refreezing" sequence. With Lewin's lead, other researchers (e.g., Logenbill, et. al., 1984) emphasized that the "unfreezing" period promoted development by liberating a person from rigid beliefs and calcified behaviors. Related investigations (e.g., Bridges 1985) note that the time of "running around" advanced development by enabling a person to reorder priorities before stabilizing at a new level of stability. As applied to Figure 1, research on chaos and change suggests that the learning process which enables a person to reduce the gap between levels of current and potential development is best patterned after a "freezing—unfreezing—refreezing" model. The learning model would portray a continual interplay between a process which pursued integration and a countervailing process which promoted confusion. Experiential learning theory

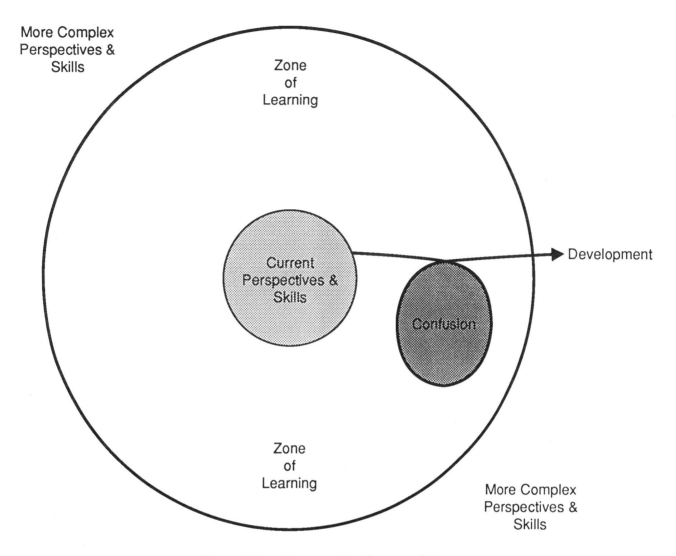

Figure 1. Learning as a Developmental Process

provides these emphases. In doing so, it provides a key to understanding the learning process promoting adult development. It also offers guidance to educators intent on using learning strategies to advance the development of older students.

Experiential Learning Theory

Experiential Learning Theory (ELT) is a useful model for understanding adult development. Roots of ELT exist in Dewey's (1938) insight that learning is a dialectic process integrating experience and abstractions, Lewin's (1951) perspective that learning derives from here-and-now concrete experiences coupled with feedback loops, and Piaget's (1951) analysis that learning involves accommodating concepts to experience and assimilating experience into concepts. Kolb (1984) synthesized these ideas into a rich framework which thoughtfully depicted learning as an active process of grasping and transforming information (Figure 2, following page).

The grasping dimension describes how adults acquire information either through immediate and direct contact with concrete experience (CE) or through detached comprehension of abstract concepts (AC). Concrete experiences, like eating a chocolate torte or engaging in a passionate kiss, are known instantaneously

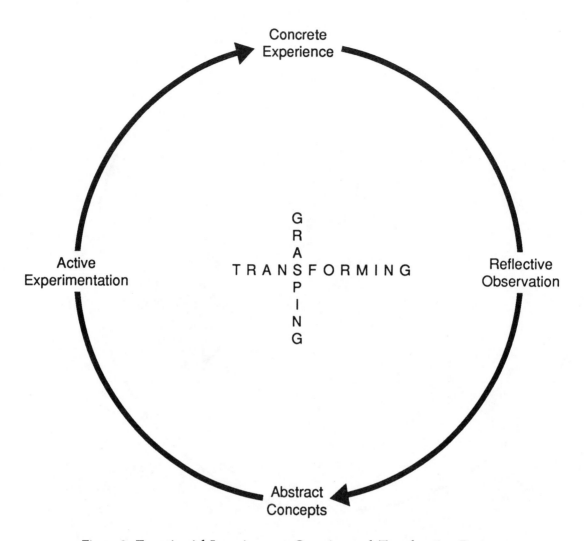

Figure 2. Experiential Learning as a Grasping and Transforming Process

without need for rational assessment. Concrete experience represents a valuing process. Using their own preferential set of perspectives and values, individuals focus on concrete experiences selected from the array of here and now stimuli. Abstract concepts, on the other hand, derive from the rational analysis of those selected experiences.

Both grasping dimensions are equal partners in the learning process. Concrete experiences provide for direct assimilation of life. They also validate hypothetical portrayals of reality. Abstract concepts play an important complementary role by ordering concrete sensations, enabling communication of experience and providing symbolic representations of the world.

Grasping initiates development. It provides disconfirming experiences or ideas which create what Bridges (1985) referred to as the "neutral zone," Lewin (1951) termed the "unfreezing process," and Logenbill et. al. (1984) called "stage II confusion." Without the stimulation of new ideas or challenges presented by unfamiliar experiences, individuals can persist in a bounded world. The grasping process provides the push for grey squirrels to start journeys across asphalt boulevards.

The transforming dimension describes how information is personalized through reflective observations (RO) or active experimentation (AE). Like the grasping dimension, transformation processes are equal partners in learning. Reflection is necessary to integrate new experiences into an adult's existing world view.

Reflection engages personal values as filters to establish salient attributes of experience which are then assimilated into abstract ideas. Active experimentation grounds ideas and experiences in the external world. Through active experimentation, ideas are tested to determine their practicality and applicability.

Transforming sustains development. It enables individuals to personalize stimulating ideas and challenging experiences which initiate development. Through reflection, individuals are able to integrate change provoking experiences (e.g., getting fired from a job) into more expansive sets of cognitions (e.g., "Now that I think about it, I could use my skills in several different professions"). Reflections can lead to abstract concepts or motivating visions which sustain development by offering perspectives of what the world will be like when the change process is completed. For example, an abstraction like "my skills are adaptable to a wide variety of professions" can sustain an unemployed worker through a prolonged job search.

Active experimentation validates the personal relevance of a provocative idea like "I could use my skills in several different professions." This calibration process enables individuals to test out the idea in personally useful situations like seeking employment in a new career field.

Without transformation, the challenges provided by new ideas or stimulating experiences would never affect an individual's core values and world views. In the absence of transformation, developmental initiatives remain isolated and ineffective since they lack personal relevance. Transforming sustains development and provides grey squirrels with the courage to complete passages to new horizons.

The grasping and transforming dimensions of the experiential learning cycle capture the dynamic nature of adult development. Experiences are filtered using personal values and then assimilated into existing perspectives—only to be tested again in new situations. New information individuals grasp through experience or abstraction precipitates confusion when it is not compatible with current ideas, concepts or values. The transforming process enables individuals to resolve the confusion and integrate ideas into current perspectives or to expand world views based upon experimentation. While grasping provides informational grist for an adult's epistemological mill, transforming engages specific milling processes to refine the experiential and conceptual wheat into ideas and actions.

For experiential learning theory to have credence as a learning process which prompts adult development, it must be able to explain a common developmental event. In the following section, the grasping—transforming process will be used to elucidate the development of professional competence.

Development of Professional Competence

The importance of the learning process in advancing adult development is magnified in discussions of professional competence (Brenner, 1984; Cevero, 1988). As depicted in Figure 3 (following page), research on professional aptitudes (Dreyfus and Dreyfus, 1986) indicates that professional capabilities spread along a continuum. Major distinctions exist among novices, advanced beginners, practitioners, professionals and experts in terms of competence, developmental focus and learning process.

Novices, for example, tend to "go by the book" in using a limited skill set. They focus on basic rules and policies to guide actions. Novices pay little attention to context. Typically their developmental focus is inflexible and involves learning more rules and procedures. Novice drivers generally fail to adapt their speed, cornering or braking to varying road conditions.

As novices learn that rules must be adapted to fit specific situations, they begin to develop integrated sets of actions and apply transforming processes to the information they grasp. These advanced beginners will change their driving behavior to accommodate to extreme weather conditions like snow or ice.

Further along the continuum, practitioners distinguish among actions based on general principles. Their development is supported by a learning process which increasingly emphasizes transforming the information they grasp. When driving a car, they are guided by general principles which enable them to refine driving behaviors in response to subtle changes in traffic and road conditions.

LEVEL OF COMPETENCE	DEVELOPMENTAL PATH	DEVELOPMENTAL FOCUS	LEARNING PROCESS
NOVICE: Can assess and adapt to deviations from basic rules and procedures	No distinction between rules & context where rules are applied	Understanding Basic Rules & Procedures	90% GRASPING 10% TRANSFORMING
ADVANCED BEGINEER: Can assess & adapt to important aspects of a situation	Actions dictated by rules TO Action dictated by situation	Developing integrated actions	70% GRASPING 30% TRANSFORMING
PRACTITIONER: Can assess & adapt to deviations from a plan	Action dictated by situation TO Action dictated by general plan	Developing General Principles	50% GRASPING 50% TRANSFORMING
PROFESSIONAL: Can assess & adjust to deviations from the pattern	Action dictated by general plan TO Action dictated by intuitions	Integrating experience into unified scenarios	30% GRASPING 70% TRANSFORMING
EXPERT: Can assess and focus on critical factors in a situation	Actions and situation are synonymous	Refining Intuitions	10% GRASPING 90% TRANSFORMING

Figure 3. Level of Competence, Development Path, Developmental Focus, and Learning Processes Used by Novices, Advanced Beginners, Practitioners, Professionals, and Experts.

Unlike novices who focus on specifics of a situation, professionals link individual events into overall patterns. They transform varied experiences into integrated scenarios which they use to guide actions in new situations. In contrast to novices, who would travel the same route regardless of traffic conditions, professionals can attune to cues from overall traffic patterns and adroitly find the fastest route across town in rush hour traffic.

At the far end of the continuum, experts, guided by intuitive perspectives, use highly cultivated skill sets. Experts isolate the critical factors of a situation by using intuitions to focus attention. Unlike their less proficient counterparts, experts' more fluid developmental focus involves refining intuitions and transforming experiences. They do not distinguish between a situation and an action. They do not "drive a car." Experts simply "drive." The act "driving" and the object "car" are integrated.

Novices, advanced beginners, practitioners, professionals and experts all require different skills to move across the zone of learning. For novices and advanced beginners, the process is primarily a grasping one. To initiate a development process, they require two sets of grasping skills. A sensitive set of valuing skills is necessary to tap the rich instructional data available in their concrete experiences. Likewise, a critical thought capacity is required to fully grasp the nuances of abstract concepts.

As individuals ascend through levels of competency, the learning focus changes. Practitioners, professionals and experts employ more transforming processes to sustain the change involved in moving across the zone of learning. Their grasping skills enable them to appreciate opportunities for development. Transforming skills enable them to establish the personal and practical relevance of development opportunities and to construct the motivating visions which sustain developmental efforts.

To effectively transform the data they grasp, these more proficient individuals require two additional skill sets. A well developed set of perceptual skills is required to reflect upon life events and appreciate the relevance of subtle differences present in varied experiences. Similarly, an advanced set of behavioral skills is required to test ideas out in practice.

The continuum of professional competence has implications for understanding the developmental process. The progression demonstrates that: (a) professional competence has a developmental component; and (b) learning is the fundamental process sustaining movement along the continuum.

Like an American driver encountering an English roundabout, development requires learning new approaches as well as cultivating old ones. A wide inventory of refined learning skills is a prerequisite for ongoing development. Experiential learning theory delineates the precise learning skills involved. Grasping skills are essential for developing the novice talents required to function in unfamiliar situations. Transforming skills are essential for expanding trustworthy approaches to accommodate increasingly complex environments.

Before accepting experiential learning as an explanatory construct underlying adult development, educators must clarify its utility for uncovering and removing impediments to development. In the following section, learning skill deficits and learning styles will be explored as impediments to development.

Impediments to Development

As previously discussed, the experiential learning process describes the chaotic expansion of the "level of current development" across the zone of learning. The grasping $\geq$ transforming perspective establishes development as a process of gaining insights and then calibrating applications within the context of personal values and world views. It also suggests that individuals adept at development possess finely honed grasping and transforming skills which enable them to assimilate experience into personally relevant abstract concepts and accommodate these concepts to new and varied experiences.

Development is impeded when individuals restrict either the grasping or the transforming process. Individuals who construct a self-reinforcing world are impervious to the change forces generated by the grasping $\geq$ transforming vector. When individuals selectively limit their engagement in new experiences or curb the diversity of ideas they contemplate, the change effects of grasping and transforming are diminished.

Figure 4 (following page) depicts the learning cycle of adults short-circuiting the grasping $\geq$ transforming process. The cycle can be easily truncated by individuals ignoring important stimuli, reflecting on events as being meaningless, considering ideas as irrelevant, or evaluating activities as useless. For example, a confirmed smoker could impede the grasping $\geq$ transforming process by ignoring concrete events like increasing shortness of breath, by reflecting on the increasing frequency of a "smoker's cough" as meaningless, by considering the research on links between cancer and smoking as irrelevant, or by evaluating activities designed to terminate smoking as useless.

Learning skill deficits and restricted learning styles contribute to bounded learning cycles. For this reason, these two factors can be considered impediments to development.

Skill Deficits

Mastery of the learning process, (i.e., the ability to grasp and transform information or experiences) impacts the capacity to develop (Sternberg, 1987). The degree to which individuals possess finely honed grasping and transforming skills represents their potential for engaging change processes. Individuals adroit at grasping and transforming information or experiences typically embrace development. Individuals who lack the skills necessary to employ fundamental learning processes tend to throttle development. From this perspective a skill deficit in the ability to learn using both grasping and transforming processes represents an impediment to development.

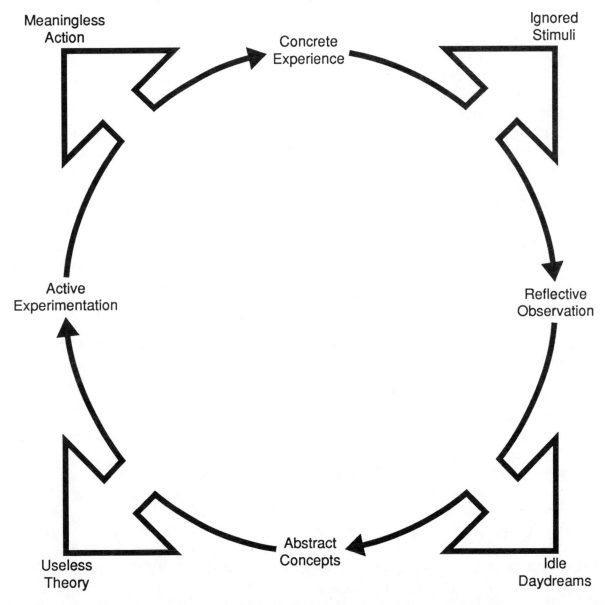

Figure 4. A Restricted Experiential Learning Cycle

Restricted Learning Styles

Movement through the chaotic development process is promoted by an integrated set of skills. Valuing skills rivet attention on concrete events, perceptual skills focus reflections on important components of experience, analytical skills extract meaning from the experience, and implementation skills establish the relevancy of concepts in specific situations. Individuals who use the four skills are adept at the development process. The degree to which individuals employ a preferred set of grasping and transforming skills to the exclusion of other skills represents an impediment to development.

The active process of experiential learning allows for individualized grasping and transforming patterns termed "learning styles." The styles function like myelinated neural pathways for acquiring new information. Figure 5 (following page) outlines the four preferential learning patterns Kolb (1984) defined as

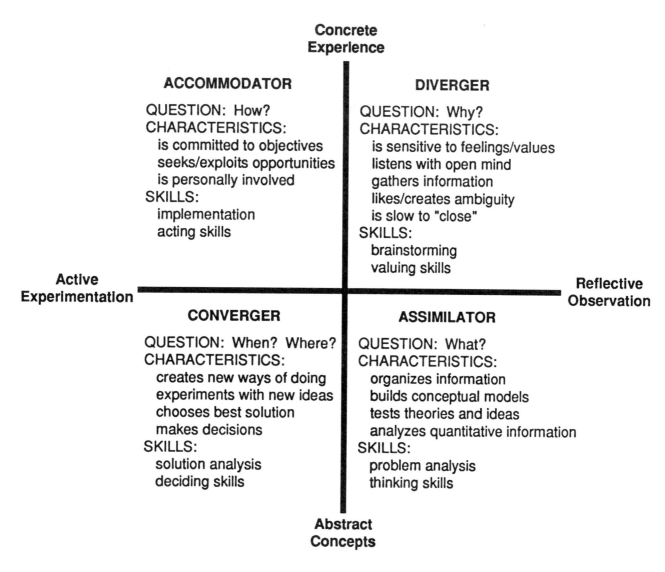

Figure 5. Grasping and Transforming Preferences

"divergers," "assimilators," "convergers," and, "accommodators." Because learning styles represent a stylized pattern of grasping and transforming, they can be termed "habits of partial learning." As such, they operate as impediments to development.

Divergers acquire new perspectives best by reflecting on concrete events. They have highly developed valuing skills and are excellent brainstormers. They diverge from a specific bit of information to develop many implications. They like to create complexity and ambiguity. Like Winnie the Pooh's friend Eeyore in search of his lost tail, they can become so lost in reflective thought that they never move into action.

Assimilators love to ponder abstract ideas and develop conceptual models. They possess highly developed abstraction and analytical skills. Occasionally, like a Walter Mitty, they can become so wrapped up in their ideas and fantasies that they lose a concrete grounding for their musing.

Convergers are excellent decision makers. They abhor complexity and seek essentials of the "bottom line." They live to place ideas and models into decisive action. Like Fred McMurray in *The Absent Minded Professor,* they can lose contact with the practical utility of their applications.

Accommodators are excellent crisis managers. They are exceptionally skilled at implementing plans. They have highly developed adaptive skills. When they get too far afield, they can become like the human chameleon in Woody Allen's *Zelig.*

Individuals rigidly adhering to a preferred style are like tennis players who engage opponents using only a forehand stroke. In both cases, the limited repertoire is maladaptive. As tennis requires a competitor to learn backhand, overhead and volley strokes, development requires a set of diverse skills.

Adapting to the world requires a diverger's valuing skills, an assimilator's thinking skills, a converger's deciding skills and an accommodator's acting skills. A learning style represents a skilled preference for one adaptive mode. It is a habit of partial learning because only selected grasping and transforming processes (e.g., reflective observation and abstract concepts) are used while others (e.g., active experimentation and concrete experience) are ignored. The preferences can also function as a psychosclerosis (hardening of the mind) obstructing adaptive function.

Educational strategies which emphasize one particular learning style facilitate rapid acquisition and use of information appropriate to that grasping and transforming process. For example, strategies emphasizing only reflection and comprehension develop conceptual models which are not always grounded in concrete reality. To promote development, learning programs must emphasize valuing, deciding, acting as well as thinking skills.

Implications

The notion that experiential learning provides a key to adult development has implications for the design of adult learning programs. Many current discussions of adult learning (e.g., Chickering, 1981) implore educational institutions to design learning programs which match states or phases of adult development. These presentations suggest that the relationship between adult development and adult learning programs is similar to the relationship between independent and dependent variables. In other words, educational institutions must determine the phase or stage of adult development and provide learning programs which are dependent upon the needs and interests of the identified developmental level.

The ideas presented in this chapter imply that the relationship between program designs and adult development could be reversed. There is an alternative to using academic course work exclusively to inoculate students with appropriate units of knowledge. With an experiential learning strategy, instructional objectives could be presented in the developmental terms depicted in Figure 1. Using experiential learning processes outlined in this chapter, educational programs could be designed to reduce gaps between levels of current development and potential development. In this design, the learning process would be the independent factor used to promote adult development.

If this process were imbedded within adult learning programs, it would be a fitting tribute to the educational philosophy Morris Keeton has advocated throughout his dedicated career.

Summary

This chapter stressed five points in discussing experiential learning theory as a key to adult development. First, it noted that development, from an adult learning perspective, involves a tumultuous movement across the zone of learning in terms of the experiential learning pathway of grasping $\geq$ transforming. The chapter also demonstrated how experiential learning theory had validity as a construct in explaining the development of professional competence. This compendium used experiential learning theory to explain impediments to development including deficits in grasping $\geq$ transforming skills and restricted learning styles. Finally, implications for developmental program design were presented.

References

Bridges, W. *Transitions: Making Sense of Life's Changes.* New York: Addison Wesley, 1985.

Chickering, A.W. "Developmental Change as a Major Outcome," in M.T. Keeton (ed.) *Experiential Learning.* San Francisco: Jossey-Bass, 1976.

Benner, P. *From Novice to Expert: Excellence and Power in Clinical Nursing Practice.* Menlo Park, CA: Addison Wesley, 1984.

Cervero, R. *Effective Continuing Education for Professionals.* San Francisco: Jossey-Bass, 1988.

Dewey, J. *Education and Experience.* Kappa Delta Pi, 1938.

Dreyfus, H., Dreyfus, S. *Mind Over Machine.* New York: The Free Press, 1986.

Gleick. *Chaos: Making a New Science.* New York: Penguin Books, 1988.

Kolb, D. *Experiential Learning.* New Jersey: Prentice Hall, 1984.

Maslow, A. *Motivation and Personality.* New York: Harper, 1954.

Lewin, K. *Field Theory in Social Sciences.* New York: Harper and Row, 1951.

Loganbill, C. Hardy, E. Delworth. "Supervision: A Conceptual Model," *The Counseling Psychologist,* 10 (1).

Loevinger, J. *Ego Development: Conceptions and Theories.* San Francisco: Jossey-Bass, 1976.

Perry, W.G., Jr. *Forms of Intellectual and Ethical Development in the College Years.* New York: Holt, Rinehart and Winston, 1970.

Piaget, J. *Play, Dreams and Imitation in Childhood.* New York: W.W. Norton, 1951.

Sheckley, B. "Adult Development: A Learning Perspective." *CAEL News,* 10 (1).

Sternberg, R. *Beyond IQ: A Triarchic Theory of Human Intelligence.* Cambridge: Cambridge University Press, 1987.

13

The Challenges of Advanced Professional Development

David A. Kolb

A *festschrift* to honor an esteemed colleague seems an ideal place for an essay on advanced professional development. This is particularly so when that person is my mentor and friend, Morris Keeton. As an advocate for adult experiential learning, the father of CAEL is our leader in moving lifelong learning from the realm of rhetorical poetry to operational reality. Personally, Morris has been both inspiration and guide in introducing me to the special challenges and wider responsibilities of mature adulthood. I would like to use this happy occasion to share some thoughts about learning and development in the second half of life. My research for the last ten years has focused on the comparative study of professions and professional education, so these reflections will be based on studies of men and women I call "advanced professionals."

Advanced professionals have specialized in their early career as engineers, physicians, nurses, lawyers, managers, educators, social workers, accountants; the list of professional specialties and sub-specialties goes on and on. They are highly educated, many with postgraduate degrees. They share an in depth, intense education in a specialized knowledge area giving them highly refined skills and a corresponding commitment to a world view that gives these skills great value. They have been educated as specialists. If the future we are concerned about is the 1990s, then 90 percent or more of tomorrow's advanced professional leaders are currently working. They are employed as individual professional contributors, functional managers and administrators, general managers, executives, entrepreneurs, political and community leaders. Many are in leadership positions of growing complexity. Their preparation for future and greater leadership responsibilities will depend on how they learn from their experiences and develop as adults in their work organizations, in their communities, and in their private lives.

My interest in adult learning and development grew out of earlier work on learning styles, where we saw that an adult's basic approach to learning is shaped by his or her educational background, and that knowledge disciplines and professions are characterized by a typical learning style. Learning styles in this perspective are higher order heuristics for learning how to learn and represent the deep structure of the knowledge that is imparted in knowledge specialties and professions. Early adult career paths can be characterized by selection into and socialization by these knowledge specialties and professions.

In 1979, Donald Wolfe and I began a series of studies to investigate adult development at mid-life and beyond. The National Institute of Education supported us in our study of advanced professional learning and development, and the Spencer Foundation helped in our investigation of the mid-life transition process in professional men and women. Over a four-year period these projects included some 20 researchers and 70 professional men and women in mid-life transition who engaged with us as co-inquirers in a continuing dialogue about their life situation and personal development. The studies also included questionnaire data, interviews and psychological testing with a cross-sectional sample of 400 professional engineers and social workers, alumni of our university in the years 1955, 1960, 1965, 1970 and 1975 (Kolb & Wolfe, 1981).

Carl Jung provided conceptual guidance. In the perspective of history, Freud's work has had its greatest impact on our understanding of child development, while Jung spoke most powerfully about the challenges and potential of adult development. What was impressive was how accurately Jung's theory described the dynamics of professional development as we observed them in our studies. Jung divided adult life into an early stage where processes of specialization and individualistic orientation were dominant, a period of mid-life transition, and a late life stage where collective integration processes dominate. This proved to be a powerful organizing framework for our data. The model fit the retrospective life histories and future aspirations of our mid-life transition panel. It also fit the "constructed" professional development stages represented in the cross-sectional sample of engineering and social work of alumni 5, 10, 15, 20 and 25 years beyond their formal professional education.

Our most significant finding was that advanced professional development presents integrative challenges to mid-life professionals that are markedly different from the specialized demands of their early careers. In addition, mid-life professionals reach this transition point relatively unprepared for the integrative life challenges that lie ahead. Most professional education programs are vocationally oriented, focused on training for entry-level, specialized, professional roles. Problems of transition from specialization to integration were most evident in the science-based professions such as medicine and engineering, where intensely specialized professional education programs seem, in some cases, to produce a dysfunctional allegiance to a specialized professional mentality, even when that approach is no longer the best way to operate (Sims, 1983).

Recently our team has been joined by Richard Boyatzis, and our attention has focused on the nature of post mid-life challenges and the mature developmental responses that advanced professional leaders make to them. This essay offers a sketch of our current challenge/response framework in the context of experiential learning theory (Kolb, 1984). The experiential learning theory of development seeks to define a trans-professional perspective on adult learning and development that identifies common life issues and work challenges across professional careers for men and women, younger and older persons. The theory has two orienting propositions:

1. *Adult careers are characterized by an early stage of specialization, a period of mid-life transition and a later adulthood stage of integration.* Our studies of professionals during mid-life transition showed this to be a major life-turning point involving changes in personal values, work and family life.
2. *Adult development is a process of learning from experience.* Growth toward the realization of one's potential comes from actively engaging with life challenges and consciously learning from the experiences.

The concept of challenge comes from Nevitt Sanford's (1981) challenge/response theory of adult development. Development occurs primarily in response to the challenges of adult life. Those who, by choice or fate, do not face these challenges are less likely to develop mature responses to them. With regard to the challenge of learning, for example, Gypen (1981) found that engineers in integrative management positions developed an integrated learning process, while those who remained engineering specialists maintained the specialized convergent learning style typical of the engineering profession. Sanford argues that self-insight is critical. The absence of opportunity for self-examination and dialogue with others about life challenges and the appropriate responses is a significant barrier to development.

We have identified eight arenas of life challenge for advanced professionals. They are overlapping and interrelated. They exist on the borderline of objective life circumstance and subjective experience; there in some measure because we wish them there. The mature, growth producing responses to challenge seem to be reflected more clearly in values and attitudes than behavior. They are less the behavioral norm than normative ideal—our aspirations for ourselves as human beings.

— The challenge of wholeness/The response of centering
— The challenge of generativity/The response of caring
— The challenge of change and complexity/The response of learning
— The challenge of time/The response of vision
— The challenge of moral leadership/The response of valuing
— The challenge of interdependence/The response of teamwork
— The challenge of ordinary life/The response of humility
— The challenge of facing challenge/The response of courage

1. The Challenge of Wholeness/The Response of Centering

It is in the life priorities of advanced professionals that the challenge of wholeness can be seen more clearly. Figure 1 (following page) compares the life priorities of early-career, mid-life, and advanced professionals in our alumni sample. For the young professionals (age twenty-four to forty), career is most important. They spend most of their time polishing their expert skills and establishing a professional identity, "making it" in their respective organizations. In mid-life (forty-one to forty-five), family gains top priority. Mid-life is dominated by a host of personal life events—marriage, divorce, parents, children, education, finances. The advanced professional brings family and work into balance with a generative priority, a desire to make a contribution to society. He or she seeks a balance among career, family, personal well being, and a desire to contribute to society.

Advanced professional work is filled with challenges for wholeness. Typically, successful young professionals rise to the peak of their professional specialty by perfecting their specialized professional skills in a work environment that is competitive and oriented toward rewarding the individual. At this peak, advanced professionals face a number of new tasks, requiring new skills—skills that in some cases are the opposite of the survival skills one has learned as a professional specialist. As Sir Noel Hall, the founder in postwar Britain of one of the first executive colleges, put it,

> Here we come to the central paradox. It is from individuals who necessarily have undergone this process of specialization, who have carried limited and restricted responsibilities that we have to draw for the higher posts those who are to be the synthesizers, the coordinators, those who have the quality of behavior which will draw other people to accept their guidance (1958, p. 9).

For professionals, these "higher posts" often come in the form of executive responsibility. The challenge for wholeness is seen most clearly as one assumes responsibility for an autonomous system—for example, as a general manager or CEO. The prime task here is to weld the functional parts of the organization into a coherent and effective whole, to give direction and purpose to the total enterprise. Advanced individual contributors, however, also experience a need to fit their specialty into the whole, to speak publicly for their profession, to mentor and lead younger professionals, and to serve society.

The process of advanced professional work is holistic, involving more synthesis than analysis. Problem solving is cooperative, typically involving integrated teamwork across different functions and professional specialties. Less time is spent solving problems, and more is spent selecting which problems should be solved, through agenda setting and priority setting. The environment outside the organization becomes more focal than the inside. The organization seen as a whole must find its place in the environmental whole. Generalized technical knowledge, the bread and butter of early professional life, must be coordinated with local knowledge— the unique situation-specific knowledge of opportunities, traps, resources, personalities, and techniques for getting things done in the organization's current environmental situation. Immense amounts of time in the executive role are spent networking, communicating, and representing in order to accumulate this local knowledge.

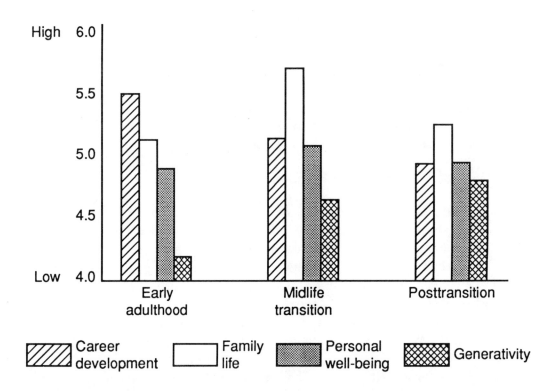

Figure 1. Importance of Major Developmental Tasks by Phases of Adulthood.

The developmental challenge to find wholeness has more personal dimensions. Finding a balance between "masculine" instrumentality/aggressiveness and "feminine" nurturance/expressiveness is often difficult in male-dominated organizations. The balance of body and mind becomes important, particularly when physical health becomes an issue or when work is heavily intellectual and abstract. Immersion in the straight lines and mechanical tools of the man-made world can cause one to lose connection with the curves and rhythms of the natural world where organic processes of growth and development thrive. Concern for self needs to be balanced with concern for and intimacy with others.

The growthful response to these challenges for wholeness is a process of centering. It requires a new attitude toward differences. Early adult development is fueled by the embrace of similarities, a process called "accentuation" because the effect of embracing similarity is to intensify and develop a particular skill or attitude—for example, by reading only opinions you agree with or specializing your performance in areas you are good at. This accentuation, unchecked by integration, inevitably leads to an imbalance, a one-sidedness, an over-investment of the person's life energies in one area. This, in turn, creates an internal need, a counter-force, to balance oneself and regain one's center.

The path to the center lies in awareness and appreciation of differences. In the embracing of differences there is not only new stimulation and interest but also a renewal process that stimulates higher-order systems thinking. Jung called this process *enantiodromia*, the Heracletian philosophical term meaning that everything turns into its opposite:

> I use the term *enantiodromia* for the emergence of the unconscious opposite in the course of time. This characteristic phenomenon practically always occurs when an extreme one-sided tendency dominates conscious life; in time an equally powerful counterposition is built up which first inhibits the conscious performance and subsequently breaks through the conscious control (Jung, 1923/1966, p. 426).

The problem of opposites usually comes up in the second half of life when all the illusions we projected upon the world gradually come back to haunt us. The energy streaming back from these manifold relationships falls into an unconscious and activates all the things we had neglected to develop. . . . in the second half of life, the development of the function of the opposites lying dormant in the unconscious means a renewal (Jung, 1923/1966, pp. 59–61).

In fully appreciating the different parts, one comes to understand the whole. With holistic thinking comes the ability to be choiceful in the way problems are selected and defined. Instead of operating by implicit assumptions, choiceful problem framing is possible. This process of choosing the perspective from which to view problems, of issue formation, becomes more important in advanced professional work than specialized functional problem solving.

With centering comes a deep sense of personal authenticity and self-confidence. It often comes with a sense of purpose, a sense of calling, in which one's past, present and future are integrated into a meaningful life plan. Jensen (1988), for example, found such a concept of centering to be characteristic of the most effective managers in his sample of physician administrators in a large clinic.

2. The Challenge of Generativity/The Response of Caring

As a species, humans have two biological functional imperatives, two basic instincts—to preserve oneself as an individual and to preserve the species as a whole. The increasing concern for generativity in advanced professionals, as shown in Figure 1, suggests that the relative importance of these objectives changes from early to later adulthood. Childhood is for the definition of self and early adulthood for the development of self. But in later life it is the collective, species perspective that gains ascendance. This view is corroborated by a recent study of professional career development by Dalton and Thompson (1986), who found the early adult career to be divided into an apprenticeship stage and an independent contributor stage. In early adulthood the primary developmental task is moving from dependence to independence. Advanced professional development is divided into an initial mentoring stage and a more advanced director stage. The developmental tasks for the mentor and director are assuming responsibility for others and exercising power. These are the challenges of generativity.

For Erik Erikson, caring is the virtue that is born from the struggle to take responsibility:

Care is a widening commitment to *take care* of the persons, the products, and the ideas one has learned to *care for*. All the strengths arising from earlier development. . .hope and will, purpose and skill, fidelity and love now prove. . .to be essential for the generational task of cultivating strength in the next generation. For this is, indeed, the "store" of human life (Erikson, 1982, p. 67).

Care is expressed in advanced professional work through caring relationships and through careful work. Caring relationships are the most concrete and intimate forms of caring. The mentoring relationship, in which one shares knowledge and skills with younger colleagues, fulfilling a need to teach and be a role model for others, is one such relationship. All relationships, in fact, prosper in the appreciative attention of care. In careful work there is a desire to create something worthwhile, to make a contribution. Generative caring is often first experienced in family life, where the natural response to care for the children is seldom experienced as self-sacrifice but more often as a fulfillment, a source of meaning and purpose. What is less widely recognized is the pervasiveness of this need to serve others outside the family arena. Recent research on the key role that mentoring processes play in organizational life has shown that advanced professionals derive much personal satisfaction from the mentor role. But focus on the mentor has somewhat overshadowed how pervasively the generative instinct is woven into the fabric of organizational life. Work itself is often motivated by this need for meaning and for a sense of contribution. Organizational hierarchies, formal and informal, receive their fundamental legitimization from identification with the generative collective view "to promote the common good." The generative social contract is: Accept responsibility for the world and you are given the power to change it. As Chester Barnard said, "In a free society the reward for good service is a demand for more service." The generative challenge for each of us is: How much responsibility will I, can I, take?

3. The Challenge of Change and Complexity/The Response of Learning

The Club of Rome in their report on global issues in human learning, described the "human gap" as humanity's most serious concern. "The human gap is the distance between growing complexity and our capacity to cope with it. . . .We call it a human gap because it is a dichotomy between a growing complexity of our own making and a lagging development of our own capabilities" (Botkin, et al., 1979, pp.6–7). The most obvious challenge for advanced professionals is to cope with this increasing change and complexity. In the rapidly evolving information society, jobs are becoming more knowledge intensive. Professional obsolescence is very real, particularly in fields such as engineering and medicine where technological change creates new occupations as rapidly as old specialties die. Change and complexity are multiplied for successful professional leaders as they take on expanded responsibilities in higher posts.

Learning is the key to managing change and complexity. Performance is not enough for sustained effectiveness in a world of change and complexity; one must develop the ability to learn from experience. The performance and learning orientations differ in four dimensions: time span, complexity, participation, and executive control. The time perspective of the performance orientation is short. The learning perspective enlarges the time frame through two processes. Protolearning, the formulation of scenarios, hypotheses, beliefs, and intentions, anticipates the future. The more articulated those expectations and models of the future are, the more quickly course deviations can be signaled. Retrolearning, the reexamination and debriefing of past experiences, establishes general operating principles, adding a cumulative quality to work and a sense of historical continuity.

High performance is often achieved by simplicity and predictability, while learning requires a search for requisite complexity—matching the complexity of one's response to the complexity of the problem situation. For example, the choice of an appropriate time span in which to view an issue is perhaps the most important decision in defining a problem and finding a solution to it. To manage a complex situation in a simple framework is like trying to clear a fog with a hand grenade. Power is not the problem; the problem is the refinement of its application. With a simple framework, actions are too crude and the time span is too short.

Participation in the performance orientation is typically hierarchical and motivated by individual reward systems. It focuses mainly on specialized professional problem solving and implementation. Participation in the learning orientation focuses on issue formulation and problem definition as well as problem solving and implementation. It is a cooperative enterprise to share ideas and develop common vision, labeled "egalitarian" by Srivastva and Cooperrider (1986).

The control process of the performance orientation is a goal-seeking, first-order feedback loop typically called "management control," where deviations from given performance targets are the trigger for management attention and corrective action. The learning orientation adds a second-order feedback loop concerned with goal selection. This defines an executive process involving strategic goal selection based on an overall system awareness. Both a performance and a learning orientation are essential for organizational effectiveness. Performance improves the efficiency of specialized organizational responses, and learning promotes integration and coordination at the strategic and developmental levels (see Table 1, following page). Successful advanced professionals have to work in both these orientations, much as a sports team moves from game to practice to game in a continuing cycle of self-development.

Table 1. Characteristics of the Performance and Learning Orientations

Characteristic	Performance Orientation	Learning Orientation
Time span	Immediate	Extended in future by proto-learning; grounded in history by retrolearning
Tolerance for complexity and uncertainty	Predictability and simplicity maximized	Development of requisite complexity
Participation	• Focused on problem solving and implementation • Competitive/independent • Hierarchical	• Focused on issue formulation and problem definition • Cooperative/interdependent • Egalitarian
Control process	Management control • First-order feedback • Goal seeking	Executive control • Second-order feedback • Goal selecting

4. The Challenge of Time/The Response of Visioning

Advanced professionals are preoccupied with time. The assumption of generative responsibilities brings a loss of control over one's personal time. To be responsible for people and projects requires responsiveness to their time demands and deadlines. Effective mentoring requires availability. The successful professional sees the financial value of his or her time increase as expertise increases. "Free" time correspondingly becomes very expensive. All this occurs at a time in life when one is more aware that one's own time is finite. Gallup's survey of successful professionals reports an average 63-hour work week, with a few top achievers working as many as 90 or 100 hours a week. It is little wonder that time management is one of the most frequently mentioned learning needs among advanced professionals.

More fundamentally, a change occurs in the advanced professional's conception and experience of time itself. It was Kurt Lewin who first observed that psychological development involves expansion of consciousness in the dimensions of time and space. The child's world is first the crib, then the room, the home, the neighborhood, and so on, in an expanding scope of awareness. Elliott Jacques (1979) maintains that a broad scope of time awareness, what he calls a long time span of intention, is the primary executive capability needed for advanced professional work. He argues that the hierarchical dimension of work, the "size" of a job, is best measured by its time span of discretion, the amount of time the person has to complete a task before his or her work is reviewed. Time span is measured by the time it takes to complete tasks in one's job role. A factory worker's output, for example, may be reviewed at the end of each eight-hour shift. An intermediate-level chief executive may take a year to introduce new machinery, or three years to open a new market, or five years to develop and market a new product. Higher-level CEOs will engage in formulation of strategic alliances and long-term projects with time spans of ten years or even more before results are evaluated.

To effectively meet the challenge of operating autonomously over long time spans requires the development of a correspondingly long time span of intentional action. With increased time discretion comes increased autonomy, and with that comes a need for intentional action skills—the ability to envision a project and carry it out. Vision is the key to intentional action. It is at once the target, the plan and the motive force for self-directed, purposeful action. To maintain intentional action over long time spans is an effort of willpower that produces continuity and stability through focused commitment and persistence. The dynamics of willpower have been no better understood than by William James. His ideomotor theory of action states that an idea held firmly in conscious focus issues forth automatically in behavior. The challenge of vision, therefore, is literally to keep the dream alive, to keep one's vision as the primary object of conscious attention.

5. The Challenge of Moral Leadership/The Response of Valuing

Eric Erikson describes the challenge of moral leadership thusly: "An adult must be ready to become a numinous model in the next generation's eyes and to act as a judge of evil and a transmitter of ideal values." The challenges of moral leadership are the most difficult in advanced professional life—to be a public person, to represent others, to serve as a model for others, to be a leader and creator of culture, to choose right from wrong in the most complex of circumstances. All these activities require the management of values, while earlier career activities focused primarily on the management of factual knowledge.

From the point of view of advanced professionals themselves, value-intensive decision making is of primary importance. In Gallup's study of successful advanced professionals listed in *Who's Who* (Gallup and Gallup, 1986), "a strong sense of right and wrong" was the personal characteristic that 67 percent of the subjects said best described themselves. Furthermore, this was true for 78 percent of the most highly successful persons in the sample.

Professional education typically has offered little preparation for this focus on value-intensive decision making. In addition, the wider social context of Western society has seen deterioration of value-forming institutions such as religion and the family. The value neutrality of positivistic science encourages leaders to avoid dialogue about value issues, while at the same time fanatical single-value movements are on the rise. Morality and ethics, the "sciences" of value choice, are seldom discussed outside religious circles.

The tasks of moral leadership are to make judgments about value priorities, to promote them in one's activities, and to preserve these values through the creation of a culture that sustains them. It is important to distinguish the growthful process of valuing from the dogmatic imposition of one's own values on others. Valuing is a creative process based on open and receptive dialogue with others. Values are the collective statements of belief generated by the valuing process. Whenever these value statements are generalized and applied outside of the context and process that created them, the danger of value imposition is present.

Valuing is the medium for caring. In caring relationships one values and prizes the other, creating value in the relationship and feelings of self-worth in the other. The goal of careful work is to create value, to make a contribution. Moral leadership is leadership in creation, promotion, and preservation of value. For Jung, the process of self-actualization that he called "individuation," was dependent on the creation of value:

> Individuation cuts one off from personal conformity and hence from collectivity. That is, the guilt which the individual leaves behind him for the world, that is the guilt he must endeavor to redeem. He must offer a ransom in place of himself, that is, he must bring forth values which are an equivalent substitute for his absence in the collective personal sphere. Without this production of values, final individuation is immoral and—more than that—suicidal. The person who cannot create values should sacrifice himself consciously to the spirit of collective conformity (Jung, 1971, p. 450).

6. The Challenge of Interdependence/The Response of Teamwork

These days I use the term "leadership" with ambivalence, for some of the images it conjures up about the nature of human relationships are profoundly misleading. To mention leadership is to emphasize the vertical power dimension of human relationships at the expense of the horizontal functions of solidarity and cooperation. Particularly in American society, the most individualistic society in the world according to Hofstede's data (1980), leadership is seen as a characteristic of individual leaders, not as a collective group process. The leader is the mythic hero, the creator and agent of action, who is given credit for success and blame for failure. That leadership is a two-way relationship where leaders are made by followers is overlooked; as is the importance of the reactive side of the leader role—reacting to the wishes of followers, receiving their communications and reflecting their values. The challenge of inter-dependence is in many ways a challenge to see through these illusions of leadership. While professionals are educated in a performance system that is individual and competitively oriented, much professional work requires cooperative team work. Entry-level professionals in our sample of engineering alumni reported this need to work as a member of a team as a major part of the "job shock" they experienced on entering the work force. As we have seen, advanced professional leadership requires effective work in muiltidisciplinary teams in order to integrate diverse knowledge specialties into a coherent plan of action.

Teamwork emphasizes the horizontal integrative dimension of leadership. In this view, leadership is the collective responsibility of the group. It is a dynamic process whereby power is given to those on the team whose capabilities best respond to the particular requirements of the moment. Differences among members are valued for they strengthen the team's capacity to adapt and create. Working together in this way, teams can produce synergy—where the product of the whole is greater than the sum of its parts.

7. The Challenge of Ordinary Life/The Response of Humility

The space shuttle Challenger disaster was a reliving of the Icarus myth where Daedalus, the master technologist, hoped to have his son fly to the sun on wings of wax and feathers. The lesson is that of all Greek tragedy—a warning of the dangers of human pride, hubris. In this case the warning is about confusing the ordinary and the extraordinary. Time magazine paid homage to the Challenger astronauts in this way:

> . . .Christa McAuliffe, the school teacher, received most of the attention. . .a reminder to everyone of what classroom experiences were or should have been. . .she called herself an ordinary person and that is how many. . .came to think of her. . .They were, all of them, human like us. Their courage and ambition took root in the familiar, sustained by circumstances and routines that everyone can recognize. On that last morning they were in preflight isolation but still a part of us. They got up and dressed, had breakfast and went to work.

The challenge of ordinary life has particular significance for advanced professionals who with highly specialized skills, enhanced by modern technology, create superhuman accomplishments. For many of these men and women the disjuncture between professional role and personal life can be disorienting; for some, work is all consuming. To become specialized is also to become special. With that sense of specialness comes two dangers. The first is a tendency to see specialized knowledge as universal knowledge, to see knowledge as wisdom. The problem with specialized knowledge is that it has no sense of priority and hence it tends to presume its own preeminence. This tendency to extend knowledge beyond its assumptions and field of application needs to be balanced by the humble recognition that begins with the discovery of the limitations of knowledge, and that confusion marks the beginning of learning. The second danger is elitism. Specialists associate with other specialists and together create a world view that gives their values priority. Others are deemed laymen, while a few are called "intelligent laymen" worthy of an occasional communication. Yet we are all laymen or women outside of our specialties. Ordinary life is important because it is the common meeting ground of all humanity. It is the source of agreement on fundamental value priorities that we all share as human beings—food and shelter, clean air to breathe, peaceful relationships with our neighbors. In ordinary life, value judgments are common sense.

8. The Challenge of Facing Challenge/The Response of Courage

The inevitable concomitant of advanced professional development is age. Age results in aging when adults disengage from social relationships and the life challenges they face. Yet it is clear that when aspirations are realistic and one stays engaged in life, learning and development continue in old age. Older adults can learn complex material such as memory mnemonics, although they are somewhat slower at it. When aged rats who have spent their lives in ordinary cage environments are placed in enriched environments, they become more active, healthier and their brains increase in the number of synapses per neuron over controls.

To face life challenges requires the courage to stay positively engaged in the social world and to find stimulation in the mastery of life circumstances. I use the term "courage" to summarize the elements of what Maddi and Corbasa call the hardiness response to stress. Their studies show that individuals who see themselves in control of their lives, committed to the world around them and challenged by life, are less debilitated by stressful life events than those who feel alienated and controlled by fate.

The rewards of facing challenge can be healing, even transcendent. Recently I saw an interview of Barbra Streisand by Gloria Steinem on the "Today Show." The interview took place after Streisand's "One Voice" concert, her first live public performance in years. She described how her increasing perfectionism and desire to exceed expectations had made it impossible for her to perform publicly. When asked how she was able to do the "One Voice" concert, she replied that she had come to the realization that the causes her singing would support were far more important than whatever personal discomfort and embarrassment she might feel. Her caring had enabled her to sing. What I witnessed that morning was not only a living example of Jung's enantiodromia and the salvation that comes by adding value, but also a numinous model willing to share her personal learning with us all.

Conclusion

The challenges described here describe a lifelong learning agenda for advanced professionals and, indeed, all adults. Surveying the developmental challenges of the second half of life, Jung raises a provocative question:

> The worst of it all is that intelligent and cultivated people live their lives without even knowing of the possibility of such transformations. Wholly unprepared, they embark upon the second half of life. Or are there perhaps colleges for 40-year olds which prepare them for their coming life and its demands as the ordinary colleges introduce our young people to a knowledge of the world?

The developmental challenges described here represent an important educational agenda for higher education. H.G. Wells observed many years ago that "Human history becomes more and more a race between education and catastrophe." Advanced professional leadership in corporations and public institutions is at the forefront of this race, facing complex issues that require not only decisiveness but creativity, not only managerial control but visionary leadership, not only the technical skills necessary to achieve the organization's mission but the integrity to resolve the value conflicts inherent in shaping that mission. While there are many new vendors addressing the lifelong learning needs of advanced professionals, the university has a special role and responsibility. Organizational education can be limited by narrow self-interest, and professional associations suffer from the myopia of specialization in their educational agenda. The university alone has the mission to universalize knowledge—to make the whole of accumulated human wisdom available to everyone. A college for 40-year olds would have to address the knowledge infrastructure neglected by vocational professional education—the arts and social sciences, literature, philosophy and history—for the wisdom of these fields bears directly on the challenges of adult development. Its campus needs to be global, probably electronic, and interwoven with the life and work of its students. It should be a community of learners dedicated to inquiry and dialogue across the special interests of age, profession, class and culture; a community actively involved in creating humanity's common future.

References

Botkin, J., Elmandjra, M., & Malitza, M. (1979). *No Limits to Learning*. Club of Rome. N.Y.: Pergamon.

Dalton, G. & Thompson, P. (1986). *Novations: Strategies for Career Management*. Glenview, Ill.: Scott Foresman.

Erikson, E. (1982). *The Life Cycle Completed*. N.Y.: W.W. Norton.

Gallup, G. & Gallup, A. (1986). *The Great American Success Story*. Homewood, Ill.: Dow Jones Irwin.

Gypen, J. (1981). "Learning style adaptation in professional careers: The case of engineers and social workers." Unpublished doctoral dissertation, Department of Organizational Behavior, Case Western Reserve University, Cleveland, Ohio.

Hall, N. (1958). *The Making of Higher Executives: The Modern Challenges*. N.Y.: New York University.

Hofsteade, G. (1980). *Culture's Consequences: International Differences in Work Related Values*. Beverly Hills, CA.: Sage Publications.

Jacques, E. (1979, September-October). "Taking Time Seriously in Evaluating Jobs." *Harvard Business Review*, pp. 124–132.

Jensen, T. (1985). "Leadership and the Physician Executive." *Medical Group Management*.

Jung, C., (1923). *Psychological Types*. London: Pantheon, 1923.

Jung, C. (1966). *Two Essays on Analytical Psychology, Collected Works*, vol. 7. Princeton, N.J.: Princeton University Press.

Kolb, D. (1984). *Experiential Learning: Experience as the Source of Learning and Development*. Englewood Cliffs, N.J.: Prentice-Hall.

Kolb, D. & Wolfe, D. (1981). Professional education and career development: A cross-sectional study of adaptive competencies in experiential learning. Final Report, NIE Grant No. NIE-G-77-0053, ERIC No. ED 209-493 CE 030519.

Maddi, S. & Kobasa, S. (1984). *The Hardy Executive: Health Under Stress*. Homewood, Ill.: Dow Jones-Irwin.

Sanford, N. (1981). "Notes Toward a Theory of Personality Development at 80 or Any Old Age." In J. Starde (ed.), *Wisdom and Old Age*. Berkeley, CA.: Ross Books.

Sims, R. (1983). "Kolb's Experiential Learning Theory: A Framework for Assessing Person-Job Interaction." *Academy of Management Review*, pp. 501–508.

Srivastva, S. & Cooperrider, D. (1986). "The Emergence of the Egalitarian Organization." *Human Relations*, London: Tavistock.

14

Residence Requirements: Inputs, Outcomes and Nonsense About the "Community of Scholars"

Urban Whitaker

The genesis of this article was in a taxi with Morris Keeton on the way to the Denver Hilton. I said something about the need for an evaluation of traditional residence requirements for baccalaureate degrees and got a typical earful from Morris. While I cannot saddle him with the blame for any weaknesses in this brief essay, he has to be credited with substantial contributions to whatever its strengths may be.

Virtually all American colleges and universities have a residence requirement for the baccalaureate degree.** Here is a sample from an actual catalog:

A student is considered to be in residence status when he/she is registered in regular Fall, Spring, Summer Session and Winter Session work on this campus. Thirty semester units (of 124 required for the baccalaureate degree) shall be earned in residence. Extension, units, credit by examination, and transfer work from other institutions are not acceptable for meeting the residence requirement.

Over the years a deep chasm has opened between what this kind of residence requirement was supposed to do and what it actually accomplishes. What was supposed to happen was: immersion in a community of scholars (that was the prescribed input) resulting in deepened appreciation and understanding of our intellectual existence (the intended outcome). That probably made sense in an era when the baccalaureate degree was pursued mostly in physical residence, on the campus, and in one four-year stretch immediately after high school. No doubt it is still true for some small minority of students in the dwindling minority of ivy-covered "ivory towers." But it is no longer true for the majority of students in the majority of colleges and universities.

What, in fact, does happen now? Too often it looks like this: students hurry from the bus or street car (or a distant parking place) to the classroom, arriving just as the session starts, and speed away afterward (or a few minutes early in order not to be late to work). They hardly notice the other members, faculty

---

**This essay is concerned primarily with the baccalaureate degree. Many of the problems discussed here, however, also apply to residence requirements for graduate degrees.

or students, in the briefly-visited "community of scholars." The professor is often on a similar schedule, getting to campus either on Tuesday–Thursday or Monday–Wednesday–Friday to conduct a class and to meet some short, mandatory office hours (that are more than occasionally violated).

Of course there are exceptions. Some students do stay on for a while to talk to the professor or perhaps to have a beer with someone else in the class. But, on the average, the contemporary campus scene is sadly lacking in both the inputs and the outcomes that are traditionally associated with residence requirements.

There are three common definitions of "residence." First, there is the place definition. It is not normally applied to the students' physical residence, that is, where they live. As a graduation requirement, "residence" refers to where the courses are taken. This definition is often stretched for the convenience of the institution so that some courses are found with the residence label even if they aren't physically taught on the campus.

Second, there is an enrollment status definition. Whether a course counts toward the residence requirement depends on whether the student is matriculated and paying regular fees, or is enrolled through extension. It is common for students to take the same course, at the same time, in the same place—but with the results certified to satisfy the residence requirement only for those classified as "regularly enrolled." (This absurd situation is often called "concurrent enrollment.") The illogical outcome of this arrangement is that an 'A' student who takes the course in extension or when he/she is on part-time status and later wants to count it as a residence course may be denied graduation. Meanwhile, a 'C' student (or even one who barely passed with a 'D') in the same course—but as a regularly enrolled student—gets residence credit.

In this Kafkaesque world, the same course may be given by the same professor and carry the same requirements both during the day and in the early evening. Those who take it during the day get residence credit; those who take it in the evening do not.

A third type of "residence" depends simply on whether it is "our" course or "theirs"—i.e., transfer credit. It is deemed to satisfy the residence requirement if it is taken from "us," but not if it is transferred from another institution. The grossly improper result of this rule is that courses taken in the old-fashioned, live-in-the-dorm-on-the-campus "community of scholars" mode doesn't count as a resident course when transferred from another institution—even from Harvard.

Clearly the residence requirement no longer has any significant relationship to the concept of a "community of scholars." The inputs that count are not related to the outcomes that matter. "Residence" tends to become a selfish fiscal concept rather than a meaningful intellectual one.

Nothing in this essay is meant to demean the value of immersion in (or at least association with) a community of scholars. I challenge neither the virtues of scholarship nor the idea that prolonged rubbing of shoulders with scholars will lead to sharing of ideas and the synergy of shared intellectual endeavor.

Nor do I challenge the need for some kind of "residence" requirement that goes beyond the completion of formal course work.

I do challenge the outmoded assumption that technical inputs such as where one lives, or where (or from whom) one learns, or how one pays tuition, have any reliable relationship to such a desirable learning outcome as intellectual sophistication.

Much has been written about the impact of technological change. The impact of demographic change may be even more important to a healthy educational system. Colleges and universities used to serve mostly an 18–22 year old student body. Now it is not unusual for postsecondary institutions to report an average age of 25–30 and to be graduating octogenarian grandparents. Only a few years ago most students were in full-time attendance. Now the part-timers often outnumber the full-timers.

It has always been true that all of us are lifetime experiential learners. But what is new—and having a major impact on the nature of campus demography—is that we are spreading out our classroom-based learning over several decades instead of just several years.

Many institutions are finding effective ways to "roll with the demographic punch." Weekend seminars and weeks—or summers—"in residence" are providing "communities of scholars" that can serve an older, part-time student body.

In time, of course, new arrangements will catch up with the new demographics. The values of the old residence requirement will be clarified, and we will find effective ways of preserving them for new generations of learners.

To speed up the transition, we need to recognize some facts:

1. one can (and many do) earn a degree on a campus without ever really being immersed in a community of scholars;
2. one can be immersed in a community of scholars in a general physical residence sense without significantly participating in much intellectual activity; and
3. the community of scholars has been dispersed so significantly by technological change that it can be found quite effectively off the campus as well as on.

We need to move, with deliberate (and probably foundation-supported) vigor, away from the contemporary nonsense about residence requirements. We need to define what it is—other than 'X' number of units completed—that constitutes the intellectual essence of a college education. We need—and I think we need this first—to specify the essential outcomes of immersion in a community of scholars. Only then can we make sense of the variety of inputs that could lead to a deepened appreciation of our intellectual existence.

15

Retention Strategies for Adult Learners: An Expanded Notion of Access

Bessie Blake

The presence of adults on college campuses has increased dramatically in the past couple of decades. This growth is probably best understood in the context of societal pressure for access, and with recognition of significant initiatives on the part of educational associations such as CAEL (Keeton and Tate, 1979), which have supported college and university efforts to recruit and enroll adults. Yet, after twenty years of growth in adult enrollment, theory formulation and program development, we continue to describe adults as a "new" population on college campuses. Perhaps it is because adults continue to find doorways into higher education where none previously existed. Their newness is also characterized by their struggle to settle in an unfamiliar setting, as well as by our attempts to understand and support them in a new environment. This struggle with newness, however, reflects a deeper challenge for colleges and universities to extend beyond initial access to the assurance of a successful college experience.

While adults bring to the education setting rich and varied life experiences that can be employed in the learning process, they are also a heterogeneous group of learners who assume multiple roles and responsibilities that place competing demands on their time. In addition, many adults have been away from formal educational settings and may be unfamiliar with academic structures or unsure of their academic potential. Clearly, access is impeded if program structures exclude or discourage adult participation due to insufficient attention to the heterogeneity and complexity of life situations and issues they bring with them.

Through the work of CAEL and other groups committed to quality academic experiences for adult learners, researchers and practitioners have developed innovative models designed specifically to support adult students in the achievement of their educational goals. These models are characterized by:

— outreach and community partnerships;
— flexibility in scheduling;
— individualized degree planning;
— student participation in shaping curricula; and,
— recognition of the value of experiential learning and the assessment of prior learning.

This emphasis on flexibility, individualization, student-centeredness and experiential learning has enabled college degree programs to facilitate adult learner success (Brookfield, 1986).

127

It is a diverse profile of adult learners who have sought to utilize these new models (Cross, 1981). Among them are students who do "not usually live in circumstances that encourage the leisurely pursuit of truth. Many commute to school from families and jobs, study part-time, drop in and out, and worry about money" (Gamson and Associates, 1984). It is this population of adult students for whom we need to sharpen the focus of access to include the notion of equity. Some practitioners, among them Taaffe and Rocco (1981), noted this dilemma nearly a decade ago. They viewed access and equity as inseparable principles that characterized the context of adult higher education; these two principles continue to define the context today. Ongoing attention to access, then, must encompass equity as an essential element of programs.

As we face yet another "new" and growing population of adult learners (women, displaced workers and the urban poor) who are underserved by current models, strategies must be developed to reduce barriers that impede their progress. This means recruitment and enrollment of adults, but it also means addressing an array of mitigating circumstances that work against their retention.

The School of New Resources is currently pilot testing a retention model for the diverse population of adults attending its adult degree program in metropolitan New York City. Since institutional cohort survival studies utilized for younger students proved ineffective in establishing patterns of retention and attrition for adults enrolled in the school, comparative studies of semester attrition were conducted over a three year period. An analysis of data revealed:

1. attrition is greater from Spring to Fall than from Fall to Spring terms;
2. on average, 83% of students are retained from one semester to the next;
3. of the 17% of students who "stop-out" in a given semester, the majority do so within the first five weeks of classes; and
4. economic and social barriers impede the progress of adults in the areas of:
   — child care needs,
   — educational funding and financial aid,
   — indirect education costs,
   — short-term financial planning and budget management,
   — interaction with social services agencies,
   — reduction of stress associated with the assumption of college studies.

Based on these findings, the school developed a retention model designed for early intervention in the disruptive processes that impede adult student progress. Activities in the areas of advisement, financial aid and planning, and other support services were consolidated in support of the following program objectives:

A. Assume an advocacy role on behalf of adult students with local social services agencies;
B. Assist adult students in addressing child care needs;
C. Assist adult students with indirect educational costs;
D. Assist adult students with stress reduction;
E. Enhance advisement and other support for adult students at risk of academic dismissal;
F. Assist adult students with financial aid processes.

Through an application of the variables associated with attrition, the pilot test identified a pool of 200 at-risk students at the school's South Bronx Campus. The pilot goal was to retain 50 of these students. Preliminary results indicate that intervention strategies have resulted in the retention of 99 students in the target group. A comprehensive evaluation of the model will be conducted in the Fall of 1989. If initial positive results hold, the model will be disseminated to the six other New Resources campuses in the Spring of 1990.

As with other academic and support services models at the School of New Resources, the retention program is an evolutionary model designed for responsiveness to changing and new clienteles of adult learners.

The assurance of access and equity for a rapidly expanding adult population demands the creation of innovative academic and support services models that are holistic, flexible, individualized and outreaching. We must assess and incorporate life experiences that enrich the learning process and, at the same time, effectively address difficult life situations that impede the admissions and retention of many adult students in college.

References

Brookfield, S.D. *Understanding and Facilitating Adult Learning.* San Francisco: Jossey-Bass, 1986.

Cross, K. Patricia. *Adults as Learners: Increasing Participation and Facilitating Learning.*

Gamson and Associates. *Liberating Education.* San Francisco: Jossey-Bass, 1984.

Keeton, M.T. and Tate, P. *Learning by Experience—What Why and How.* San Francisco: Jossey-Bass, 1979.

Taaffe, T. and Rocco, T. "Access to Higher Education for Adults," in *Providing Access for Adults to Alternative College Programs.* Scarecrow Press, 1981.

Part IV

Towards the Learning Society

16

The Road to the Learning Society

K. Patricia Cross

Yesterday, a new book, entitled *Making Sense of Experiential Learning,* arrived on my desk. "Making sense," I decided, wouldn't be a bad thing to do so I opened the book to discover that experiential learning means different things to different people—very different things.

The authors of the book, Susan Warner Weil and Ian McGill, wrote from the experience of the first international conference on experiential learning held in London two years ago. They discovered, during that conference, four different meanings to experiential learning. Because meanings and people tended to cluster into four quite distinct groups, they referred to each cluster as a village: The four villages of experiential learning that they identified are these:

1. Village One is concerned particularly with assessing and accrediting learning from life and work experience as the basis for creating new routes into higher education, employment and training opportunities and professional bodies.
2. Village Two focuses on experiential learning as the basis for bringing about change in the structures, purposes and curricula of higher education.
3. Village Three emphasizes experiential learning as the basis for group consciousness raising, community action and social change.
4. Village Four is concerned with personal growth and development and experiential learning approaches that increase self-awareness and group effectiveness.

Morris Keeton has probably done more than anyone else in the world to provide leadership to the inhabitants of Village One. Although his writing and speaking have reflected the perspectives of all four villages, he has managed to do what few academics ever do—bring about significant change in the perceptions and practices of educators. To his everlasting credit, he has put Village One on the worldwide map, and in effecting such change, has made an enormous contribution to Village Two. It is far more difficult to say who has done what in Villages Three and Four. There are many immigrants to those villages who came from other lands other than experiential learning.

*Prepared for the Second International Conference on Experiential Learning, Sydney, Australia, July 3–7, 1989. This paper contains portions of a paper entitled, "The Changing Role of Higher Education in the United States," presented in Stockholm, May 20, 1987.

I don't perceive myself to be a native of any particular village in the Weil/McGill definitions. Rather, I seem to be more like an itinerant salesperson traveling from village to village, interested primarily in what each is doing to encourage lifelong learning for all people.

Thus I decided that rather than look at any single village in this paper, I would look at the road of lifelong learning that connects the villages. You may expect a description of the road traveled to emphasize what is common to all four villages of experiential learning, but my metaphor is more realistic and less figurative. Roads traveled may connect villages that have little in common, and certainly roads are not made up of pieces of villages. So I shall simply define the road I am traveling as a route to the destination of the learning society.

I expect that each of the villages of experiential learning will be cordial to lifelong learning; each will nourish me in my route; each will add to my understanding of lifelong learning and the learning society which I seek. But I won't tarry long in any single village. I seek rather to determine what each has to offer to the destination of the learning society.

The concept of the learning society has two interpretations. One refers to a society which is dependent on knowledge. In this interpretation, learning is an adjective, used to describe a society that makes its living by its wits. In an earlier age, we talked about an agrarian society to describe a society that made its living from the land. Then came the "industrial society," which became, in short order, dependent on machines to do the work of society.

Now we enter the learning society in which information and know-how are the driving forces of the economy. A good idea can be worth millions today—more than land and more than manufacturing power. This learning society runs on brain power. Human resources, unlike natural resources, have the advantage of being non-depletable and of increasing the more they are developed and used. Thus, one view of the learning society shows a society that cultivates and depends on people who can use their minds and knowledge to think creatively and constructively.

The second interpretation of the learning society refers to the pervasiveness of the activity of learning. When learning spreads beyond schools and colleges to pervade the work place, senior citizens' centers, and commuter trains, and when people of all ages and from all walks of life participate in learning activities, then we can legitimately refer to the society in which all of this takes place as the "learning society." In this view, learning is an active verb, describing a major activity of the members of the society.

Thus, I know what I am looking for. My road to the learning society will take me to a destination in which human resources are the capital assets of the society and in which all people are engaged in lifelong learning for self-development as well as for the economic and social development of the society.

The industrialized nations of the world have already traveled some distance down this road. Because my travels in lifelong learning have been largely in the United States, I should like first to trace a bit of history in the United States to illustrate the steady push of history in the direction of the learning society.

If the purpose of education is to serve the society which creates and maintains it, then when the needs of society change, the services of educational organizations should change. There are those who would argue that formal education is slow to respond to the changing needs of society, and others will argue that education should do more than respond; it should take the lead in preparing for the future. History will show, however, that pressures for change come largely from forces external to the formal educational system. In the United States, pressures for change in higher education have come largely from the triple forces of social pressures for equal educational opportunity, economic pressures for maximum development of human capital, and demographic pressures created by the aging of the population.

Gradually, higher education in the United States has been shifting from a privilege to a right. Most students today are not especially grateful for the opportunity to attend college; they feel that it is their right and that sweeping away the barriers to college attendance is a responsibility of society. Thus, the piece of the road already traveled is the shift in the stance of higher education from exclusiveness to inclusiveness. That moves us, in my definition, part way down the road toward the learning society.

Gradually at first, and then with increasing momentum, the barriers to college attendance have been falling. In the early days of private colleges, it was primarily the children of well-to-do families that attended college. The criteria for admission were social and financial. Those excluded were primarily those from families that lacked money for tuition and expenses.

With the advent of land grant colleges in the United States, the meritocratic phase of higher education appeared, and higher education was offered to those who "merited" it by virtue of their past performance in school. Those excluded were those who lacked the high school grades and/or test scores to suggest academic promise. Ultimately, it became clear that most barriers to higher education were highly interrelated, operating to exclude quite consistently certain groups of people.

The call for equality of educational opportunity brought the establishment of low tuition, open-admission community colleges at the rate of one new college per week throughout the late 1960s. Then higher education began actively recruiting previously excluded poor people, ethnic minorities and women. Now colleges are seeking to abolish all other exclusionary practices, including discrimination because of age, part-time student status and geographical isolation.

Higher education in the United States today is largely non-selective. Most of the decisions made about where to go to college are made by students rather than by colleges. Only 16 percent of all American colleges can be considered "selective," and it is estimated that two-thirds of all freshmen attend colleges that accept all or almost all applicants (OERI, 1986). That includes some 1300 open door community colleges that enroll more than four million students—a majority of all college freshmen and sophomores in the United States.

In recent years, new options plus pressures for equal opportunity have resulted in significant growth of populations that were under represented in higher education in the 1950s. Between 1972 and 1982, for example, the rate of growth for women was 61 percent, compared to 15 percent for men; minority enrollments increased 85 percent, compared to 30 percent for whites; students 35 and older increased by 77 percent, compared to 23 percent for students 18 to 24 years of age, and part-time students increased by 66 percent compared to 19 percent for full-timers (NCES, 1983).

These rather dramatic changes in the constituency of higher education are moving us inevitably toward the learning society as people of all ages and from all walks of life participate actively in learning. I make a point of talking about the expansion of higher education because participation in the formal educational institutions of society influences in a powerful way participation in lifelong learning (Cross, 1981). A college graduate is three times more likely to participate in adult education than a high school graduate. Education is habit forming; the more people have, the more they want.

The notion of offering education to everyone who wants it has a profound effect upon the design of higher education. In this sense, our road to the learning society travels through Village Two of experiential learning which desires to bring about change in higher education. Selecting students who are predicted to succeed in the type of college education that we happen to offer is a very different task from educating all who come. Under selective admissions, the emphasis is on admitting those who are predicted to succeed in college. If a student fails, we look for more accurate measures of predicting success. The questions we ask are these: How can we enter measures of motivation into the prediction equations to make them more accurate? Do admissions tests predict performance as well for minorities as for Caucasians? How can we recruit the kind of student who will succeed in college?

These are the questions of the meritocracy. In contrast, the big questions in egalitarian higher education are not how can we predict motivation, but how can we create it? Not how well tests predict grades, but how well they diagnose learning strengths and weaknesses. Not how to recruit those who will be successful, but how to make successful those who come. The goal of access to higher education affects open admissions colleges directly, of course, but a national mission of equality of educational opportunity has considerable impact on all higher education, as well as on our conceptualization of educational systems.

The sign that I want to post on this part of the road to the learning society is too simple to capture its full impact on changing the structures and purposes of higher education, but for the sake of brevity, I shall call it the historical trend toward student inclusiveness. While there are many miles yet to go on this road, substantial progress has been made in increasing the sensitivity of colleges to the advantages of inclusiveness and diversity.

The next portion of the road traveled toward the destination of the learning society, I shall label campus-expansiveness. Geographically, as well as conceptually, colleges are reaching out to include a broader community. Early in the history of higher education, colleges were deliberately located in small towns. Faculty lived around the campus and students lived on the campus, and college was a community unto itself—its geographical isolation a symbol of its removal from the worldly concerns of the masses.

Things are quite different today. Colleges pride themselves on being very much a part of the real world. College professors serve as mayors, and students run for city council; hotels abound with visitors from every corner of the earth, and airports bustle with professors off to consult with business and government about solutions to very practical problems. Not only have colleges moved from campus into town and more broadly into the world, but the new strategy is to take the colleges to the people either by locating them in population centers or by extending them into rural areas.

Where off-campus learning facilities do not exist naturally, they are created through imaginative use of technology. Talk-back television permits isolated learners to join in class discussions conducted hundreds of miles away. Cable television is reaching into a majority of American television homes, and video disks and personal computers are spreading information more rapidly than we can absorb it.

The trend is as clear as it is steady. The college campus has burst explosively from its boundaries, and decentralization of learning is a major trend of our times. The demographics of the birth rate, combined with the explosion of knowledge in the information age, are pressing even thoroughly traditional colleges into looking for new clienteles to serve and new locations of operation. Thus, one of the consequences of the decision to include rather than exclude people from postsecondary learning opportunities is the expanded campus that takes learning to the people.

The two historical movements that I have described as people-inclusive and campus-expansive are portions of the road already traveled. While they concern pressures and changes in formal higher education, they provide the background for the continuation of our journey into the learning society. The road I wish to travel now is not very clearly marked since it lies in the future. Directions to the learning society are mixed, and it is possible that we will lose our way. But I see three trends emerging:

> The first and most vigorous trend into a full-blown learning society is the move toward increased options for adult learners. We have come a long way since Ezra Cornell stood on a hill overlooking Lake Cayuga and staked out the mission of Cornell University. "I would found an institution," he said, "where any person can find instruction in any subject." That was a farsighted and egalitarian view for the mid-1800s, but I wonder if he had any idea of what that would mean some hundred years later. Did he know that he was founding an institution where a 50-year old grandmother could study hotel administration if she wished? Did he know that someday his dream of egalitarian education would be expanded to say, any person can study any subject, anywhere, anytime, by any method, for any purpose?

Shortly after Cornell expanded the options of the curriculum, Governor LaFollette of Wisconsin combined forces with President Charles Van Hise of the University of Wisconsin to expand the concept of "campus" by proclaiming that, "The boundaries of the campus are the boundaries of the state." Today's University of Wisconsin would find the boundaries of the state limiting rather than expansive. For the University of Wisconsin and most other universities, the boundaries of campus are no more. The world is the campus.

One thing that limited the vision of Ezra Cornell and the original "Wisconsin idea" was that they assumed that the university should provide the many options for education that they advocated. Wouldn't they be astounded now to see the variety of providers of education? Higher education today provides just about a third of the organized learning opportunities for adults; the remaining two-thirds is provided by a vast array of schools and noncollegiate providers, many of whom offer everything colleges do and more. They may offer credit, degrees, education leading to promotion, licensure, personal fulfillment, intellectual stimulation and practical skills. Industry, for example, spends 30 billion dollars annually on the education and training of employees (Carnevale, 1986). That means that business currently allocates more money for education and training than the 23 billion dollars that all 50 states combined allocate for higher education (Lynton and Elman, 1987). Aetna, Xerox, IBM, and other corporate giants have built campuses with classrooms and residence halls that rival anything offered in our most exclusive and expensive colleges. Some corporations have the largest teaching forces in the nation. IBM employed 6,000 full-time instructors last year, and the banking industry offered 1.3 formal courses for every employee (Carnevale, 1986).

Professional associations, too, are becoming the builders of vast educational networks. The American Management Association conducts 3,200 programs annually and enrolls 100,000 learners, but even they have no corner on the market for the most popular of all adult education courses—business. It is estimated that 3,000 different providers, many of them private entrepreneurs, conduct some 40,000 public business seminars each year.

Added to these providers are the military services, which provide education and learning for 4 million students, and government which claims 15 million workers, half of whom undertake some form of organized instruction each year (Hodgkinson, 1985).

The largest village on the way to the expanded options of the learning society is Village Number One, which is concerned primarily with assessing and making legitimate the various forms of learning. The people of this village are not concerned so much about how people learn as with whether they continue to learn and how much they can contribute to the society of which they are a part. The inhabitants of Villages One and Two are neighborly; the legitimization of experiential learning, the major interest of Village One, does a great deal to bring about changes, sought by Village Two, in the structures, purposes and curricula of higher education.

The next portion of our road to the learning society takes us past experiential learning Villages Three and Four—not so much through the middle of the villages, I think, as through some outlying streets, and perhaps across some uncultivated land.

While Village Three is interested in experiential learning for community action and social change, and Village Four is interested primarily in personal growth and development, it is not at all clear what vehicles the people in Villages Three and Four will use to reach the learning society.

The functions of the various providers of educational services used to be fairly clear. Employers offered training related to work and careers. Colleges offered liberal education designed, according to their catalogues, for self-development, cognitive growth, and the enhancement of intellectual and cultural appreciations. YMCAs and senior citizens' centers offered instruction in hobbies and the use of leisure time. Adult schools offered basic skills and literacy education. Academic credit was granted for college courses, certificates for trade schools, career advancement for training provided by employers.

In the learning society that lies just over the next hill, it is no longer clear who offers what or which courses merit academic credit. The distinction that we used to make between the education offered by colleges and the training offered by industry is difficult to maintain when applied to providers. Colleges today are heavily involved in training as well as in education, and the programs of many corporations contain as much emphasis on theory, research, and personal development as those of any college. Consider, for example, this description of IBM's Systems Research Institute:

The institute's educational philosophy is in many ways that of a university. It stresses fundamental and conceptual education and allows students to choose those courses that will best nurture their own development. The intent is to stimulate and challenge, to teach the theoretical and the practical, to discuss and argue differing viewpoints, to broaden the individual, focusing on his or her special skills (IBM Systems, 1981, p. 6).

Contrast that broad educational philosophy with this course description taken from a college catalogue. The course is called Airline Reservations and carries three academic credits. The description reads as follows:

Prepares students for airline employment opportunities through a familiarization of the procedures involved in airline reservations, the use of official airline guides, and airline route structures.

If one were given a blind sample of course descriptions today, it would be hard to tell whether they came from industry, colleges, museums, labor unions, or professional associations.

A related blurring of educational functions occurs in the distinction between credit and non-credit learning. Within higher education the waters have been muddied by some shifting of non-credit, non-funded courses to the credit, funded side of the ledger. Outside of higher education, non-colleges are beginning to offer not only fully legitimate credit courses, but full-scale degree programs.

A 1985 study (Eurich, 1985) identified 18 corporation-founded institutions in the United States that have been accredited (or have applied for such status) and granted permission to give academic degrees. Most grant bachelors and masters degrees, but they range from associate degrees through doctorates. Education and training within large private sector corporations in the United States have, according to the author of the study, "become a booming industry" (p.1).

While the image of academic degrees offered by these corporate colleges is still mildly sensational, the movement of collegiate institutions into the realm of non-credit instruction is now commonplace. Between 1968 and 1978 more than a thousand colleges introduced non-credit programs on—or more likely off—their campuses. Today it is the norm rather than the exception for degree-granting colleges to be involved in non-degree instruction. This includes prestige research universities. At the University of California, for example, there are more than 350,000 students enrolled in continuing education courses, and more than 3/4 of these students already have college degrees (Stern, 1983).

But whether a course was originally taken for credit is not especially important today; it is increasingly easy to convert non-credit learning into college degrees, thanks to Morris Keeton and his neighbors in Village One. Just a decade ago only about a third of American colleges granted credit if students could demonstrate on standardized examinations that they knew the material; today 93 percent of all colleges grant credit by examination, and 90 percent accept GED test scores as the equivalent of a high school diploma. Ten years ago, only 14 percent of the colleges would consider granting credit for experiential learning; today more than one-third do (Stadtman, 1980; Hexter and Andersen, 1986).

Historically, colleges have been reasonably generous in accepting credit from other colleges; today they are increasingly likely to endorse learning regardless of its source. More than three quarters of all colleges grant credit for courses offered by the armed services, and 38 percent grant academic credit for courses conducted by business and industry (Hexter and Andersen, 1986). The American Council on Education's Office of Education Credit lists over 2,000 courses offered by more than 180 corporations and government agencies. College and university faculty members conduct site visits in order to verify quality and recommend credit.

Illustrations of the blurring of once distinctive functions in adult education could be extended, but my point is that the frontier of the learning society is very large, and the roads leading to it are many and varied, as are the vehicles used to travel the roads leading to the learning society.

Finally, I want to look specifically at the rocky road facing Village Four. The problem for the inhabitants of Village Four is that while they toil on their rocky road to personal development through education, others are building a superhighway to the learning society which may bypass their village altogether.

The notion of education as a formative, developmental process, which is the major interest of the inhabitants of Village Four, has virtually disappeared as people rush from option to option, seeking education as a product. Like shoppers at the mall, they select from a beautiful array of offerings whatever they need or want at the moment. Education has become a marketable commodity. People want it, preferably nicely packaged, delivered, and certified; they are willing to spend time and money to get it. And it is beginning to sound like a product.

Let me illustrate the shopping mall mentality:

Some adults, visiting our hypothetical educational shopping mall, will pick up anything on sale. If the schedule and price are right, why not take a course or two?

Some do comparison shopping at the mall. The options are many, and the careful shopper can usually find something a bit cheaper, a little easier, or perhaps just more convenient. Some shoppers are uncertain and timid and will take whatever the salesperson is pushing at the time. If courses on ecology are "in" this season, why not take that?

Some come to the shopping mall to get the job done. They go to the nearest purveyor, pay and do whatever is necessary to get the product, and depart. The product is typically a certificate or degree.

Some come to the mall with careful instructions from someone else about what to get and where to get it. Their task is to return to the sender with the certifiably correct product.

Relatively few—and they are usually frequent shoppers—are becoming careful consumers. They analyze their needs, question various purveyors to determine how their needs can be met, check out the quality, and become ever more sophisticated in their pursuit of education.

If Village Four wants the road to lifelong learning to go through their village, they need to begin to move the metaphor from shopping mall to fitness center. A fitness center sells a process rather than a product. A person gets out of it what he or she puts into it. While a skilled staff can diagnose and provide equipment, programs, and exercises, it is clear from the beginning that the benefits derived depend as much on the energy and commitment of the customer as of the staff. The process of becoming and remaining fit is lifelong, interactive, personal and individualized, and it changes over time. People come to a fitness center for renewal, for development, for self-improvement—to effect changes in themselves, not to purchase a product.

Morris Keeton, through his writings and through personal example, has demonstrated that learning can take place anywhere. The measure of learning lies in what has been learned by the person, rather than in what has been offered by the provider. Morris Keeton has left his mark on all of the villages of experiential learning; he has not only traveled the road to the learning society, but has left it well-marked for others.

References

Carnevale, A. P. "The Learning Enterprise." *Training and Development Journal.* January 1986, 18–16.

Cross, K. Patricia. *Adults As Learners.* San Francisco: Jossey-Bass, 1981.

Eurich, Nell P. *Corporate Classrooms.* Princeton, N.J.: Carnegie Foundation for the Advancement of Teaching, 1985.

Hexter, Holly and Andersen, Charles J. *Admission and Credit Policies for Adult Learners*. Washington, D.C.: American Council on Education, 1986.

Hodgkinson, Harold L. "Demographic Imperatives for Education" in *Proceedings: National Meeting of the Labor/Higher Education Council*. Washington, D.C.: American Council on Education and American Federation of Labor and Congress of Industrial Organizations (AFL-CIO), 1985.

IBM Systems Research Institute Bulletin. New York: IBM Systems Research Institute, 1981.

Lynton, Ernest and Elman, Sandra. *New Priorities for the University*. San Francisco: Jossey-Bass, 1987.

National Center for Education Statistics. *Digest of Education Statistics 1983–84*. Washington, D.C.: U.S. Government Printing Office, 1984.

Office of Educational Research and Improvement. "Projected Declines in College Enrollments Not Materializing." *Statistical Highlights*, December 1986.

Stadtman, Verne A. *Academic Adaptation*. San Francisco: Jossey-Bass, 1980.

Stern, Milton R. "How Can We Keep Them Educated?" Paper delivered at the University of Michigan, Ann Arbor, March 22, 1983.

Weil, Susan Warner, and McGill, Ian. *Making Sense of Experiential Learning*. Philadelphia: Society for Research into Higher Education and Open University Press, 1989.

17

"Any Theory is the Autobiography of the Theorist"

— What am I Doing
Bruce Chatwin, 1989.

Norman Evans

The Learning from Experience Trust is, not to put too fine a point on it, the British equivalent of CAEL, with allowances made for socio-cultural and political differences. Youth Access is the most recent government initiative with which the Trust is associated. It was invited to write a feasibility study paper and currently it is helping to vet proposals submitted for funding. It is an operation a bit like FIPSE, except that the Trust wrote the scheme in the first place and is now helping to decide who is fit to undertake it.

Morris Keeton could well have written the brief. Certainly, he could have done a better feasibility paper. But the essentials of Youth Access are consistent with the principles and practices articulated through CAEL, with one essential difference: it concerns youth not adult learners. Not that the transposition poses significant conceptual problems for the purpose of this chapter, which attempts to show how many of the initiatives associated in the U.S. with Morris Keeton and CAEL are echoed within one initiative in Britain.

The brief from the training agency of the Department of Employment was as follows:

Youth Access

1. RATIONALE

Demography

The demographic changes in the 16 to 18-year age group over the next few years will have far reaching implications for employers and educational institutions alike. Indeed, whilst it was not examined in detail by "Young People and the Labour Market," the effects of the fall in population on educational institutions were recognized by that report.

The most immediate implications are in tertiary education and in particular on colleges of further education and other vocational education and training agencies. With the impact of demographic changes, the traditional "client" base of tertiary education may be eroding ("Young People and the Labour Market," National Economic Development Office, July 1988, p. 3).

141

A similar problem will be faced by institutions of higher education, which will find it increasingly difficult to recruit sufficient students from a diminishing pool of 17–18 year olds. Such changes in demography might well produce a shortage of highly skilled people on the labour market. Moreover, such skills are necessary to develop a competitive economy.

An innovative method of providing access to higher education is one means through which the nation might secure sufficient high level skills in its work force for the last decade of this century and the early part of the next one.

Academic Underachievement

The recent period of youth unemployment has made many education and training providers recognize that the traditional academic curriculum has not provided the equality of opportunity for many young people that would enable them to develop potential skills and cognitive abilities. The implementation of such programmes as Technical and Vocational Education Initiative, Combined Penal and Vocational Education, and Youth Training Scheme has shown that a more practical and experiential approach to learning, as well as relating the curriculum to the needs of the work place, can motivate young people who had not responded to a subject-bound curriculum.

Hence, the needs of higher educational institutions to broaden their recruitment base, and the underachievement of young people who may have the innate ability to pursue a higher education course, require an examination of alternative modes of entry into higher education. This paper seeks to propose a new method known as Youth Access.

The Nature of Youth Access

In essence this would parallel the recent compacts between employers and students, with the guarantee of a place at a higher educational institution if the student maintains certain standards and achieves certain outcomes prior to entry.

2. CONTINUITY AND SUPPORT

Youth Access will, if it is to be successful, need to involve not only the young person and the higher education institutions, but also the further education provider and the employer. . .

The Young Person

Many of the young people who might benefit from youth access will be disaffected by the world of education. They may also have very negative perceptions of their own ability and potential. It is likely that they will not see the benefits of higher education, even if they consider themselves capable of following a higher education course. There would, therefore, be a need to market Youth Access to young people and to persuade them of the benefits of higher education. Conversely, they may see getting a job as an immediate priority, and anything which is not an obvious means of enhancing employment prospects as an irrelevance. . .

The target group for youth access will, in the main, be those young people who have not responded to the traditional school curriculum. . . .

That was the essential part of the brief.

The Trust's Response

The Trainees

Now you can only make sense of that brief if you take seriously the characteristics of the young learners. What the Trust said was as follows:

Young people in the lower social and economic groups in the Registrar General's classifications who have the latent ability to study successfully in higher education are likely to have
- relatively to utterly negative views about formal school education
- strong motivation towards earning money through work
- powerful cultural influences to reinforce that view
- a low self-esteem generally
- a scant sense of "deferred gratification"
- indications of possible higher education success which are not readily recognized or valued by most school staff

And they may well be concentrated predominantly in urban inner cities.

Comment

In their essentials, these characteristics simply echo those of many of the adult learners who have been CAEL's particular concern throughout, and more recently are the essential characteristics of many employees engaged in various forms of Joint Ventures programmes in the United States.

The Curriculum

Trying to invent a curriculum which will engage and hold young people with these characteristics begins by accepting two clear requirements. Any programme needs to be learner-centered and experientially based; work-based learning needs to be the center-piece of a Youth Access curriculum. In its turn, that means some form of individualized learning programme, and it probably means organizing individual learning programmes on the basis of learning agreements.
The curriculum design set out by the Trust had five components:

- An orientation period on entry
- A negotiated work-based learning programme
- A seminar programme to complement that programme
- A core curriculum
- A programme of work-related studies.

The programme, handled on a seminar basis, would attempt to offer opportunities for Youth Access students to get a better sense of their own worth, leading to "delabeling and relabeling," and to thinking about ways of learning. If the taster idea within employment was added, and something under the general title of Life and Career Planning leading to the first stage of the negotiated learning agreement was included, there would then be a natural arena for coming to terms with various modes of learning and how to use them.
Because the first two years of a Youth Access programme are to be on an individually negotiated basis, the seminars and core will provide the anchor base for the entire enterprise.

The purpose of the seminar programme is to enable participants to articulate what they are learning from their work-based assignments and thus to learn from one another and to act as a checkpoint for general progression along the lines of their negotiated programmes.

The core curriculum is designed to develop the participants' abilities and skills, both oral and written, to handle and interpret information and work effectively with others.

Seminars and core could easily overlap.

The work-related studies relate specifically to the work-based learning programme and could be provided by the education institution, either on an individual learning programme basis, or through attending regular classes, or by the employer if suitable provision is available.

Each work assignment must be both an employee's work task, undertaken within normal employee working conditions, and such that it can be a source of planned intentional learning.

The nature of the task, its length and duration and its level is bound to vary according to the occupation. Some tasks might be lengthy, some might be relatively short, say moving around different departments. The balance of the various components is such that the proportion of time spent weekly on the work-based learning and the work-related study programmes will alter, with the emphasis over the two years shifting from the former to the latter.

Comment

This approach to curriculum is simply a version of the approaches to adult learning programmes as propounded by CAEL. It is also an echo of the Keeton/Dewey assertion that "experiential education is superior education." It is consistent with the dictum that "Experiential learning refers to learning in which the learner is directly in touch with the realities being studied." (New Directions in Experiential Learning, No. 1).

Institutional Change

The Trust set out the requirements for schools, further education colleges, higher education institutions and employers as follows.

Schools

Partnership in a YA scheme means that a school will need to have:

— a positive recruitment policy for YA
— willingness to adjust the curriculum for YA recruits if desirable
— an existing working relationship with the further education college

Further Education

Partnership in a Youth Access scheme means that the further education college will need to be able to:

— handle Learning Contracts as an effective mode of learning
— have contracts with employers over a broad range of occupational areas

— provide work-related study as required in the requisite occupational areas
— have an academic organization which can enable YA students to study in mainstream courses if required
— be able to identify staff suitable for working in the YA programme
— accept that staff will be recruited by the manager to the program in agreement with the college rather than being assigned to it by the college
— have an established relationship with a higher education institution

Higher Education

Partnership in a Youth Access scheme means that a higher education institution will need to:

— accept in principle that the results of students on the YA programme will be considered as equivalent to A level performance (school examinations for those aged eighteen) provided that the standards are appropriate
— accept in advance the possibility that YA students would have a choice between full-time, part-time, periodic, deferred or Learning Contract style higher education
— have existing working arrangements with a number of employers who might be partners in the YA partnership
— be prepared to nominate a member of staff to give continuing support and pastoral care to YA students

Employers

Partnership in a Youth Access scheme means that the employer is going to bear the responsibilities which are clearly marked out in four categories:

— job opportunities for YA students at a succession of stages and a guaranteed job at the end of higher education
— recruitment with care of appropriate line-managers as YA staff
— the time commitment of line-managers in relation to on-site negotiation and supervision of YA students and a liaison with a coordinator for learning agreements
— the inevitable, unforeseen costs (staff loss of time, etc.) of having YA students under employment conditions, sometimes for four days a week, sometimes three days a week, etc., when YA students cannot possibly be fully productive.

Comment

But if educational institutions are to be involved in Youth Access with that kind of curriculum, then considerable changes are implied for the role of academic staff. This is an echo of CAEL's original Institutional Development Programme and involves many of the points established and propagated through the Commission on the Adult Learner which was concerned with making institutions more "user friendly." The implications are not all that different from the Positioning Workshops for institutions who wish to get involved in Joint Ventures activities with business, labor and government.

There is an additional set of implications, and that is for employers. If work-based learning is the centre piece for the curriculum and has considerable implications for the role and style of work by academic staff in educational institutions, then it also has far reaching implications for employers. Work-based learning presupposes planning for intentional learning through work. For a start, that is likely to be a new role for most supervisors of young trainees. Moreover, it will be an additional role. One way or another, Youth Access is implying that employers are becoming teaching colleagues with academic staff from educational institutions. How far Joint Ventures has moved or can move employers significantly in this direction is an interesting question.

There is no doubt about the importance of this implication for employers. Thoughtful industrial and commercial employers will commonly agree that the central training, retraining and updating problem is to get line managers to accept, as a day-to-day part of their responsibilities, the nurturing of those whom they supervise. The most high powered team of a company's trainers, equipped with the most ample conditions, can at best make a contribution which is doomed to relative ineffectualness unless line managers are day-to-day trainers and accept this as part of their occupational role. Involving work placed supervisors in the active "teaching" of young trainees can thus become a lever for effecting institutional change in employment.

Some Principles

Underlying the Youth Access idea are some important principles. The first is absolutely consistent with CAEL's view of the relationship between learning and experience. That view is put with admirable clarity both in Keeton's introduction to the recent CAEL publication by Urban Whitaker, *Assessing Learning: Standards, Principles and Procedures,* and in Whitaker's preface to the same work. Indeed it is a major theme of the book. Assessment is concerned with learning. Experience may be a source of learning. Confusion between the two is not only bound to produce invalid assessments, it is simply unprofessional. Youth Access is concerned with learning. Experience matters as an arena for learning.

The second vital principle is quality assurance. Since the Youth Access programme is designed to encourage more young people from the lower socio-economic groups to enroll in higher education, the standards achieved by Youth Access students must be acceptable to higher education admission requirements. The implication there is that the full battery of quality assurance measures which are to be found in each and every university, polytechnic and college of higher education in Britain will come into play for Youth Access students.

The third underlying principle is the integrity of recognition of learning achievements however they have been acquired. This is another way of making the point which again comes out clearly in Urban Whitaker's book of the need to always draw a tight distinction between procedures for learning and the learning acquired. What Youth Access will be concerned about is the learning outcomes, and it is an attempt to devise an additional route to learning outcomes. It is not seeking to change the quality of learning outcomes themselves.

Some Implications

There are three significant underlying implications of this government initiative. It is important to recognize that this is not a specially funded additional program. It is a set of ideas being piloted in some institutions on a pump-priming basis with a view to discovering how to insert the Youth Access approach into the mainstream activities of the educational institutions themselves. So it is that the first underlying implication is for institutional change. There is no conceivable way in which a Youth Access scheme could be introduced to the work of an existing education institution without its having profound potential requirements for institutional change.

The second underlying implication, which is consistent with government policy, is to seek different forms of collaboration between employers and education. This is a double-barrelled shot; it is an attempt to persuade, cajole and encourage employers to take greater responsibility for the education and training of their own employees; and financially the intention is to get employers to pick up larger and larger proportions of the financial costs.

The third underlying implication is more nebulous—cultural shift. In Britain, as is well-known, shamefully so, the participation rate in postsecondary education is woefully inadequate. Going back to the characteristics of the potential learners for Youth Access, some means has to be found of engaging and holding greater proportions of those men and women in the business of learning for a longer time. How far Youth Access can act as a lever for this kind of climatic cultural change is unknowable. But at least the intention is there.

In many ways, the exceptional interest of the Youth Access initiative stands as an example of the way senior permanent civil servants in government departments can produce imaginative proposals and obtain authority from ministers, in this case the Secretary of State for Employment. Each of the principles and implications referred to here was fully accepted by the Training Agency, as indeed was the entire feasibility study.

Commentary

It's been a long journey from the introduction to my English colleagues of the idea of assessment of prior experiential learning (APEL) to the founding of the Learning From Experience Trust. A long journey from Keeton's first Study Tour of England in the spring of 1980 to the Youth Access scheme.

So it seems, in a different context and in a different culture, Youth Access epitomizes so many of the practices and principles enunciated in the professional work of Morris Keeton.

"Any theory is the autobiography of the theorist."

18

The Class of 2000:
A Workforce at Risk

Elinor M. Greenberg

Ever since *Workforce 2000: Work and Workers for the 21st Century*, a study by the Hudson Institute's Herman Kahn Center in Indianapolis, was made available in 1987 by the U.S. Department of Labor, my attention has focused on the "Class of 2000."

The opening lines of the Executive Summary of that landmark report state, "The year 2000 will mark the end of what has been called the American Century" (viii). The summary goes on to say, "Four key trends will shape the last years of the twentieth century":

- The American *economy should grow* at a relatively healthy pace, boosted by a rebound in U.S. exports, renewed productivity growth, and a strong world economy.
- Despite its international comeback, *U.S. manufacturing will be a much smaller share of the economy in the year 2000* than it is today. Service industries will create *all* of the new jobs, and *most* of the new wealth, over the next 13 years.
- The *workforce* will *grow slowly, becoming older, more female, and more disadvantaged*. Only *15%* of the new entrants to the labor force over the next 13 years will be native white males, compared to *47%* in that category today.
- The *new jobs in service industries will demand much higher skill levels* than the jobs of today. Very few new jobs will be created for those who cannot read, follow directions, and use mathematics. Ironically, the demographic trends in the workforce, coupled with the higher skill requirements of the economy, will lead to both higher and lower unemployment, *more* joblessness among the least skilled and *less* among the most educationally advantaged.

Six challenges to policy makers are then set forth, as follows:

1. Stimulate *balanced* world growth.
2. Accelerate *productivity* increases in *service industries*.
3. Maintain the dynamism of an *aging workforce*.
4. Reconcile the conflicting needs of *women, work* and *families*.
5. Integrate *Black* and *Hispanic workers* fully into the economy.
6. Improve the *educational preparation* of *all* workers.

These six challenges clearly link America's future to education.

Following on the heels of that national report was a Western Regional report[1] which showed that in five southwestern states (AZ, CA, CO, NM and TX) minorities will comprise close to 50% of the populations by the year 2000, compared with less than one-third in 1980. Currently, in these states, less than 11% of all baccalaureate degrees and less than 8% of all graduate degrees are awarded to minorities. These figures occur at a time when we know that an increasing number of jobs in the 21st Century will require higher level skills, more complex thinking and increased ability to be flexible in an ever-changing number of careers throughout one's lifetime.

The report's recommendations clearly linked the Western Region's future to education.

In my own state of Colorado, with a population of 3.43 million people, the majority (1.72 million) of the population is now female. Women become the majority in the 45–50 year old age cohort, rising to more than double the male population by the time they reach the 80–85 year old age cohort[2].

Colorado's economy faltered in the mid 1980s, along with that of other "boom and bust" western states; and out-migration exceeded in-migration for the first time since the "gold and silver rush" days. Just at this precarious time, women were projected to become more than 55% of the workforce by the year 2000; and minorities in the workforce were projected to increase, overall, to nearly 20%.[3]

When I thought about the Colorado Territory, in 1860, before statehood—when there were only 34,277 residents, of whom only 1,586 were women and 46 were free Blacks—my perspective on "a century of change" was significantly altered.

These Colorado reports' recommendations to the governor clearly linked the State's future to education.

On September 19, 1988, *Business Week* magazine captured the attention of the American business community with its "Special Report on 'Human Capital,' " which showed how changing American demographic patterns related to jobs, skills, business, the economy and education. The dramatic graphics in that article showed that, in 1985, the American labor force was "dominated by U.S. born white males" (47%). That graphics' caption stated that this particular male group will play "a smaller role in the future," comprising only 15% of the new entrants to the workforce by the year 2000. The companion graphic showed that U.S. born white females will comprise 42% of the workforce in 2000; and American born minorities and immigrants will total 43% of new workers—a total of 85% of all new workers!

The *Business Week* special report clearly linked the future of American business to education.

These vast amounts of data were beginning to show a pattern and tell a story. The picture that began to form in my mind was one of a two-humped camel: the front hump, slightly smaller than the back hump, was made up of minority and female youth; while the larger, rear hump was made up of men and women of all ethnic groups, over the age of 45, with older women far outnumbering the men. In the middle was the trough, the smaller dip, made up of relatively youthful U.S. born white males, between the ages of 18 and 45, who will increasingly bear both the public and private responsibilities and burdens of our society. By the year 2000, this shrinking group of young white American men will need to run the corporations, invent the new products, create the new technologies, build the highways and bridges, pay the taxes and protect the country—all by themselves—with heart attacks coming earlier and earlier—unless we do something very different in the coming decade than we have been doing in the past. Clearly, I thought, the 1990s cannot be a "business as usual decade," if America is to remain strong and healthy and maintain both its political leadership and economic competitive edge as we move into the 21st century.

During our own lifetimes, the face of America has changed dramatically. We are becoming a very different kind of country than we historically have been.

But, what do we know of this new terrain? How can we prepare to meet its challenges? How can we ensure that our own sons and daughters will not inherit a burden that they can neither support nor sustain? What new roles will each sector of our society play in the coming transformative decade of the 1990s?

And, if the quality of the workforce in our state, our region and throughout the country is clearly linked to the quality of our schools, what must *education become* and what must *educators do* in order to provide solutions to our dilemmas, not merely add new problems to an already complicated situation?

At the center of this new picture of our country is, literally, a "workforce at risk," both younger and older adults who are not now being well prepared either to drive the economic engines or to maintain the high standard of living and quality of life to which we have become accustomed during the latter half of the 20th century.

Are our children and grandchildren destined to live lives of downward mobility? Will they live in an America that ranks third, or even tenth, in world leadership? Will our American, communal, pioneer, "can do" spirit be replaced by a lethargic, victim, "me first" mentality?

Have we, Americans of the twentieth century, witnessed "the rise and fall" of the first democratic civilization on the face of the earth?

As I wrestled with these ultimate questions, it became apparent that our efforts need to be redoubled and become more focused and sophisticated than they have been in the past if we are to turn the corner during the 90s and greet the year 2000 in good shape.

In my mind, I retraced our contemporary history:

— The early 1900s focused on westward expansion and industrialization.
— The 1920s brought the early European immigrants into the mainstream.
— The 1930s crashed the economy, rendering our country depressed, and created new social policies to ensure the future security of our workers.
— The 1940s brought us to victory in World War II by employing Rosie to rivet and Johnny to march.
— In the 1950s, we built Levittown, created a broad middle class with the GI Bill, and fired up a mighty peacetime economy.
— The 1960s created access for minorities out of the Civil Rights struggle.
— The 1970s honed equity out of the Feminist Movement and the Vietnam tragedy.
— The 1980s focused on the quality of managing our schools and industries, as other nations rose to become friendly, and not so friendly, competitors.

I concluded that the 1990s would need to be the "decade of leadership," transformative leadership (Burns, 1978), as we confronted the new realities of the Information Age and the new American demographics, in the context of a competitive, global economy. If we are going to be saved at all, or better yet, if we are to be able to save ourselves, we, as a nation and as a society, will have to take a harsh, critical look at ourselves and at all our institutions.

Whereas, in the past, it was necessary to argue for minority access, women's equity and adult programs in postsecondary education on essentially "humanitarian" grounds, like equal opportunity and altruism, these arguments are no longer sufficient.

Whereas, in the past, we could afford to spend five or ten years debating academic policies in the faculty senate, this time frame is no longer tolerable or realistic.

Whereas, in the past we could point to social evolution as the primary force for generational change, this strategy will no longer suffice.

In short, I believe that we have just a little more than a decade, about ten years, to turn around our major American institutions, if we are to be able to move into the 21st Century with a well-educated, productive, competitive, quality workforce that can maintain and advance our own high standard of living and our nation's leadership position in the world.

During the late 1980s, it became apparent that it was the business community, not the education community, that was fully aware of these conditions. Enlightened businesses were also worried about the

"Class of 2000" and they were beginning to do something about it. Partnership was the mode; speed was the essential ingredient; and the wise, focused use of scarce resources was the key strategy.

Still, the schools slept.

High school drop-out rates for minorities rose, while test scores fell. Fewer Blacks and Hispanics were awarded graduate degrees; while more Asian and Middle Eastern immigrants and foreign students completed American masters and doctoral programs in mathematics, the sciences and business; and many returned to their native lands to use this training to compete against us.

Still, the schools slept.

Young girls continued to avoid mathematics, while teenage pregnancies rose. More young women entered college; and still without adequate guidance or mentors, fewer graduated. Women seeking to reenter the workforce lacked the skills needed in increasingly computerized offices, while Women's Centers continued to be abolished or under-funded. Both younger and older women increasingly found themselves alone and heads of households, while their average yearly earnings continued to lag at less than 70% of that of males.

Still, the schools slept.

Americans continued to live longer, while mandatory retirement policies remained in effect. Older adults filled our dreary nursing home facilities, while medical science increased the quantity of life, but not the quality of life. Senior men with mature work experience were "put on the shelf;" while senior women, often single, were dependent on their meager savings and social security payments in the face of inflation and a work ethic which excluded them.

Still, the schools slept.

Colleges and universities admitted and collected tuition from millions of older, diverse, working adults, mostly women, while maintaining their pediatric policies and campus environments, designed in another era for another class, gender and age group. Competencies and skills acquired outside the classroom were still considered irrelevant by most institutions; while business and industry developed billions of dollars worth of in-house training programs, as it became apparent that they could not rely on established schools to provide them with skilled workers quickly enough.

Still, the schools slept.

Then, as the decade of the 1980s reached its mid-point, a new phenomenon began to appear on the scene. Trade unions, once the bastions of job security and self-interest, began to stir. Deep down in their gut, unions like the United Auto Workers (UAW) and the Communications Workers of America (CWA) began to link future employment security to education. Training and retraining opportunities were collectively bargained in the automobile and telecommunications industries. Millions of workers returned to college, often the first in their families to do so. Blue collars were worn simultaneously with back packs and mortar boards. Pink collars showed up alongside computer terminals and volumes of Plato's *Republic*.

While the schools slumbered on, CAEL got busy. The "Class of 2000" was beginning to arrive on the campuses. And, CAEL was at the clock tower to meet it, guide it through the academic maze, and applaud it to the sounds of "Pomp and Circumstance" at commencement.

Out of the Mid-West region came the College and University Options Program (CUOP), created by UAW/Ford and CAEL, which enabled thousands of auto workers to go back to school with the support of career counseling, consumer information about the schools and pre-paid tuition.

Out of the Mountains and Plains region came the CWA/IBEW/U S WEST Communications program, PATHWAYS to the Future, which attracted 7,986 telecommunications workers in seven states, 29% of the workforce, over a three year period (1986–89).

Out of the Eastern region came similar programs for Scott Paper Company, the Bricklayers and Allied Craftsmen, the United Food and Commercial Workers, the AT&T Alliance, state and federal government agencies—all designed and managed with the assistance of CAEL, whose commitment to adult learners found new avenues of expression.

The reach of these innovative "employee growth and development" efforts began to extend into the deep South (Alabama, Mississippi and Florida), into the wooded Northwest (Oregon and Washington), and onto the beaches of Southern California.

Adult workers—men and women in their middle years, many of whom had been successfully employed for long periods of time (fifteen years average), who felled trees in the chill of Maine winters and the sweltering heat of swampy Mississippi summers, along with Montana telephone operators, Arizona linemen, Pennsylvania electricians, California bricklayers and Colorado managers of all sorts—exchanged quiet evenings at home with their families and weekend fishing excursions with their buddies for the classroom. They became adult students.

They planned with counselors, discussed their fears in workshops, agonized through prior learning assessment regimens and waited in the registration lines in more than 1000 schools and colleges all across America. Unbeknownst to most of them, they were becoming the "Class of 2000."

And, still, many schools slept.

CAEL's role in these efforts was often invisible—training hundreds of counselors; writing dozens of manuals; organizing endless meetings; moving thousands of pieces of paper through tedious, detailed processes; paying never-ending invoices; and learning how to become part of the Information Age, as its own sparsely staffed offices hummed with computers, printers and fax machines.

Behind the scenes, Morris Keeton, the ultimate Quaker missionary, encouraged exhausted staff, wrote lengthy position papers and listened carefully.

On the front lines, the directors and program managers learned to be anthropologists in foreign, sometimes alien, lands. We learned how to speak the language of managers and union members. We became colleagues of grey-suited CEO's and overalled local union presidents.

And, still, many schools slept.

While business and union leaders (collectively and agonizingly) bargained hundreds of millions of dollars for "training and retraining" programs, which were quietly creating the "Class of 2000" to ensure that "Workforce 2000" could cut it in the fiercely competitive global marketplace of the 21st century—the colleges and universities of our country were being dragged, kicking and screaming, into the decade of the '90s.

To some in CAEL's constituency, it was unclear what was meant by these "joint ventures." Some members, who represented academic institutions, thought that CAEL was abandoning them for the "strange bedfellows" of the corporations and labor unions.

Other practitioners, who had worked tirelessly for the acceptance of prior learning assessment in their schools, thought that CAEL was abandoning them for quick-and-dirty on-the-job counseling.

Some of those in charge of adult degree programs thought that CAEL was no longer interested in them, in the liberal arts or in quality academic education and was becoming an advocate for crediting trade union apprenticeships and in-house corporate training.

A few in the CAEL family, those whose work focused on research and publications, thought that CAEL had abandoned them and their long-term scholarly pursuits, replacing them with fast-track, quick-buck, revenue-generating projects.

The women thought that CAEL was led by the men; while the men pointed to the number of women on CAEL's staff.

CAEL's small ethnic minority contingent could find little evidence of the organization's overt commitment to equal opportunity and access, as Assembly attendance remained, essentially, white and Anglo.

What some of these well-meaning, but tunnel-visioned, friends of CAEL did not recognize was that by joining hands with the powerful business sector and by becoming colleagues with the politically savvy organized labor sector, together we could exercise influence in the slow-moving postsecondary education sector on behalf of adult learners and all that CAEL stood for, far beyond our present small membership and limited power base.

Through a series of accidents, serendipitous events, economic shifts, historical conditions and a few personal and professional relationships, we had stumbled onto the rather obvious fact that the adult learner was one and the same as the adult worker.

White, middle-class housewives were still returning to school, but so were Black, Hispanic and White "first-generation," female clerical workers.

White, middle class Vietnam-era drop-out men were returning to school, but so were Black, Hispanic and White "first-generation" male linemen, computer programmers and assembly line workers.

It soon became apparent that CAEL's adult learners were not only those familiar, self-motivated men and women who had found their own way to the hard-to-find, on-campus Admissions Offices, but also those who were too busy at their jobs, too weary raising their children alone, too far away from the campuses, or too alienated and confused about if and how to return to those formal learning environments we call schools.

It also became obvious that if we in CAEL, most of whom came out of the academic community, albeit often holding maverick positions in that community, could play anthropologist well enough to learn the language, mores and cultures of the business, labor and governmental sectors, we could combine our political forces, resources, expertise and common interests to achieve our mutual goals.

After all, businesses needed a competent workforce in the year 2000; labor needed employment security in an ever-changing workplace in the year 2000; and schools and colleges needed adult enrollment, as the youth population shrank, by the year 2000. Mutual needs were becoming mutual goals.

The formula rapidly became this: unions bargained for training and retraining; employers supplied the funding for counseling, workshops, assessment, tuition, fees and books; and CAEL supplied the expertise to access and work with the educational institutions to deliver appropriate personal support services and quality curricula to adult learners/adult workers.

It was a win-win-win situation, a three way partnership—designed on behalf of adult learners/adult workers, who comprised that portion of the "Class of 2000" that was already in the workforce but in jeopardy of becoming obsolete, displaced or just plain left behind as the global technological clock ticked ever faster and louder.

For me, the "Class of 2000" is not an abstract concept; it has become real. The names of this class are in our fast-growing database and on our thousands of file folders. Their faces and life stories are part of my daily experience:

- *Julia*   from Albuquerque, who graduated from the University of New Mexico, after dropping out of school twenty years ago when she lost her fiance in the Vietnam War;

- *Jim*   from Helena, who holds a baccalaureate degree in Soil Science and is completing a Computer Science Certificate at Carroll College in order to be ready for the Information Age;

- *Leissa*   from Missoula, who has attended eight Montana institutions, as she is transferred around the state to install telephones, and who yearns to go to law school, one day;

- *Steve*   from Salt Lake City, who once thought of himself as an academic failure, but who now knows that he can own his own business, someday, after achieving straight A grades at Salt Lake Community College;

- *April*   from Tucson, who now climbs telephone poles with her heavy tool belt around her hips, and who hopes to complete a degree in Counseling at the University of Arizona so she can do something about the drug problem.

— *Joe*   from Denver, who, although totally deaf, is working toward a Computer Programming Certificate at Front Range Community College;
— *Martha*   from Boise, who, in her fifties, looks forward to receiving her bachelor's degree from Boise State University in the year 2000; and,
— *Sharon*   from Cheyenne, who discovered that she was good in science at Laramie County Community College and plans to continue her education at the University of Wyoming.

As in all adult education programs, the stories of our students' lives are poignant. They reflect the diversity of their backgrounds and the ecstasies and agonies of everyday life—hopes, dreams, goals and celebrations, as well as disappointments, failures, confusions and funerals.

Be it through the vehicles of Joint Ventures, Universities Without Walls, Adult Degree Programs, Assessment Centers or Corporate Training Centers—it is *the individual adult learner/worker who remains at the center of our work and commitment.*

But, we cannot do our work and meet our commitments alone. CAEL, like all other sectors in our society, must use the decade of the 1990s to create partnerships and to collaborate with others, if it is to be successful.

We are in good company: the U.S. Department of Labor and other federal agencies; the regional compacts, like WICHE; the states, like Colorado; the corporations; and the unions.

It is now up to CAEL to wake the slumbering schools.

I, for one, do not yearn for the "good old days"—the days when we were alone in our quest—trying to persuade the faculties, arguing with the curriculum committees, being polite to the presidents and, often, cowed by the legislators.

Today, we stand on the ledge of the window of opportunity—and we are not alone. Our new partners and colleagues are those in the great corporations and unions of our country who know full well that if we do not produce a superb, competent, open-minded, diverse "Class of 2000," comprised of men and women of many ethnic groups and backgrounds, our great United States will sink slowly, but surely, into the history books as a nation with a dream that went unrealized and a promise that remained unfulfilled.

I, for one, now live my life in our future, in the year 2000—when the schools and colleges of our country will know, in a deep and abiding way, that learning is lifelong and that "learning can be to education what justice is to law" (Greenberg, 1981); but that, like justice, the focus on learning and the individual learner must be won in every generation—over and over again.

Morris Keeton has always been ready for yet another battle, another conference, another committee meeting.

The most significant legacy we could leave to him now is to carry on his work, his mission and his commitment—throughout the 1990s—so that the "Class of 2000" will be made up of 18-year olds, 22-year olds and older adults of every age, ethnic background and persuasion that make up that wonderful diversity we call America.

For it is in our diversity that we will prosper and become the nation of learning and justice about which we all dream and for which we all strive.

Footnotes

1. "From Minority to Majority: Education and the Future of the Southwest," Western Interstate Commission for Higher Education, WICHE, (1987).

2. "Colorado Women: The New Majority," a report to the governor, *Colorado Women's Economic Development Task Force* (August 1987).
3. "An Overview of the Colorado Economy," *Jobs for Colorado's Future* (August 31, 1988).

References

Burns, James MacGregor. *Leadership*. New York: Harper & Row, 1978.
Greenberg, Elinor M. *Quality Lifelong Education: New Perspectives on Design and Administration*. University of Northern Colorado. University Microfilms International, Ann Arbor, Michigan, 1981.

19

Some Social Policy Implications of Joint Ventures Programs

Lois Lamdin and Pamela Tate

An earlier version of this article was begun in the wake of the 1988 presidential campaign. In that dismal performance, both Democrats and Republicans claimed the right to be the party of education, and all four candidates for national office came out squarely for the high priority of training and retraining in our efforts toward economic revitalization. However, neither the party platforms nor the speeches of the candidates ever began to define how this training and retraining would take place. Nor have the years since the campaign provided any enlightenment. It still remains to be seen who will provide training, who will fund it, how it will be structured, and what we will train people for. And even more important, there is still, as of 1991, no visible national effort under way to convene the players to begin the planning.

Despite general agreement that this country's economic well being depends upon a well trained and highly adaptable workforce, and despite constant references to the demographics which remind us that at least 80% of the workforce of the year 2000 is already out of school and working, and despite our further understanding that this workforce is ill-equipped for meeting the escalating skill demands of industry, including even high school level literacy, despite all this, the basic mechanisms for building worker skills and competencies are not yet in place.

Moreover, none of the present high level thinking seems to have taken account of the major stumbling block that militates against the success of such current training programs as the Job Training Partnership Act, the Private Industry Councils, others at state and local levels that provide public or private funding for training people for jobs.

The Problem

The stumbling block is simply that these programs ignore the needs of the trainees themselves. Most of them begin by looking at the job market, at the current and local needs of industry and business, and at the near term economic forecasts for the region. The best of them have tried to determine how many jobs are likely to open up in which sectors and what skills will be called for by those jobs. States, cities,

157

counties are spending thousands of dollars gathering and interpreting workforce data and, if there is any money left over, putting it into short-term training programs that may or may not bear some resemblance to the actual needs of the workplace by the time the participants graduate.

What programs are *not* doing is addressing the intended recipients of the training to find out in what ways their attitudes and life situations may be blocking their taking advantage of training opportunities; how their interests skills and values may determine the kinds of training in which they will succeed; what life and career goals they have or can be encouraged to think about.

The real question isn't just what courses or programs workers should be taking. The real question (as Morris Keeton has taught us) is how to help workers determine which choices are valid for their individual situations in a changing job market.

Faceless workers, moved about from program to program like counters on a checkers board (we rejected the chess metaphor as too deliberate), may or may not succeed in completing their training, may or may not find new jobs, may or may not be able to function successfully in those jobs, may or may not find their new skills still in demand five years out, but they are hostage to forces outside their control. Unfortunately, current attempts to forecast which skills will be necessary a few years from now, or even to define the evolving nature of new jobs, are based on rather fuzzy thinking. We don't really know for certain what specific knowledge and skills we should be acquiring. The likely result of many current attempts to solve the training conundrum is further fragmentation of our most valuable economic resource—the American workforce.

Solutions

There are signs that the solutions to this dilemma may come not from government or from postsecondary education or even primarily from the business world but from the American labor movement. For the American labor movement, despite continual reports of its demise, is currently beginning to assume a leadership role in the area of workforce training.

After labor's long history of fighting for job security, health benefits, occupational health and safety assurance and higher wages, union leaders are now looking beyond these and realizing that they are no longer enough. As in Maslow's hierarchy of values, beyond security, benefits, safety on the job and good wages, there lie other needs which may have seemed unthinkable fifty years ago but which are currently critical. Primary among these is access to training which is relevant both to workforce and to individual needs.

As unionized industries hit the 1980s, the benefits and values for which they had fought were no longer sufficient because of changes in how business operated. Out-sourcing, leasing a workforce, using multiple vendors to do jobs that had previously been done in-house or sending some of the work overseas has enabled companies to cut their workforce radically. Job security has become a thing of the past.

And indeed, as changing technologies and manufacturing techniques have changed the skill demands of jobs and have enabled one worker to do the job of five or six, the concept of permanent employment in the same company has become obsolete. As a result, massive layoffs have occurred in many major industries where job security had been a given.

A salient example is Bell Telephone. In the past, once one got a job with Ma Bell (the affectionate nickname was appropriate to the role it played), the job was assumed to be for life. Now, with radical changes in the nature of communications, complicated by the newly competitive stance of the post-divestiture Baby Bells, that is no longer true. And similarly, jobs in the steel and auto industries, except for temporary layoffs and strikes, also used to be seen as fairly permanent. However, in the past fifteen years, thousands of steel and auto workers have had to face an unemployment that won't go away.

In significant ways, the new needs of business and labor intersect. Labor needs to attract and maintain its membership. It needs to find new ways to reward members' loyalty and to demonstrate its commitment to their growth and development. And business needs to find ways to make certain that its workforce has the flexibility and competency to adjust to new technologies, new jobs. Since there are already premonitory shortages of workers in both entry level and highly skilled jobs, both unions and employers need to recruit and maintain the workforce. Some companies have joined the unions in thinking about their efforts to educate workers as a strategy for creating what Morris Keeton has called "employment security." Others see it as a strategy for giving them the competitive edge in hiring and retention.

Given this series of complex and interlocking problems, the Council for Adult and Experiential Learning (CAEL) has begun to find a way to define and support the career and education needs of the individual worker through joint ventures among business, labor and postsecondary education. These joint ventures are designed to bridge the gaps between the needs of industry for productivity based on a skilled workforce, the desire of workers for employment security, and the resources of the existing education institutions.

In 1984 CAEL began to turn its attention from adult learners in the classroom to adult learners in the workplace. Keeton and Pamela Tate, who was then lead consultant for the UAW/Ford National Development and Training Center, were given the task of defining and delivering a workforce-based employee support and education program for UAW/Ford.

UAW/Ford provided an ideal situation for an experiment in creating workers' employment security in a volatile economic climate. Ford had, between 1980 and 1982, laid off half of its hourly workforce. It was generally acknowledged that even if the auto industry were to recover, increasing automation and other structural changes made it unlikely that Ford, or any of the other American auto makers, would ever again need such a large workforce.

However, a safety valve had been created. In the historic 1982 bargaining agreement between the company and the union, five cents had been set aside for every hour worked, to be applied toward a variety of support programs for union members. This "nickel fund" had grown enormously by 1984. The joint company/union group (NDTC—National Development and Training Center) delegated to manage it was hoping to create a support system that would enable Ford employees to take advantage of the education and growth and development opportunities it could make available.

CAEL happily accepted the challenge of creating a new model for employee growth and development that would build on its expertise in adult and experiential learning. The success of this first CAEL/UAW/Ford program has led to a number of similar "joint ventures" between industry, unions, education, and state and local governments to support industrial, service and technical workers. The goal of all of these programs is to broaden and deepen workers' skills and competencies, to connect them with appropriate learning resources, and to foster their flexibility and employment security in an increasingly chancy job market.

Since 1984, CAEL's joint ventures concepts have led to contracts with, among others, several Bell companies across the country, Scott Paper, The AT&T Alliance, and such major unions as the Communication Workers of America, the International Brotherhood of Electrical Workers, the United Food and Commercial Workers, the International Union of Bricklayers and Allied Craftsmen, and a number of federal and state agencies, including the federal Departments of Agriculture and Education.

These joint ventures rest on a few seemingly simple principles which have had consequences that could radically change conventional thinking about worker education and training. These principles are: learner-centered education, pre-paid tuition, supportive counseling, and active involvement of the schools in planning as well as delivery of services.

Learning-Centered Education

Although CAEL's programs take into account the needs of the sponsoring company, union or state, primary emphasis is given to the needs of the individual worker. In other words, CAEL-designed programs rest on the assumption that learner-centered education is the most effective education.

When one looks at the industrial, service and technical workers who are the target of most education and training programs, one finds a predominance of people who have not been well served by the current educational system. There is a high rate of functional illiteracy among what used to be called blue collar workers. Even among those who have managed to negotiate the system successfully and receive a high school diploma, education all too often has negative connotations of oppression, coercion, inefficiency. Too many working adults tend to discount what they learned in the twelve years or so of their incarceration and, unlike their more highly educated peers, they are not eager to go back for more of the same.

Moreover, frequently the family or peer culture offers neither precedent nor support for continuing education. The mental and psychological adjustments necessary to think of returning to the classroom in this situation are awesome to contemplate, particularly if one's earlier educational experience has left a bad taste.

The current mass migration of adults back to school is almost exclusively a middle class phenomenon. Study after study has shown that the more education you have, the more you want. The middle manager at the bank or the housewife who finished a year of college before she got married is far more likely to consider going back for a degree or for a specific course than is the brick layer or the telephone linesman or the assembly line worker.

Recognizing these barriers, the first thing CAEL did for UAW/Ford was to design a "Returning to Learning"® workshop to deal with the real and perceived barriers that adults face in going back to school and to help them make informed choices of education and training. The result was a twelve hour workshop using highly participative, experiential techniques to explore:

a. *self-assessment*—a close look at the individual's own skills, aptitudes, values, needs;
b. *the economic context* in which the individual is currently functioning: a reality testing of the immediate and projected environment with emphasis on the job market, hot and cold sectors, etc.; and a crash course on how to spot trends and do job research;
c. a look at *how colleges and other schools operate*, their language and culture, the increasing numbers of adults in the classroom (message: you won't be the only one on campus with graying hair and a mortgage); a look at the difference between the school experience for young people and adults; a brief rundown on the existing structure of degrees, certificates, non-degree study; a look at some non-traditional options; defining one's own needs and demands on the educational institution; becoming familiar with specific schools in the immediate geographic area to see which ones offer the programs and other resources each individual needs;
d. an exploration of *people as non-stop learners*; how and what we learn outside the classroom; how this informal or experiential learning helps us in more formal situations and how it may even, in some cases, be translated to college credit; why we should feel good about our learning; means of measuring and assessing learning;
e. a guide to *adult survival in school*: building a personal support network of family and friends, study skills, time management for the working student, using the resources of the school, the hidden costs of education in time, money and stress.

This original workshop formula has been redesigned for different clients in ways that may alter order, time, and even content, but in all versions, the emphasis remains on empowering learners to make informed decisions about their own careers and education.

By the end of the "Returning to Learning"® workshop, each participant is expected to have completed a preliminary action plan which includes: choices of vocational areas to be pursued, based on self-assessment data; long term goals (e.g., getting a high school graduate equivalency degree or completing a certificate program in data processing or taking a course in business writing); and "next steps," a list of the immediate things that must be done to begin to put the long range plan into action.

Counseling Support

Clearly a twelve hour workshop alone cannot answer all of people's questions, allay all their anxieties or solve all their problems. Ideally, the "Returning to Learning"® workshop is followed up by anywhere from one to six hours of one-on-one career and education counseling designed to further explore the implications of the self-assessment exercises, sharpen the connections between what has been learned and one's own realistic career goals, and assist people in making informed choices about what they will study and where they will go to do so.

Unlike the usual situation where counseling is available to a student only after registration in a college or vocational school, this counseling is accomplished *before* registration by counselors who are "neutral" (that is, who are not favoring their own institutions) and who have been trained to understand the practical needs and special psycho-cultural situation of worker/students.

Pre-Paid Tuition

Traditionally, companies wishing to support their employees' aspirations for further education and training have done it in one of two ways:

One, on-site at the company's expense, either by company trainers or by bringing in a vendor—a school or private consultant.

Two, by reimbursing the tuition costs upon successful completion of a course or courses taken outside the company. A 'C' grade or above is the usual criterion, although some companies specify a graduated scale of reimbursement depending upon the grade.

On-site, company-sponsored training may be useful for both company and worker, but typically it is centered more on the needs of the former, dealing with skills and competencies useful in increasing productivity and bearing directly on the bottom line. Moreover, such training is usually highly practical and lacks the theoretical dimension that would make the intended learning transferable to other situations.

As for tuition reimbursement, it is not a viable option for many working people. Consider the single mother at $15,000 per year with bills piling up and a son needing orthodontia. Or the father of five who must decide between Mary's piano lessons and his taking a course in introductory accounting. For such people, the promise of reimbursement cannot make up for current deprivation. Moreover, thanks to one of the less enlightened IRS policies, tuition reimbursement is now considered a taxable benefit, so that when the check arrives, part of it becomes a burden to contend with the following April 15th. Is it any wonder that the national average for employees taking advantage of tuition reimbursement has hovered between three and five percent?

In contrast, pre-paid tuition has proved to be a powerful motivator for workers at all levels of the pay scale, lifting the percent of participation dramatically to more than 21% of the workforce (one company's participation has soared above 30%).

Moreover, concerns about workers taking frivolous courses because they are "free" or of not completing those for which they register have not materialized. Since approval for pre-paid tuition in all of the CAEL programs utilizing this option is dependent upon whether the specific course or program is part of the individual's action plan, each registration is scrutinized, and deviations from the plan must be explained. To date, available data indicate that workers' completion and success rates in pre-paid programs seem to be somewhat higher than in company-sponsored reimbursement programs.

Involvement of Schools, Colleges and Universities

A crucial element in the success of the entire "Returning to Learning"® process is CAEL's insistence that local education institutions be involved from the beginning in the planning and delivery of educational services. In each community in which CAEL has contracted with companies and/or unions and government agencies to deliver a "Returning to Learning"® program, the local colleges, universities, vocational and high schools have been encouraged to form a cooperative association for the provision of education and support services. These associations have consisted of anywhere from two or three to as many as forty institutions.

Clearly, the schools' first concern is how many students the program may generate for their classrooms, but gradually, over time, more farsighted administrators come to recognize that there is more at stake here than a numbers game, and at that point, the quality of cooperation rises and issues of economic development take the floor.

Meanwhile, CAEL undertakes to train a few counselors from each participating school who will serve as facilitators for the workshop and as post-workshop counselors. In many cases, CAEL also offers "Prior Learning Assessment" workshops to faculty and administrators who wish to institute programs that can assess and credit workers' non-school learning. And finally, CAEL also offers a "Positioning" workshop for administrators wanting to learn how to form and manage joint ventures for their schools on their own.

All of this cooperative activity has pitfalls, of course. Institutions don't stop thinking in competitive terms overnight, and they are frequently discouraged by the lag time between first discussion of the program and the time when workers in significant numbers actually begin appearing on their campuses. Nevertheless, the rate of shared activities and the numbers of institutions sticking the course are encouraging.

Conclusions

CAEL's joint ventures programs have, in the less than six years of their existence, impacted upon thousands of employees' lives, enabling working class men and women to access education and training that will directly affect their ability to accommodate to a changing job market.

An extensive evaluation program is underway, which can track participants' further progress in continuing their educations, their subsequent job histories and their sense of satisfaction with their lives. Preliminary data are encouraging.

Participants in the program have gained not only the narrow, technical skills needed to do their present jobs better, but have begun to acquire more broadly generic cognitive skills in analyzing, synthesizing, critical thinking, planning and decision making, marrying practice and theory, adapting more easily to change, and others that are the mark of the educated human being. Their working lives have been enhanced, but so have their growth and development as individuals, family members and citizens.

The CAEL joint ventures programs have demonstrated some success factors that could serve as guidelines for policy planning at the national and state levels. If this country believes that workforce training is crucial to its successful navigation of the economic shoals of the 1990s and beyond, policymakers might well ponder the following experientially-derived guidelines:

> Programs should begin with individuals' needs, i.e., they should be learner-centered.
> Adults are more likely to engage in meaningful educational experiences if they are given the tools to make informed decisions and choices.
> Programs that are driven by the immediate needs of the marketplace substitute short range for long range goals; the former fluctuate unpredictably and do not usually provide a wise basis for making career and education choices.

The development of broad, generic skills that enable the worker/student to respond flexibly to changing job requirements pays off better than teaching narrowly job specific skills.

Utilization of existing education resources is more cost effective than the creation of new resources. Given the opportunity and encouragement, most schools and colleges are capable of responding to a new student population and can become more flexible regarding issues of scheduling, delivery systems and even content.

Pre-paid tuition is a powerful incentive for worker participation in education, training and retraining programs.

While the CAEL "Returning to Learning"® programs clearly do not solve all of the current problems related to educating and training the workforce, they do provide a new direction and a funding strategy which would seem to hold promise. Most important, they are empowering working men and women to take charge of charting their own education and career paths and to take responsibility for their own futures.

The Contributors

George Allen is a professor of Psychology and director of the Clinical Psychology program at the University of Connecticut. He has served as a faculty member at five National Institutes on Adult and Experiential Learning. His research activities focus on the multiple dimensions of "wellness."

Bessie W. Blake is dean of the School of New Resources at the College of New Rochelle. She is also a member of the executive committee of CAEL, the advisory council of Graham Windham, and the Middle States Task Force on Off-Campus Instruction, a regional group that develops guidelines for accreditating off-campus adult and non-traditional programs. In addition, she has lectured widely on issues affecting adult and minority students.

     Dr. Blake received her masters degree in English and History from North Carolina Central University, her Ed.D. from Teachers College, Columbia University, and has done post-doctoral work at Harvard University's Institute for the Management of Lifelong Education.

Arthur W. Chickering is currently professor in the Department of Educational Leadership and Human Development, College of Education and Human Services, George Mason University. From 1977 to 1988 he was distinguished professor and director of the Center for the Study of Higher Education at Memphis State University, and before that, as the founding vice-president for Academic Affairs, he played a major role in creating Empire State College.

     Chickering's publications include *Education and Identity, Commuting Versus Resident Students*, and *The Modern American College*, as well as a number of other books and articles. He holds an M.A. degree in teaching English from the Graduate School of Education, Harvard University, and a Ph.D. in school psychology from Teachers College, Columbia University.

     Recognition of the impact of Chickering's research and publications has included an honorary degree from the University of New Hampshire as well as awards from the American Educational Research Association, the National Association of Student Personnel Administrators, the American College Personnel Association, and CAEL. He has served on the editorial boards of the *Journal of Higher Education* and the *Journal of Higher Education Administration*.

K. Patricia Cross is the Elizabeth and Edward Conner Professor of Higher Education at the Graduate School of Education, University of California, Berkeley. She is a psychologist with research interests in the adaptation of institutions of higher education to changing student populations and to the changing role of education in society.

Cross is the author of six books and more than one hundred articles, mostly about adult learners, community colleges , the future of higher education, the improvement of instruction, and nontraditional education. She has been a teacher of high school mathematics, dean of students at Cornell University, Distinguished Research Scientist at Educational Testing Service, and professor and department chair at the Harvard Graduate School of Education.

Professor Cross has served as president of AAHE, vice chair of the American Council on Education Commission on Women in Higher Education, commissioner of the New England Association of Schools and Colleges, and a board member of numerous professional associations. She is currently on the editorial boards of the *Journal of Higher Education, Change Magazine, Higher Education Abstracts* and *Journal for Higher Education Management.* She has traveled with study commissions on education to UNESCO, the Soviet Union, France, Germany, Japan, Denmark, Sweden and Australia.

Norman Evans has been, since 1986, the founding director of the Learning from Experience Trust, a kind of (pale) CAEL. This followed six years as a senior fellow of the Policy Studies Institute, working on the early stage of the Assessment of Prior Experiential Learning in Britain. Previously he was research fellow at the Cambridge Institute of Education, principal of Bishop Lonsdale College of Education and headmaster of a secondary school.

Since 1979 Evans has been closely associated with CAEL as British Liaison, drawing heavily on its experience as he sought to promote APEL through polytechnics, colleges, in employment, youth training, social work and nursing with increasing emphasis on work-based learning, and now with a representative group of five universities. He has written numerous articles and several books, the next of which will be published in 1991 as *Experiential Learning: Assessment and Accreditation; Linking Personal Learning with Public Recognition.*

Zelda F. Gamson is founding director of the New England Resource Center for Higher Education and professor of Sociology at the University of Massachusetts at Boston, as well as a former professor at the University of Michigan.

A long time student of change and innovation in higher education, Dr. Gamson has written *Liberating Education* and *Higher Education and the Real World: The Story of CAEL.*

Elinor Miller Greenberg is the executive director of PATHWAYS to the Future, the training/retraining program that serves 40,000 U.S. West Communications employees in fourteen states. She is also the executive director of Project LEADERSHIP, which is partially supported by the Weyerhaeuser Family Foundation, and serves on numerous government, community and non-profit boards.

Founding director of the University Without Walls (1971-1979), she has also had prior careers as faculty member, administrator, community development director and speech pathologiest.

Ellie's doctorate is from the University of Northern Colorado, and she has honorary degrees from Saint Mary-of-the-Woods College (IN) and the Professional School of Psychology (CA). She is the co-author and editor of three books, as well as 150 articles and pamphlets on lifelong education, leadership and institutional change.

James W. Hall is the founding and current president of Empire State College (SUNY) and a past president of CAEL's Board of Trustees. Dr. Hall has written extensively about reform and innovation in American higher education. Most recently he authored *Access through Innovation: New College for New Students.*

Hall holds the Ph.D. in American Civilization from the University of Pennsylvania and has taught or held administrative positions at State University of New York and Cedar Crest College.

Joan Knapp is president of Knapp and Associates in Princeton, NJ, a research and development firm specializing in the assessment of professional competence. Her clients include organizations that represent a diversity of occupations and professions from arthroscopic surgeons to nurse anesthetists to classroom teachers.

Dr. Knapp was formerly the Executive Director of Health Certification and Licensing Programs in the Center for Occupational and Professional Assessment at Educational Testing Service. Her last year at ETS was spent in developing an interactive videodisc training and assessment certification system for nurse assistants in long term care facilities. The system is in use at nearly 1500 long term care institutions across the country. In the 1970s, during CAEL's initial period of development, she was involved in the creation of procedures and a methodology for the assessment of prior experiential learning.

Malcolm Knowles is Professor Emeritus of Adult and Community College Education at North Carolina State University. Previously he was Professor of Education at Boston University, executive director of the Adult Education Association of the U.S.A., director of Adult Education for the YMCAs of Boston, Detroit and Chicago, and director of training for the National Youth Administration of Massachusetts.

Dr. Knowles received his A.B. from Harvard in 1934, and his M.A. and Ph.D. from the University of Chicago in 1949 and 1960 respectively. Since his retirement in 1979, he has been actively engaged in consulting and conducting workshops for organizations in North and South America, Europe, Australia, and the Far East.

Dr. Knowles is author of eighteen books, including *The Modern Practice of Adult Education* (1980), *Andragogy in Action* (1984), and *The Making of an Adult Educator* (1989), and over 200 articles.

David A. Kolb is professor and chairman of the Department of Organizational Behavior in the Weatherhead School of Management at Case Western Reserve University. Dr. Kolb received his Ph.D. in Social Psychology from Harvard University and honorary degrees from the International Management Center, Buckingham, U.K. and from the University of New Hampshire.

Dr. Kolb has authored numerous books, articles, and monographs in the field of organizational behavior. His latest book, *Experiential Learning: Experience as the Source of Learning and Development*, is an integrative statement of 15 years' research on learning styles and the learning process. He has also recently completed the revision (5th edition) of *Organizational Behavior: An Experiential Approach to Human Behavior in Organizations and Organizational Behavior: Practical Readings for Managers (with I. Rubin and J. Osland)*.

Jackson Kytle is president of Goddard College in Plainfield, Vermont, a small, liberal arts college that follows the traditions of progressive education. Before Goddard, he served Antioch University in a variety of faculty and administrative roles for fifteen years. The last position was as vice president and provost. His B.A. in English is from Middlebury College, followed by a Ph.D. in Social Psychology from Columbia University. His research interests are: mental health and social change, the limits of planned change, and experimental education.

Lois Lamdin is co-director of the Business Development and Training Center in Pennsylvania and New Jersey, chairman of the Board of Dusco Community Services Inc., publisher of the *Great Valley News*, and consultant in adult learning issues.

Lois's Ph.D. is from the University of Pittsburgh, and she has taught at Carnegie-Mellon University, chaired the English department at Hostos Community College (CUNY), and served as associate dean at Empire State College and as executive director of CLEO, a consortium of 37 colleges and universities.

Dr. Lamdin has written extensively in the fields of literature and experiential learning, does a monthly column for the GVN, and is currently finishing up the revised edition of *Earn College Credit for What You Know* as well as working with Morris Keeton on a book on employability.

Elana Michelson is chair of the Master of Arts program in Culture and Policy Studies at Empire State College (SUNY), where she has also served as a faculty member at the Harry Van Arsdale Jr. School of Labor Studies and as director of the Empire State College program in Jerusalem.

Elana is the co-author of *Portfolio Development and Adult Learning: Contexts and Strategies* and has worked extensively as a writer and consultant in the field of adult higher education. She holds a Ph.D. in English Literature from Columbia University.

Barry Sheckley is an associate professor of Education at the University of Connecticut. He has worked closely with CAEL over the last decade as a senior regional executive officer and staff research associate. He has also directed six National Institutes on Adult and Experiential Learning. His current research activities focus on how experiential learning fosters adult development in workplace settings.

John H. Strange received his B.A. degree in Political Science from Duke University and his M.A. and Ph.D. degrees in Politics from Princeton University. He has taught at Princeton, Duke, the University of North Carolina, Johns Hopkins University, Rutgers University, the University of Massachusetts at Boston and the University of South Alabama.

At the University of Massachusetts at Boston, John founded the College of Public and Community Service, a non-traditional college for adults based on the evaluation of competencies acquired through prior learning and the attainment of new knowledge and skills through experiential learning. John served as the dean of the College of Public and Community Service for six years, following which he was vice president of CAEL.

John became interested in the impact of technology on education in 1981. Since that time he has written widely on that and related topics. He is currently professor of Educational Technology at the College of Education of the University of South Alabama. He also serves as director of the University's Center for Retraining and Educational Development in Technology and Telecommunications.

Pamela Tate is president of CAEL, an organization with which she has been actively involved since 1976 as executive vice president, editor of the *New Directions in Experiential Learning* series of books, editor of the organization's quarterly newspaper, member of the board of trustees, designer of CAEL's joint ventures models, speaker and consultant.

Tate has been in academic administration and involved actively with experiential learning for almost twenty years, including serving as assistant vice chancellor for Lifelong Learning and Alternative Education for the central administration of the State University of New York. Among her previous positions she was associate director of the Compact for Lifelong Educational Opportunities (CLEO), president of the Society for Field Experience Education (SFEE), and director of the Innovative Studies Department at SUNY, New Paltz.

Tate is nationally recognized for her work in creating joint ventures between higher education, labor, government and business and for her work in assisting colleges and universities to develop systems of prior learning assessment.

John R. Valley was at Educational and Testing Service from 1954 to 1984 where he had the opportunity to conceptualize, implement, and administer assessment services directed to recognizing and credentialing learning, first through the Advanced Placement Program, then the College Level Examination Program, and later Cooperative Assessment of Experiential Learning, the forerunner of CAEL. He also worked to enhance arrangements for recognizing learning through professional organizations such as the International Association for Continuing Education and Training, and by serving on various educational boards and commissions.

Since his retirement from ETS, Valley has maintained his professional involvement with education as a consultant, author and member of community higher education commissions and committees. He is currently a founding member of the board of directors of the Hilton Head College Center.

William H. Warren is a consultant in continuing and higher education, residing in Vermont. Most recently, he served as vice chair and executive of the Commission on Higher Education and the Adult Learner of the American Council on Education. Previously he was vice chancellor of the University of Maryland University College and senior vice president of Antioch College.

Warren received his doctoral degree from the Harvard Graduate School of Education and his A.M. from the University of Chicago.

Urban Whitaker earned his Ph.D. in Far Eastern Studies and Political Science at the University of Washington. He was professor of International Relations (1954–68) and dean of Undergraduate Studies (1969–79) at San Francisco State University until his early retirement.

Dr. Whitaker has been active in numerous CAEL activities since the organization was founded and is author of *Assessing Learning: Standards, Principles, & Procedures* (1989).